The Center for South and Southeast Asia Studies of the University of California is the unifying organization for faculty members and students interested in South and Southeast Asia Studies, bringing together scholars from numerous disciplines. The Center's major aims are the development and support of research and language study. As part of this program the Center sponsors a publication series of books concerned with South and Southeast Asia. Manuscripts are considered from all campuses of the University of California as well as from any other individuals and institutions doing research in these areas.

RECENT PUBLICATIONS OF THE CENTER FOR SOUTH AND SOUTHEAST ASIA STUDIES

JOHN LARKIN
The Pampangans:
Colonial Society in a Philippine Province

MURRAY J. LEAF
Information and Behavior in a Sikh Village:
Social Organization Reconsidered

DANIEL S. LEV
Islamic Courts in Indonesia:
A Study in the Political Bases of Legal Institutions

DAVID G. MARR
Vietnamese Anticolonialism, 1885–1925

GORDON C. ROADARMEL
A Death in Delhi:
Modern Hindi Short Stories

SOCIAL RELATIONS IN A
PHILIPPINE MARKET

This volume is sponsored by the

CENTER FOR SOUTH AND SOUTHEAST ASIA STUDIES,

University of California, Berkeley

Social Relations in a Philippine Market

Self-Interest and Subjectivity

WILLIAM G. DAVIS

University of California Press

BERKELEY, LOS ANGELES, LONDON

UNIVERSITY OF CALIFORNIA PRESS
BERKELEY AND LOS ANGELES, CALIFORNIA
UNIVERSITY OF CALIFORNIA PRESS, LTD.
LONDON, ENGLAND
COPYRIGHT © 1973, BY
THE REGENTS OF THE UNIVERSITY OF CALIFORNIA
ISBN: 0-520-01904-0
LIBRARY OF CONGRESS CATALOG CARD NUMBER: 71-145783
PRINTED IN THE UNITED STATES OF AMERICA

To

NANCY, ROXANNE, AND JOCELYN

For the family times this replaced

Contents

MAPS

TABLES

Preface

This essay is intended as a critique of some points in the continuing controversy in anthropology concerning the nature of, and the most useful ways of analyzing, the non-Western economic systems with which anthropologists typically work. The results of the study, which appear in these pages, were, however, somewhat unanticipated. The original intent was to investigate a Philippine marketplace economy in order to determine what mischief impersonal, competitive market organization was working on "traditional" forms of social and economic organization. I was particularly interested in assessing the degree to which conflict within the local community could be attributed to economic change introduced by the market. What I found and recorded here initially came as a surprise. For what impressed me most about the sociology of the marketplaces of the Southern Cordillera region was the degree to which exchange relations characterized by a high degree of reciprocal and conscious social obligation were carried forward into the marketplace. This organizational feature, above all, I have sought to describe and interpret, and to relate to wider conceptual problems in anthropology.

The investigation which produced these data was conducted between May 1963 and April 1964. It consisted of two principal phases. There was an initial three-month survey of the main areas from which the marketplace in Baguio City

xi

drew its produce. During this time the flow of goods to and from the marketplace was investigated. The remainder of the time was allotted to the sociology of marketplace relations themselves.

The research was supported by a grant from the National Institute of Mental Health and was conducted under the direction of Professor Robert F. Murphy, who was the principal investigator on the grant. I am grateful to Professor Murphy both for his scholarly assistance and his (sometimes perhaps overly) cheerful support while I was in the Philippines. In addition to Professor Murphy, I appreciate the effort and patience invested in my training by Professors William C. Beatty, George M. Foster, Clifford Geertz, David Plath, and Paul Wheatley. I also wish to acknowledge a special intellectual debt to Professor Sidney W. Mintz, who generously corresponded with me during the field phase of the study, and whose suggestions I found always to be particularly insightful and valuable. Additionally, thanks are owed to Professor Alice G. Dewey for the many hours spent discussing mutual problems and interests, and to Robert Jay for listening to me and offering sound advice. I am deeply indebted to Katherine Keysor Davis and Philip W. Knopp for the considerable effort both of them invested in editing the form and content of the manuscript, and I can hardly thank them enough for their assistance, support, and encouragement. Mrs. Susan Alcala did an excellent job typing the manuscript in spite of often being obliged to work her way through pencilled, interlinear notes. Finally, gratitude is owed to the students in my graduate seminars at the University of California, Davis, for helping me to sharpen ideas.

In the Philippines I received assistance from Mary Hollnsteiner, Frank Lynch, and John Carroll, all of the Institute of Philippine Culture, Ateneo de Manila University. I am also greatly indebted for insights provided by Dr. Milton Barnett and Professor Henry T. Lewis, Jr. Likewise, I wish to acknowledge obligations to Charles Kaut, F. Landa Jocano, Dan Scheans, and William Henry Scott. In the Baguio City area I owe everlasting gratitude to Frederico M. Mirasol, who was not only of assistance in arranging interviews for me, but who was also a good friend and an enjoyable companion. Additionally, I was helped in important ways by Cecile Afable, Joaquin Bogayong, Vicente Chan, Marcelino Contemprate, John Dimalanta, Henry Fernandez, Councilor Gaudencio Floresca, Crispin T. Mendoza, Councilor Ricardo Paraan, Ramon Resurrection, Jacinto Riellera, Felix Tagtag, Fabian Tiongson, and Isabelo V. Valdez. Many other local people took me into their confidence, and in appreciation of that fact it has been my wish to delay publication of much of this material until there is no longer any possibility of violating trusts or of embarrassing or offending any of them.

Finally, I am particularly indebted to Professors James N. Anderson and Neil J. Smelser of the University of California, Berkeley, for their careful and thoughtful reading of the original manuscript. Professor Anderson has earned my special thanks for taking time during a busy period in his own life to read my work with meticulous care. Both of these gentlemen made suggestions which were especially incisive and sensible, and most of them have been incorporated into my work. I am, of course, responsible for interpreting the advice and suggestions received from these many sources.

Chapter One

The Transcultural Relevance
of Economic Theory

INTRODUCTION

"Every society has an economy," writes Manning Nash, "and in principle the economy can be marked off from other spheres of action like the polity or the family" (1966:3). Because to ensure survival every human population must routinely obtain, distribute, and husband goods and resources, this logic runs, every society must embrace "an economy." If this assumption is correct, an observer should be able to isolate a specifically economic universe of behavior, describe it, analyze it, and compare it to corresponding areas of action in other societies.

However, almost as quickly as scholars turned to the cross-cultural investigation of economies, disputes about the nature of the economy arose (e.g., Boeke 1910). This controversy has questioned which conceptual framework is most productive for such studies and the content of the "economic" sphere of action. In recent years, especially following the publication of Karl Polanyi's *Trade and Markets in the Early Empires* (1957), controversy has intensified and now has crystallized in anthropology into two major opposing views. Scott Cook has done us the service of attaching convenient labels to the polar camps; he terms them the "substantivist" and "formalist" positions (Cook 1966). Because this essay is intended as a critique of some central issues in this debate, it is useful to review the major points of argument.

Until somewhat more than a decade ago nearly all contributions to the literature of economic anthropology drew heavily on the general theory (if not the statistical methods) of economics, thereby holding implicitly with Goodfellow that "if economic theory does not apply to the whole of humanity, then it is meaningless" (1939:3). This view of the general relevance of economic theory was strongly challenged in 1957 by several theoretical papers in the *Trade and Markets* volume edited by Professor Polanyi and his associates. Although the title of the work suggests an exclusive interest in archaic economies, several contributors devoted considerable attention to a critique of attempts—largely by anthropologists—to apply the principles of formal economics to analysis of the economies of contemporary primitive and peasant societies. They concluded that the concepts of formal economics are inadequate as general theory, and they proposed instead what they believed to be a new conceptual scheme (substantive economics), which they claim is more adequate for the study of economies in all times and places.

In the intervening years, substantive economics has enjoyed considerable popularity among anthropologists and sociologists, as the nearly unanimous approval which recently received a review paper by one of the leading spokesmen of the position indicates (Dalton 1969). Partly, no doubt, substantive theory has appealed to the noneconomist because it appears to be a major exposé of ethnocentricism in the statistically oriented, nonhumanistic discipline of economics. Partly substantivism is attractive because it seems to represent an uncommonly sound variety of common sense. Whatever the attraction, the substantivist persuasion in the anthropological study of economies at present has a large group of followers who have contributed an approximately equal share to the existing literature in the field. Since Polanyi's death in 1964, George Dalton has been the most consistent, articulate, and outspoken proponent of this viewpoint, and any assessment of the substantivist approach must first be directed to his work. But Dalton's general position is joined by Conrad Arensberg (1957), Walter Neale (1957a, 1957b, 1964), Paul Bohannan (1959, 1962, 1963), Marshall Sahlins (1960, 1965), and David Kaplan (1968), among others. Among those in anthropology who have defended the cross-cultural utility of more traditional economic concepts are Raymond Firth (1939, 1946, 1959, 1964a, 1967), Melville Herskovits (1952), Richard Salisbury (1962, 1968), Edward LeClair (1962, 1968), Cyril Belshaw (1965, 1967), and Scott Cook (1966, 1969).

THE SUBSTANTIVIST POSITION

In general terms, the substantivist-formalist argument revolves around the utility of applying theory and methods derived from the study of modern industrial capitalist economies to the primitive and peasant economies which traditionally have been of more concern to anthropologists. As Dalton (1967) has phrased the issue, one's viewpoint hinges upon whether he regards economies as sufficiently like modern industrial economies for the same theoretical assumptions to be equally useful in understanding both. As the substantivists formulate the problems, there is no logical basis for such an assumption.

According to Polanyi (1957) and Dalton (1961), two distinct meanings of "economic" have in the past been confused: a "substantive" meaning and a "formal" one. The substantive meaning is derived from empirical fact and "from man's dependence for his living upon nature and his fellows" (Polanyi 1957:243). "Economic" used substantively refers to "the provision of material goods which satisfy biological and social wants" (Dalton 1961:6), not to a system of deductive logic. All human populations have biological and social wants, and depend for existence upon "the sustained provision of material items" (Dalton 1961:6), and in this material sense all human societies (and other populations of organisms, too) have an economy.

But as Polanyi and Dalton have put the matter, the formal definition of "economic" is quite different. It is not given in nature and empirical conditions, but is an expresson of particular kinds of deductive logical assumptions. The character of these special assumptions, they claim, seriously impairs the usefulness of formal theory in analysis of non-Western economies.

First, there is the assumption concerning the availability of resources, or the "scarcity postulate." As Dalton explains the formal view, economists assume that human wants are insatiable, and therefore that means will be inadequate to satisfy the entire range of wants. If wants are infinite and means are finite, scarcity is by definition a universal condition of human populations.

The second assumption of formal theory is that means are capable of alternative output uses. A given set of means is not limited in use to a specific end; it can be employed more or less interchangeably to attain any of several ends in the value

4

hierarchy. The limited and interchangeable nature of means implies that goals "compete for" means, a formulation which is an important aspect of the formal theory.

Third, it is assumed that human beings desire more than a single end or goal. However, these are not of equal value to actors, but are ranked into an order of priority, a "value schedule." It is assumed, therefore, that actors know what they want.

Finally, because by definition means are insufficient to attain the entire range of wants, actors must apply means to attain as large a proportion of priorities as possible. This judicious use of means the economist calls economizing, and the economy is then thought of as the area of behavior characterized by economizing action. The substantivists wish to establish that economizing in this sense is the result of a syllogistic chain based on logical assumptions concerning the scarcity of means and the capacity and will of individuals to choose among alternative ends. Thus in the formal theory economizing behavior becomes a special kind of rational action.

But throughout their respective discussions both Polanyi and Dalton operate with an implicit assumption of their own: they represent both their own and the formal position as defining an economic sphere of action in terms of a presumed orientation of behavior toward the "material." This assumed relationship is explicit in their definitions of the substantive economy, and nearly as explicit, if somewhat more confused, in their references to formal theory. For example, Polanyi speaks of the substantive economy as "an instituted process . . . which results in a continuous supply of want satisfying *material* means" (1957:248, emphasis added). In a similar manner, the formal position is viewed as formulating the economy in material terms, except that here goals themselves are assumed to be material: "Time and again it was argued [by formal economists] that 'economics' should be based upon the whole range of man's *material* want satisfaction" (Polanyi, Arensberg, and Pearson 1957:241, emphasis added). Continuing the line of thought, Dalton attributes to formal theory the formulation of the "economic" problem as dealing with both material means and ends. He first notes that the assumption of purely economic motivation was especially significant in the work of classical economists and then characterizes the syllogistic chain which typifies formalist assumptions in the following way: "... man's material wants are infinite, his material means are finite ... maximum material acquisition therefore requires economizing calculation" (1961:5). Moreover, Dalton interprets the formal theory to assume not only that individuals economize, but that when they do they express "materially *self-gainful* economizing" (1961:9). In brief, although there is some confusion over whether it is material means or material ends which the economist employs to abstract his domain of data, the leading substantivist scholars seem unanimously to agree that "economic" is to be equated with "material." Furthermore, the view of formal theory which one extracts from the substantivists' discussions is that it assumes that self-gainful material ends have the highest priority. Only in respect to this particular view of formal economics can one understand why Polanyi and Dalton believe themselves to be attacking formal theory when they point out that economizing behavior may also involve the "non-material" (cf. Polanyi 1957:245–246; Dalton 1961:7).

Any theory based on such special assumptions as the substantivists claim characterize formal theory will be useful only to the extent that those conditions empirically exist. The substantivists' claim, of course, is that the conditions postulated by the formal theory have a limited distribution among human populations. As it happens, logically enough, the economies in which these conditions exist empirically, and to which formal theory is therefore relevant, are those which have existed in the past two centuries in the Western world. Not surprisingly, these are the economies which the formal theory was called into being to explain. In these economies affairs happen to be so arranged that the formal (logically defined) economy and the substantive (empirically defined) economy are congruent, and formal theory is useful. But to the extent that other economies are organized in different ways, empirical conditions are not likely to approximate those assumed by the formal model, and the formal theory has no analytical utility.

Instead of assuming that all economies are organized in terms of the economizing choices made by individuals, Polanyi has argued for an approach which emphasizes the "process and institutedness" of the economy: that is, how the flow of economic goods and services achieves "unity and stability" in any particular time and place (1957:248–250). This inductive method makes it immediately apparent that the organization of resource flow which typifies Western economies is unique. In substantive terms, most economies do not exist as unifunctional institutions, discretely organized and separate from other social forms, but are "embedded" in other social institutions; the social units which carry the economic process are the basic units of the social order itself. Another way of putting the matter which seems consistent with Polanyi's intent is that in non-Western settings roles are likely to be "involuted" (Nadel 1957); that is, each individual relates to any other alter in terms of more than one role, and not solely in terms of economic roles. Thus economic roles are affected by other dimensions of the relationship: the institutional setting exerts significant influences on economic organization, and proper abstraction of the economy must at the same time consider the institutional setting. It would seem that there would exist in the world a large number of ways of producing a routine flow of goods and services ("institutedness"), but empirically Polanyi and his associates have isolated only three, although they do not claim to have exhausted the possibilities. Polanyi refers to them as forms of economic integration, while Dalton refers to them as transactional modes. Specifically, they are termed *reciprocity, redistribution, and integrative exchange* (Polanyi 1957:250).

Reciprocity, as defined by Polanyi, "denotes movements [of resources, goods, and services] between correlative points of symmetrical groupings." Dalton further explains the idea as "material gift and counter-gift giving induced by social obligation derived typically from kinship, as in the case of the Trobriand Islanders" (1961:9). In sum, for reciprocity to be the main principle of economic integration, social organization must consist of a series of discrete groups which are more or less structural equivalents of one another. These groups pass goods and services back and forth between one another, but they do not exist solely as economic units, like the firm or enterprise characteristic of the Western economy. Rather, they have many other concurrent social functions. The transfers of goods and services are only one aspect of a multidimensional relationship obtaining among the groups involved. Further, the motivation for the exchange is viewed as being in sharp contrast to the Western case, for the impetus is custom and the goal is solidarity, not profit. Some pragmatic utility may result from reciprocal exchanges, but utility is subordinate to socially-defined ends. And because the transactions are constrained by custom, individual choice is excluded and bargaining for advantage violates the ethics of the "reciprocity setting."

The type cases of reciprocal integration are the *urigubu* and *kula* exchanges of the Trobriand Islanders described by Malinowski (1922). In the *urigubu*, for example, a man gave the bulk of his garden produce to his sister's husband, rather than keeping it for himself, and in turn received garden produce from his own wife's brother. Because in the Trobriands a man and his brother-in-law are necessarily members of different matrilineages, Polanyi interprets these exchanges as occurring between matrilineal units. Thus Polanyi, like Mauss (1950) before him, places his interpretive emphasis on exchanges between *groups* as he seeks to interpret exchange systems of the reciprocal type. Individuals are significant only to the extent that they represent institutionalized forms ("correlative points") in acts of exchange.

Polanyi defines redistribution as "appropriational movements towards a center and out of it again" (1957:250), and for redistribution to be the mode of economic integration, "some measure of centricity" must be present in the institutional setting. Dalton, apparently deferring to the criticism of Polanyi's scheme by Neil Smelser (1959), elaborates by referring to redistribution as "a channeling upward of goods or services to socially determined allocative centers (usually king, chief, or priest), who then redistribute either to their subordinates at large by providing community services, or in specific allotments to individuals in accordance with their political, religious, or military status" (1961:9). Thus in redistributive systems goods and services are collected by a power center, then apportioned to individuals or marshalled for social purposes. The chief distinctions between reciprocal and redistributive systems appear to be that the former is nonhierarchical and governed by social obligation, while the latter supports a power hierarchy and is integrated by public authority. Neither is seen to be motivated by self-interest, and neither offers the opportunity for individuals to make economizing choices. Empirical examples of redistribution include many of the classical riverine civilizations (e.g., Egypt, Sumeria, and Babylonia), African *kraals*, Hebrew patriarchal families, and "any large peasant household where grain is not marketed" (Polanyi 1957:254).

In application redistribution becomes a troublesome category, for any economy which can be described as redistributionally integrated may also be analyzed in terms of a series of reciprocal relationships. An element of power is, after all, inherent in most social relationships, so centricity becomes a nebulous basis for establishing a type. Sahlins, in fact, specifically refers to redistributive systems as aggregates of "pooling" relations which involve considerable reciprocity (Sahlins 1965). In practice, therefore, distinctions between reciprocity and redistribution are difficult to maintain. For example, Neale in his analysis of the Hindu *jajmani* system meets the problem by classifying *jajmani* relations as reciprocal in terms of services, but redistributive in terms of goods. However, both reciprocal and redistributive systems are viewed as being "embedded" in the basic units of social structure and therefore are not integrated in terms of self-interested choice.

Exchange, the last of the forms of economic integration dealt with by Polanyi, refers to "vice-versa movements taking place as between 'hands' under a market system" (1957:250). There are, however, several kinds of exchange, two of which are significant enough to be described. First there is "decisional exchange," or exchange at set rates, rather than bargained ones. But decisional exchange cannot, in itself, be a form of integration, for where exchange at set prices takes place, the mechanisms which integrate the economy are the forces which establish the exchange rates and not the acts of exchange themselves. Because the only possible sources of rate-fixing forces remaining are reciprocity and redistribution, it follows that decisional exchange is only another expression of one of these arrangements. It seems, therefore, that the matter was raised only to demonstrate that some transactions which seem to be of the

10

market type turn out, under closer scrutiny, not to be organized by the market principle at all.

Of the several forms of exchange organization, only integrative exchange has the capacity to integrate an economy. A distinctive quality of integrative exchange is that transactions take place at bargained rates, so that the acts of exchange themselves establish the rates of exchange. Furthermore, bargaining implies that actors are free to make choices and that they are seeking to optimize self-interest.

Polanyi and his colleagues repeatedly caution us that none of these forms of integration emerge from the random transactions of individuals. Individual acts are results of an institutional-level organization in operation. Thus integrative exchange, too, is the product of a particular institutional setting: a system of price-making markets. Where bargained exchange is supported by a market system "which tends to spread the effects of prices to markets other than those directly affected" (Polanyi 1957:255), integrative exchange has the capacity to organize the economy. Integrative exchange, therefore, is what is conventionally known as free exchange, or market organization.

The substantivists claim that market organization does not occur commonly in time and space. In fact, economies in which the principle of bargained exchange is the most prominent form of resource allocation exhibit some special features. First, there tends to be a relatively high degree of specialization of labor. This in turn results in a high degree of mutual interdependence among the participants, and a correspondingly heavy emphasis upon the principal distributional mechanism, the market. All participants depend upon selling something to the market and purchase from it what they want, need, or can afford. The market, therefore, becomes the mechanism which transacts the entire purchasable range of goods and services.

11

Resources, labor, capital, talent, and manufactured goods all flow through the same distributional channel.

Second, in ideal terms, the market is decentralized and free from the "irrational restraints" (embeddedness) of authority, custom, and sentiment. In theory it is a specifically economic institution, whose sole purpose is to allocate resources among alternative uses. In this setting exchange rates are set by the acts of exchange themselves, and become the chief organizational mechanism. Because prices are free to reflect conditions of supply, demand, and advantage, they may operate to redirect the flow of resources to areas of the economy in which they are desired. Thus, through the influence of supply and demand, as these are reflected in price changes, the market becomes a self-regulating institution, serving to allocate and reallocate the factors of production. The market "disembeds" the economy by removing allocation from the jurisdiction of custom and public authority, consigning it to the mechanical "laws" of supply and demand. As Heilbroner (1961:7–8) notes, the market game involves a delicate balance of interdependence. Polanyi and Dalton suggest that not all societies have wanted to play it.

Finally, and perhaps most importantly for the substantivist position, the free market form of economic organization not only *permits* an expression of self-interest, it *requires* it. Where the market exists, each individual must have the minimal interest necessary to realize enough profit to sustain himself and his dependents; each man must enter the market to seek bargains and gain. Thus social relations in the market are not bound by commensal goals and a system of social ethics internalized through habitual association; rather, they are highly competitive, casual, and impersonal. "Exchange at fluctuating prices," remarks Polanyi, "aims at a gain that can be attained only by an attitude involving a distinctive antagonistic relation-

12

ship between partners" (1957:255). Moreover, because social life in the market setting must be arranged appropriately to facilitate the market order, the attitudes and ethics appropriate to the market may come to pervade all aspects of life. It is therefore proper in such cases to speak of a "market society" (Dalton 1961:3).

Not surprisingly, substantivist scholars view the market principle as typical only of Western economies after the Industrial Revolution, with reciprocity and redistribution typical of all others. In the primitive economy land and labor are rarely for sale at all and tend to be allocated in terms of the social statuses which persons occupy. Furthermore, the reciprocal-redistributive economies are so bound by social restrictions that they offer little opportunity for individuals to exercise gain-oriented choice-making, the *sine qua non* of formal theory. Appropriate to this position, one of the original contributors to the *Trade and Markets* volume, Walter Neale, has taken the astonishing position that nonmarket economies are "so organized by tradition, religion, or authority that economizing choices are *absent*" (Neale 1964:1302, emphasis added). Thus in the substantivist view, as Sahlins (1960) has summarized the argument (with an interesting use of definitions), the economy is one thing, economizing another; the two do not necessarily correspond.

Polanyi and Dalton do not end their considerations with economic organization. They also imply that particular kinds of ethical systems are appropriate to the main forms of economic organization. Their ideas have in common with the schemes of many evolutionists a concern for the *quality* of the human relationships which characterize different kinds of economic organization. They suggest that where reciprocity and redistribution obtain, strong subjective elements impinge upon economic relationships: in these cases economic relations are not only social, but socially valued and sociable. Economic relations do not express a spirit of competition and self-interest but of social solidarity and cohesiveness—the near reverse of the market situation. Bargained exchange, however, can only threaten the "fount of solidarity" which other forms of economic integration establish (cf. Polanyi 1957:255).

In the substantivist view, then, modern market-oriented economies and their counterparts are similar in few dimensions: organization, ethics, goals, social solidarity, and economic "mechanisms" (e.g., media of exchange) are all very different. If one accepts these assumptions, it follows that the market organization of the United States' economy, as opposed to the reciprocity-redistribution economy of the Trobriand Islands, *"makes the differences in economic organization and processes between the two more important than the similarities"* (Dalton 1961:10, emphasis in original), and that: "Primitive economy is different from market industrialism not in *degree* but in *kind"* (Dalton 1961:20, emphasis added). Therefore, there is no compelling reason to believe that formal theory has anything to offer toward the development of a general economic theory. "The relation between formal economics and the human economy is, in effect, contingent. Outside a system of price-making markets economic analysis loses most of its relevance as a method of inquiry into the working of the economy" (Polanyi 1957:247). Or as Dalton sums it up: ". . . there is a gulf between the Western and the primitive; types of economic organization do not shade imperceptibly one into another; and it is not impossible to say where the usefulness of economic theory ends" (1961:18). Thus, to assume that formal theory, based as it is on a special set of assumptions, has anything to offer the student of non-Western economies seems an outrage to common sense. Accordingly, it is tempting to conclude that: "The real task is nothing less than the building of a cross-cultural economics based on the substantive problems of production and distribution rather than on the formal problems of choice" (Fusfeld 1957:354–355).

SUBSTANTIVISM, SOCIAL ORGANIZATION, AND THE PROBLEM OF CHOICE

It is neither necessary nor desirable to become mired here in the polemics of the substantivist-formalist controversy in economic anthropology. As Matthew Edel (1969) concludes, and as the substantivists suggest, there is no reason to believe that an analytical focus on decision-making is the best way to approach all social data, or that the entire range of concepts employed in the formal theory have functional analogs in primitive societies. However, some of the points raised to counter the substantivist viewpoint are pertinent to the present discussion.

Both Polanyi and Dalton attacked the scarcity postulate; as they understood it, the formal theory postulates that scarcity arises from insatiable human wants. Both held that scarcity is a phenomenon of the particular social organization at hand, induced in some societies by the patterns of ownership and division of labor. Several scholars have responded to the substantivist argument on this point. Smelser (1959), one of the gentler critics, chides Polanyi for too strongly dichotomizing between scarcity and the other trappings of the market, and no scarcity at all. That economies are institutionalized, he points out, does not ensure that sufficient means to realize social goals will flow automatically from the environment. Therefore, he concludes, we should not abandon the concept of scarcity and its corresponding inducement to rational calculation, but should repair it so that it is generally useful (1959:176–177).

The critics who have dealt specifically with Dalton's discussion of scarcity, notably LeClair and Cook, have been less kind. Both LeClair (1962:1184–1185) and Cook (1966:334–335) reject without qualification Dalton's contention that economists assume human wants to be insatiable. They suggest that formal theory simply assumes that human aspirations typically exceed the readily available means to attain them. LeClair then shows that formal theory has actually refined the notion of scarcity through the concept of marginal utility, which permits consideration of varying degrees of scarcity. Several contributors to a recent volume edited by Raymond Firth (Firth 1967) also treat scarcity, and the resource management practices which follow from it, as an assumption important to the analysis of the primitive and peasant economies with which they are dealing. In sum, as the notion is used in analysis, the concept of scarcity seems sensible and useful, particularly when examining the behavior of populations which utilize marginal technologies. It also seems that as technical knowledge expands, we learn to want more.

A second problem raised by the substantivists has to do with the nature of ends formalists allegedly have given priority, and which define the economic field of action itself. Both Polanyi and Dalton regard formal theory to stress the maximization of material ends and means. A number of formalists object. Burling (1962), for example, has noted that this is a singular procedure: it is quite different from the way that economists themselves define their field; it raises some problems of its own (e.g., what about nonmaterial values); and it is ethnocentric in the bargain. Joy's remarks are as explicit: ". . . whatever economists implicitly assume, they would almost universally deny the existence of 'economic ends.' The choice of ends is not a subject of study to the economist . . . Profit maximizing is certainly not a necessary postulate for the analysis of producers' behavior" (1967:32–33). Similarly LeClair (1962:1181) quotes George Stigler on the "economic": "The concept of the 'economic man' does not imply (as almost all critics state) that the individual seeks to maximize money or wealth, that the human soul is a complex cash register. It does not affect formal theory ...in the least whether the individual maximizes wealth, religious piety, the annihilation of crooners, or his waistline" (1946:63–64). Thus, the formalist critics have consistently argued that the formal theory does not distinguish between ends which are *sui generis* economic and those which are not. The theory seems capable of dealing with the interdependences which exist between material and nonmaterial dimensions of human behavior. Oddly enough, in recent intellectual history the anthropologists (e.g., Herskovits 1952:3–4; Nash 1966:3, 1967:525) and especially the economic historians (e.g., Polanyi and Dalton), not those more familiar with contemporary economic theory, have most insisted upon the definition of an economic sphere of action on the basis of material criteria. It is also, as Frank Knight comments (1956:145), curious to note the repugnance among scholars to the notion that human beings calculate costs and gains in choosing among behavioral alternatives.

In this controversy the problem of choice emerges as a central issue, with great significance not only for the cross-cultural study of economies, but for social theory more generally considered. In his most recent programmatic paper, Dalton puts the matter concisely, drawing attention to the two ways of viewing an economy:

...one [way] is to concentrate on economic "behavior" of individual persons and the motives that impel the individual behavers, so that the economy is seen as a cluster of individual actors and their motives. ... The other approach is to perceive the economy as a set of rules of social organization (analogous to polity and political rules), so that each of us is born into a "system" whose rules we learn. It is from observing the activities and transactions of participants that we derive these systematic rules (1969: 66). . . . All societies of record—those studied by anthropologists, historians, and economists—have structured arrangements to provide the material means of individual and community life. It is these structured rules that we call an economic system (1969:72).

Obviously, the substantivists opt for the second of these two approaches, for in their view nonmarket economic processes are so thoroughly embedded in cultural rules and social organization that the exercise of individual choice, and the use of analytical strategies that focus on choice, are not possibilities. The tribesman's "decisions" are specified for him by traditional role behavior, and he has few options. Organization is therefore such that he may not exercise self-interest. In fact, he may not wish to, for he has unconsciously learned to associate his own ends with those of society, much as language is acquired: "In subsistence (non-market) economies, the question of choice among real alternatives does not arise in such explicit fashion [as it does for American farmers]. A Trobriand Islander learns and follows the rules of *economy* in his society almost like an American learns and follows the rules of *language* in his" (Dalton 1969:67). On the other hand, in the market economy individuals must choose among alternatives, and in ways consistent with material interest; they are free to, and anxious to, pursue material gain.

The immediate theoretical significance of the claim that formal theory is concerned exclusively with the profit-maximizing choices of individuals now becomes more apparent: it is an attempt to establish an inevitable relationship between making choices and material self-interest. Much as in the scarcity issue as formulated by Polanyi and Dalton, the reader is offered an all-or-nothing choice. One is asked either to reject the "choice-making" level of analysis entirely, or to accept it with the stipulation that choices made by individuals will be guided by a strategic priority upon material advantage. Because human beings do not in all cases act to optimize material gain, the basis seems to exist for banishing from general theory analytical procedures based on individual choices in favor of those which stress "rules" and institutions.

Dalton's concern is over which analytical concepts are best suited to the interpretation of "real world processes and institutions" (1969:63), which seems to imply that his principal interest is in behavior, as opposed to ideals. Therefore, his preference for treating the economic sphere of action as "a set of rules of organization" is curious and open to fundamental criticism. But Dalton's emphasis on the form which social relations assume in the aggregate is a logical continuation of the preference, expressed by the editors of the *Trade and Markets* volume, for "the reality of society," in opposition to "atomistic individualism" (Polanyi, Arensberg, and Pearson 1957:239). It is also a familiar view in anthropological models of sociocultural phenomena other than economic data.

Anthropologists have conventionally recognized three distinct but interrelated levels of social phenomena in human populations (cf. Radcliffe-Brown 1940, Leach 1945). The first level is the behavior of individuals. The second level is derived from the first, and consists of the general pattern, or "average" pattern, which is expressed in the behavior of many different individuals, and which is often referred to as the norm. The third level is the "ideal." It consists of the principles which are reported by the actors themselves to govern conventional behavior, and is often referred to as the level of "rules." Often informants also express the opinion that the rules will be enforced by the application of sanctions,[1] though this may not prove to be the case. Leach (1945:60) indicates that because we must rely in the field on a limited number of informants and observations, we are especially likely to confuse levels two and three (norms and ideals), though in practice behavioral patterns typically are but approximations (and often remote approximations) of the "structured rules."

Societies are of course composed of individuals, and group relationships themselves may, after all, be expressed only through the actions of individuals. Thus, even if we derive the "systematic rules" which govern economic behavior by *"observing* the activities and transactions of participants" (Dalton 1969:66, emphasis added), to consider the behavior of individuals remains necessary. Therefore, to assume that to ground theory on the actions of individuals is strategically improper implies either that we are concerned solely with the rules and norms, or that one of two additional assumptions is being made. Either the external social constraints which channel individual behavior in directions specified by the ideal rules are functioning to near perfection, or, alternatively, these constraints have ceased to be external and have become perfectly internalized by actors, so that individual and societal goals are identical. Dalton seems to imply the latter by comparing the learning of economic "rules" to those of language.

Now, this is the set of assumptions that Dennis Wrong (1961) has characterized as the "oversocialized conception of man" in modern sociology, and it's the same set which typifies Polanyi's "reality of society." The evidence, however, indicates

---

[1] Experiences with informants suggest that it might also be useful to distinguish a fourth level. Informants often offer their own interpretation of "actual" conditions which differ from the ideal, from observed behavior, or from the average or general pattern.

that none of these assumptions is matched by actual conditions in any society, including primitive ones. Variations from the rules of social organization exist in all areas of behavior, including language usage, wherever anyone has bothered to look for them.

The oversocialized view of primitive peoples has led to one of the more spirited attacks on the substantivists' assumptions, that launched by Scott Cook (1966, 1969). Cook suggests that the substantivist portrayal of primitive society amounts to a romanticized set of misinterpretations. Specifically, Cook notes that in primitive societies many opportunities for choices occur, and there, too, the expression of self-interest may lead to conflict. For example, one may lay on strong obligations of indebtedness through reciprocal transactions, and the failure to reciprocate may itself lead to contention. We are therefore only deluded when we deal exclusively with the rules of economic organization. The reader may see something of the problem in "the most minutely described case in the literature" (Dalton 1969:72) on primitive economies, Malinowski's Trobriand Island studies. Malinowski carefully describes the ideal rules which govern kinship and the complex network of exchanges in which Trobrianders participate. But he also offers discussions of particular situations in which actual behavior is described, and we see the discrepancies. There is, he notes, an ideal of solidarity in the matrilineal descent group, but as it turns out this ideal:

...is by no means forcibly expressed on its economic side. The right of inheritance, the common participation in certain titles of ownership, and a limited right to one another's implements and objects of daily use are often restricted in practice by private jealousies and animosities. In economic gifts more especially, we find here the remarkable custom of pur-

21

chasing during lifetime, by instalments, the titles to garden plots and trees, and knowledge of magic, which by right ought to pass at death from the older to the younger generation of matrilineal kinsmen (1922:192).

Thus in spite of his polemical arguments to the contrary, Malinowski's own data show that in this "typical tribal economy" self-interest breaks through the rules of the moral order.

In anthropology and sociology the dominant societal paradigm has for some time been the "functionalist" one, commonly associated with Radcliffe-Brown and his students in anthropology, and with Talcott Parsons and his students in sociology. Generally speaking, the functionalist position presents society as a system of subsystems which exist in equilibrium with one another and with the external world. Social relations are more or less consistent with cultural ideals and jural rules, and all operate to produce personalities appropriate to the system at hand. The social system may occasionally become disorganized, divided by conflict, or disturbed by disharmonies, but the mechanisms of social control generally have the capacity to reinstate the equilibrate condition. In fact, conflict may be viewed as a purgative, maintaining the social organism in good health. But functionalists assume that a single, ordered set of relationships (*the* social structure) and—though these may be selectively distributed among particular situations—a single set of values exist.

A consequence of this formulation of "the reality of society" has been a concentration upon ideological rules and normative patterns and inattention to statistically less significant deviations from these. In kinship studies, for example, descriptions of patrilineal or matrilineal *societies* are not unusual, even though the behavior of significant numbers of persons by no means adheres faithfully to the rules of descent. This set of

assumptions renders it difficult to deal with "real world processes": "In the approach of Radcliffe-Brown, Evans-Pritchard,
and Fortes, with regard to descent systems, the possibility of
establishing correspondence rules that link theoretic constructs with behavioral systems is limited. This is due to an
exclusive concern with the system of jural constraints which
structure the basic cultural framework" (Buchler and Selby
1968:102). Radcliffe-Brown took the extreme view that descent systems were classes of a "natural kind"—that there existed
in nature only a few forms of social structure which would be
exposed if only proper discovery procedures could be developed (Radcliffe-Brown 1957).

The most common criticisms offered of the functionalist
paradigm are directed at the failure of the model to deal adequately with the varieties of expressed behavior, and especially
with the problems of conflict and change. In the functionalist
society, "process" characteristically refers to the dynamics of
the social order as it reproduces itself, and therefore tends to
be interpreted as cyclical in nature: for example, the life cycles
of individuals, the developmental cycle of domestic groups, or
the fissioning of lineages. Because the emphasis is on norms and
rules, and not upon the decisions made by actors in social situations, problems related to statistically significant behavioral
deviations from norms, or competing sets of values, or other
changes with sources internal to the social system are difficult
to formulate. Functionalist models of society deal best with
the forces of change which emanate form *outside* the social
order, such as the "acculturation" situations which once occupied much anthropological attention (van den Berghe,
1963). As one of the chief antagonists of functional theory,
Ralf Dahrendorf, puts it: "By no feat of the imagination, not
even by the residual category of 'dysfunction,' can the inte-

grated and equilibrated social system be made to produce serious and patterned conflicts in its structure" (1965:216).[2]

The substantivists' conceptualization of the primitive society and economy is strikingly similar to the variety of functionalism which has been prominent elsewhere in anthropology. Both views stress a high degree of consensus on values and the norms and rules which structure the basic cultural context,[3] as opposed to a concern for the behavior of individuals (and collections of them) in culturally-defined situations. The forms of integration—reciprocity, redistribution, and integrated exchange—exist at the same level of abstraction as rules of descent —patrilineal, matrilineal, and cognatic; and they are no better predictors of real behavior. In consequence, as in the case of functionalist models, the substantivists' framework does nothing to encourage precise consideration of the "events of change" (Barth 1967a). Only by extrapolation may we account for the processes by which reciprocal economies become redistributive ones, or by which either is converted to a market system. It is no accident that Dalton argues that significant socioeconomic changes must emanate from outside the primitive society: ". . . local community change or development

[2] This is, however, not an entirely satisfactory view, for several different sets of ideas have been referred to as "functionalism." Cancian (1960) reviews some of the more common forms of functionalist theory and shows that these differ widely in their capacities to deal with change.

[3] It is ironic that Polanyi derives his terms—"substantive" and "formal" economics—from Max Weber's discussion of substantive and formal rationalism (Weber 1947:184–185), for in this passage Weber seeks to deal with universal elements of conflict. Weber sees substantive rationality as the rational application of means to ends governed by a "given set of ultimate values," and formal rationality as the application of means to ends subject only to the criteria of efficiency. Weber's point is that "formally rational" individual interests exist in a constant state of tension with the normative order and are always a potential source of conflict.

seems never to be a 'natural' process of immanent expansion
... but rather the local community's response to incursion from
outside itself" (1969:76). Thus he formulates the two central
problems in economic change as: "... *what is the nature of
the initial incursion which starts the processes of socio-eco-
nomic change, and to what extent does the character of the
initial incursion shape the sequental changes that follows* [sic]"
(1969:76, emphasis in original).

Because functionalism and substantivism share a number of
fundamental—and contentious—assumptions, they are in large
measure subject to the same conceptual difficulties and criticisms. Hopefully, putting matters this way may help to
clarify the significant points at issue in the substantive-formal
controversy.

A massive reaction to the problems inherent in the functionalist paradigm was not long in coming, and by the early
1950s it was well under way. One of the popular forms this
reaction has taken is a strong tendency toward concern for
individuals and the choices they make (e.g., Firth 1954, Leach
1954). Firth argues that: "A theoretical framework for the
analysis of social change must be concerned largely with what
happens to social structures. But to be truly dynamic it must
allow for individual action. As a member of society, each
separate individual is striving to attain his ends, interacting
with other members in the process" (1951:83). He speaks of
social organization as: "The processes of ordering of action and
of relations in reference to given social ends, in terms of adjust-
ments resulting from the exercise of choices by members of the
society: (1964b:45). In Firth's work, the intent of organizational analysis is: "... to extract the regularities from the social
implications of the process of decision-making and allied processes" (1964b:60). Similarly, Alan Howard writes that: "Instead of conceiving society as having a social structure ... we

conceive of social behavior as being structured by participation in given activities within which behavioral choices are regular and predictable" (1963:409). And to return to Buchler and Selby, they feel that to deal adequately with kinship behavior, as opposed to descent ideologies, it will be necessary to: ". . . develop adequate measures for these constructs and consider the optimization problems and interlinked decision processes that are characteristic of classes of systems and the conceptual transformations that map one structure onto another" (1968:102–103). But perhaps the most succinct demonstration of the problems of ignoring decisive action strategies emerges in a seminal paper by Goodenough (1956). He shows that residence "rules" derived from behavior fail to predict actual residence behavior precisely because the elements of strategic choice which were manipulated by the actors are not given sufficient weight in the analysis.

More recently Homans (1958), Barth (1966), and Belshaw (1967) have suggested the advantages of viewing social behavior itself as self-interested exchanges, or transactions, in which individuals calculate gains and losses as they determine courses of action.[4] However, the "individuals" portrayed in these formulations are not the "atomistic individuals" which the formal theory is alleged to propose, but individuals behaving in culturally-defined situations, constrained by rules and norms, and the power and interests of others, while seeking a variety

[4] Dalton (1969:67) suggests that the use of analytical strategies which stress choice-making is not possible in the investigation of primitive economies for yet another reason: the lack of standardized prices renders assessment and calculation too difficult for the natives themselves. The lack of standardized prices may render calculation less precise, to be sure. Nevertheless, all of us calculate, and this computation occurs in many areas of behavior in which quantification is difficult: for example, in choosing between conflicting obligations to kinsmen (e.g., van Velsen 1967).

of culturally-defined values. Rules and norms are significant influences in action, and probablistic predictions of behavior would be impossible without a knowledge of them. The problem which both functionalism and substantivism face is that to deal exclusively, or primarily, with the "rules of social organization" is to do no more than describe the context of social and cultural opportunities and constraints in which choices are made and "real world processes" expressed. The rules are not the processes themselves, and to define the goals of economic anthropology as Dalton does moves against a strong empirically-grounded current in the development of social theory and methods of analysis.

MARKETS AND THE RULES OF SOCIAL ORGANIZATION

The remaining portions of this essay deal with two central problems. First, how adequate is an analytical strategy which focuses on the "rules of social organization" as a procedure for understanding economic action? Second, are the economic relationships expressed in market settings unique?

The rules of economic organization are important, but to deal with interaction and strategy remains necessary if we hope to understand real behavior. The latter procedure allows us to explain a wider range of cases: not only the rules, but also variations of them and violations of them. The rules exert powerful influences over behavior, and they are a prominent reason why human behavior is, in the first place, "patterned" and amenable to systematic investigation. Therefore, it may matter a great deal whether individuals operate under rules of reciprocal economic organizations rather than those of the market. But we cannot assume that the behavior patterns of individuals are any more than an approximation of the rules, or that the behavior of significant numbers of individuals doesn't deviate from the norms at any given point in time. For a more satisfactory view of behavior, we must also consider interaction among individuals and the associations they form. Unfortunately, we know little about the ways in which societies vary from one another at this level, for the emphasis in anthropology has for so long been placed upon aggregate patterns (van Velsen 1967).

Given the substantivist view of the consensual nature of primitive economies, and the corresponding limitation on the distribution of interested choice to market economies, the market emerges as an unique economic institution. In fact, it is so different that a "gulf" exists between it and other forms of economic organization. Thus, the introduction of the self-interest, antagonism, and materialism of the market is disruptive to the moral order of traditional societies (Polanyi 1944, 1947; Dalton 1969), and relationships in the market are less "meaningful" or "immediate and crucial" than corresponding relationships in primitive societies (Dalton 1965b:16). Bohannan goes so far as to speak of the "conflict of economies" (1962:259–263), and Francisco Benet, one of the contributors to the *Trade and Markets* papers (Polanyi, et al., 1957), argues that in Berber society the market principle is so disturbing to social harmony that situations in which interested choice is permissable are kept separate in community life from those in which it is not:

No allowance is made at the villages for a disrupting bargaining behavior.... That both these contexts of Berber life are institutionalized into physically separate spheres of action, village and market, is important indeed. If they were not, those contraries would come to a head on collision.... Markets are here external places for exchanges between individuals who are shedding the corporate personality of which they were a part within township and village (1957:212–213).

In these claims the organizational rules of the economies involved are abstracted to create a set of ideal-type constructs which are then contrasted (e.g., the ideal primitive economy versus the ideal market economy). This procedure, as Weber (1949:90–93) makes clear, is calculated to stress at the analytical level differences which at the empirical level may be slight. Accordingly, ideal-type comparative procedures can tempt the investigator to attribute to the differences which emerge entirely too much concreteness and power to motivate action. Thus, Dalton discusses the market not as an ideal type but as an empirical form which recently existed in a pure state: "The economic man of the 19th century was not a myth, but the succinct expression of this institutional fact: the necessity for each of the atomistic units in an impersonal, market exchange system to acquire his livelihood through market sale" (Dalton 1961:2).

The position assumed here is that when attention is directed to the interaction level, many of the social relational differences alleged to distinguish market from nonmarket economies tend to be greatly reduced in magnitude, in some cases nearly disappearing. For what Weber (Parsons 1947:10, 30 ff.) termed "subjective" factors (those sociocultural factors which have meaning for the actors being observed) intrude upon the ideal structure of the competitive market. Thus, many "primitive" elements of sociability exist in the market and there is no great "gulf" between market and nonmarket behavior. The test case is the sociology of a Philippine marketplace economy.

Chapter Two

Physical and Social
Environments

The existence of markets is an index of interdependence both within and between locales, for a wide variety of factors motivate individuals and firms to exchange resources, labor, and outputs. Regional ecological variation, local economic specialties, and the division of labor within communities may encourage the development of markets. Markets, however, don't constitute a single, uniform type but vary with the social and physical settings of which they are part. Therefore, in discussing any specific network of market relationships, to make the data useful for comparative purposes, we must consider the local physical and sociocultural features which impinge upon market relationships. The intent in this section is to describe external conditions which have relevance for the social interaction I shall describe.

THE REGION

The marketplace which is the principal source of data for this essay is in Baguio City, in the region known until recently as the subprovince of Benguet in the southernmost area of Mountain Province, northern Luzon. Mountain Province is the political-administrative unit which encompasses the greater portion of three mountain ranges (the Malayan, Central, and Polis) which together constitute the principal highlands of northern Luzon, an area usually referred to on maps as the Cordillera Central. Because of these highlands, the climatic patterns characteristic of the region, and the ethnic groups which inhabit the area, this district as a whole is distinctive in the Philippines.

The Cordillera Central ranges rise abruptly from the Central Plain of Luzon, beginning roughly 100 miles north of Manila. They reach their highest elevation to the south, then fall away irregularly to the South China Sea, approximately 200 miles to the north. By world standards none of these mountains is particularly high. For example, Mt. Pulog, located in the Polis range just north of Baguio City, is only 9600 feet and yet is exceptional for the Luzon highlands. However, what the Cordillera lacks in elevation, it compensates for in the broken nature of its terrain. These formations are of geologically recent age and are, in consequence, relatively lightly weathered and steep (Huke 1963:9). The Cordillera is a major obstacle to east-west travel and communication along the whole length of northern Luzon, and it nearly isolates the Cagayan Valley to the east.

The north coastal plain lies to the west of the Cordillera and contains the "Ilocos Provinces"—Ilocos Norte, Ilocos Sur, and La Union. This plain is narrow, ranging in width from thirty

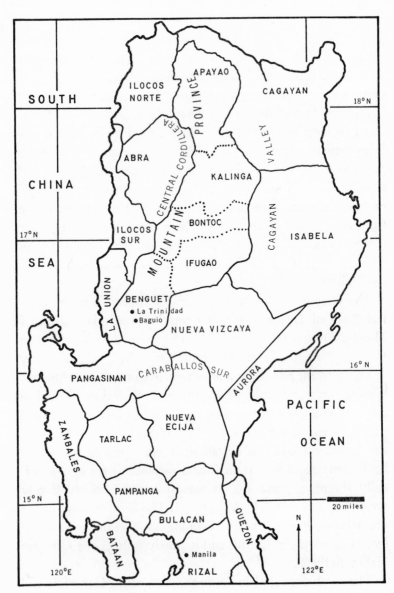

MAP 1: North and Central Luzon

miles at its widest point to only a few hundred yards in those areas where the mountains nearly meet the China Sea. Populations in the Ilocos areas have apparently been *in situ* for many centuries with the result that through time and expanded numbers land holdings have become severely fragmented and reduced in size (Lewis 1971:18, see Table 1). That soils in this

TABLE 1

Nutritional Densities of Selected
Provinces in Northern Luzon

Region	Province	*Persons/Sq. Mi. Cultivated Land*
I. Central Cordillera	Mountain	78.8
II. Cagayan Valley	Cagayan	128.1
	Isabela	107.4
	Nueva Vizcaya	51.4
III. West Coast	Ilocos Norte	218.9
	Ilocos Sur	339.4
IV. Central Plains	Pampanga	733.1
	Pangasinan	542.4
	Tarlac	361.9
V. National Average	–	224.3

SOURCE: Wernstedt & Spencer 1967: Table 13.

coastal region are not especially fertile has made land pressure more serious. In spite of the reputation of its Iloco speaking inhabitants for thrift and hard work, therefore, the Ilocos coast has long been a food-deficient area, and "Ilocanos" have emigrated from the homeland provinces of Ilocos Sur and Norte in large numbers. Iloco speakers are now the numerically dominant portion of the populations of such adjacent areas as La Union, Cagayan, and Isabela Provinces, and they constitute nearly half the population of Pangasinan Province to the south. In the Mountain Province they constituted 20 percent of the population at the time these data were collected (1963–1964) and outnumbered the largest single population of indigenous mountain peoples (Bontoc speakers, approximately 75,500) by nearly 10 percent. In Baguio City, at the southern end of the Cordillera, they are again the most numerous ethnolinguistic group, and there are significant numbers of them in most of the larger settlements throughout Mountain Province. In Mountain Province, the larger the settlement, the larger the proportion of Ilocanos in the population.

On its eastern side the Cordillera is bounded by the valley of the Rio Grande de Cagayan, a nearly level lowland much larger than the plain of the northwest coast. Administratively, the Cagayan Valley contains Cagayan and Isabela Provinces, and the lowland portions of Nueva Vizcaya. Because several rivers drain this and the surrounding hill regions, the Cagayan Valley contains high quality alluvial soils. These soils, together with a relatively sparse population, have permitted farming in larger, more economical units than are found on the northwest coast, and the valley of the Cagayan is important for its agricultural exports—notably tobacco, maize, and rice. For example, Cagayan rice is significant in the diets of Ilocos and Mountain Province populations.

The Cagayan area is still a frontier region in the Philippines; it remains relatively sparsely populated and undeveloped in terms of transport and communications. However, the region's role in the Philippine economy is potentially great if reasonably priced transport can connect the Cagayan to marketing areas. To the east the Cagayan is bordered by the Sierra Madre Cordillera ranges. To the south the Caraballo Sur range connects the Sierra Madre Cordillera to the Cordillera Central, forming yet another obstacle. Roads over the Caraballo connect Cagayan with the central plain, and others lead into the Mountain Province, but these roads are rough and narrow. Water transport is equally difficult to develop, for the rivers of the Cagayan region are not navigable by commercial-sized watercraft, and choppy seas to the north hinder regular shipments from its major port, Aparri (Wernstedt and Spencer 1967:320). Most of the rice shipped to the Ilocos area travels along Highway Three, which follows the north end of the island and connects with the coastal highway in the west, but this highway is not passable all year round due principally to the lack of adequate bridges. However, lumbering and milling industries and large agricultural holdings have encouraged the development of several market towns which serve not only the surrounding Cagayan Valley areas but also adjacent mountain communities.

South of the Cordillera Central is the Central Plain of Luzon, the largest lowland plain in the Philippines, which contains the "rice basket" provinces of Nueva Ecija, Pangasinan, Tarlac, Pampanga, and Bulacan. This intensively cultivated agricultural region is the focal area of lowland Philippine society, in terms of its products, its population size and density, and its cultural impact on the nation. Land ownership in these provinces tends to be concentrated in the hands of a few wealthy operators, but farmstead sizes suggest the pattern of land fragmentation encountered on the northwest coast. The Central Plain is the region of the Philippines which has long been noted for a high proportion of share tenancy and absentee landlords, with attendant social problems (Rivera and McMillan 1952:116). In spite of the significance of the Central Plain for the nation as a whole, the commercial economy of the Mountain Province tends to look for its markets beyond the plains to the "Greater Manila" manufacturing region. Nevertheless, locally important trade between the Cordillera and Central Plain lowlands exists, with the mountains exporting vegetables and importing fish, meat animals, and fowl from the lowlands. The marine and pond fishing industries of the Pangasinan area are especially important to the people of Mountain Province, and dried fish and fish sauces from the lowlands are widely traded throughout the Cordillera Central.

CLIMATE

Nearly the entire upland region of north Luzon expresses some climatic features which contrast sharply with those characteristic of the Philippine lowlands. The contrast is especially sharp when consideration is limited to the southern end of the Cordillera, where the mountains are highest. Much of the southern area from the town of Bontoc south to Baguio City— a region largely incorporated by the old subprovincial boundaries of Benguet—is over 5,000 feet in elevation, and the floor of the Benguet Valley is 4,800 feet.

Aside from the lower slopes, the climate of the Benguet area is generally more temperate than that of most of the remainder of the Mountain Province, and is much more temperate than the lowland Philippines in general. For example, Laoag (on the northwest coast) has an average annual temperature of 81°F, with monthly averages that vary only 6.8° from the warmest month (May, 83.4°) to the coolest (January, 76.6°). Similarly, Dagupan City and San Fernando, which lie roughly in the same latitude as southern Benguet but are in the lowlands, both average 80° annually (temperatures are conversions from the Centigrade scale presented in Huke 1963). With an average annual temperature of 64°, Baguio City (4,860 feet) is roughly 15° cooler, month by month, than any of these lowland stations of similar latitude. Moreover, temperature variations increase at the higher elevations. Daily highs in Baguio City often exceed 80° in May and early June, and lows may drop to 42° in January. Regions above 7,000 feet may experience occasional frosts during December and January. The differences are obviously due to orographic cooling, of which the southern Cordillera area is an extreme Philippine example.

A second significant feature of the climate of the southern Cordillera is the amount of precipitation which occurs in several forms throughout the year—rain, dew, fog, and occasional frost. In this region only December, January, and February are really dry (less than one inch of rainfall). From February on rains grow in frequency and intensity until they peak during August. The seasonal peak is marked. For example, at Baguio City, where the annual rainfall averages 170 inches, 62 percent falls in July, August, and September. During a 47-year period the average rainfall was 42 inches for the month of August (Annual Climatological Review 1956).

In addition to the irregularity and unpredictability of rainfall, northern Luzon lies astride a major typhoon track. Although only a few storms strike the area directly, the Cordillera is so exposed that the presence of a storm center anywhere within several hundred miles may produce appreciably heavier local rains. Thus although rainfall patterns are seasonal, they are likely to occur within a few periods of great intensity instead of being evenly distributed throughout the season. The most dramatic recorded example of this tendency occurred on July 11 and 12 in 1911 when 45.99 inches of rain fell on Baguio City in a single 24-hour period.

Cultivators, like other organisms, are more likely to be affected by extremes than by averages, and the local climate is noteworthy for its extremes. In this sense local cultivators must come to grips with many climatically-induced problems more commonly associated with temperate zones than with tropical ones, as well as with problems typical of tropical areas. Therefore, even an experienced cultivator can easily decide to plant the wrong crop, or plant too closely against the last storm of the season. After a heavy rainfall, particularly one accompanied—as often happens—by high winds, whole fields whose crops have washed away completely or whose foliage is shredded by wind-driven rain are not unusual.

Attempts made by local populations to solve these problems are many, varied, and frequently labor-consuming and ingenious. The artificial construction of level fields (terraces) which are at least potentially irrigable (or which, alternatively, will hold run-off for some time) represents one such attempt, and the steady diffusion of terracing in the southern Cordillera region shows that it offers some advantages. However, terrace construction requires enormous amounts of labor, relative to the amount of land constructed, and is in itself no thoroughgoing solution to local conditions. The long-term effectiveness of terracing is directly related to the nature of the water supply. They may flood and wash out in heavy rains or dry out as the streams which water them diminish, much as unterraced fields do. However, terraces hold moisture better than sloping fields, they tend to preserve soil, and they render watering by hand much more convenient if such drastic means become necessary.

A second common response is to rely on crops which are less sensitive to conditions of temperature, wind, and water. Popularly-grown crops fitting this description include sweet potatoes, yams, maize, and *galyang*, a local variety of taro which is said to be especially drought resistant. However, though "safer" to cultivate, these crops are not in as great demand on the market, so their cultivation is not potentially so profitable. They are "subsistence-oriented" crops. But neither of these attempted solutions reduces risks substantially, and agriculture in the southern Cordillera remains a risky venture, though one which has the potential to provide attractive rewards. Therefore, technological "conservatism" (i.e., the reluctance to convert to cash crops or try new cropping techniques) is as well explained by the ecological problems which local cultivators face, and about which they must make rational decisions, as by attributing to them a mental disposition toward a "fear of the market."

Even a relatively small region in the southern Cordillera is not likely to form an homogeneous ecological zone. Where variation in landform is so dramatic, mineral content, temperature, rainfall, exposure, and drainage—and therefore soils themselves—exhibit a correspondingly wide range of variation. The general configuration, then, is of a large number of varied microenvironments and results in a wide variation in the flora of the region. This flora is a complex mixture of tropical and temperate species, the dominance of one sort over the other correlating closely with exposure, altitude, and the extent of human modifications of the local environment. Thus, for example, at Sablan (located at 2500 feet on the sheltered eastern side of the Cordillera) rainfall averages approximately 85 inches per year and temperatures are 10° warmer than concurrent temperatures at Baguio City, only 20 kilometers away. In this foothill zone natural floral species are still essentially lowland types (hardwoods, bamboo, and other monsoonal forest species), and the principal crops are "dry" hill rice, pineapples, bananas, and other fruits commonly found in the lowlands. But from approximately 4,000 feet and higher virtually all evidence of lowland floral species fades away to pines and fern trees. At these higher elevations wet rices replace the dry varieties, and temperatures are too cool for pineapples, bananas, papayas, etc., to do well. This marked ecological diversity obviously encourages trade.

Despite the wide variety of soils in the southern Cordillera, the local climate has had such a profound impact on their development that a few generalizations can be made about them.

In the first place, they tend to be thin, badly weathered, and "patchy in occurrence" (Wernstedt and Spencer 1967:345). In the wet tropics constant warmth and the presence of surface water in excess of evaporation generally produce a soil maturation process variously termed "laterization" (Dobby 1960:77), "ferralization" (van Riper 1962:414), or the more recent term, "latozation" (Wernstedt and Spencer 1967:66). The end result of this process are "lathosols," soils whose basal colloids have been leached by the warm water (now converted to a weak acid solution) which has percolated through them. Under maximal conditions of "latozation," the resulting soils are brick red (from the high proportion of iron oxides that remain undissolved), structureless, deep, and infertile. Water penetrates them easily, and they dry rapidly, so they have the advantage of being tillable soon after heavy rains, but they are also friable and easily eroded unless well covered by vegetation.

Conditions in the southern Cordillera region are not ideal for the formation of lathosols, because the marked dry season periodically reverses the downward flow of percolating water, and because temperatures are not uniformly high enough to create soil acid solutions of substantial concentration. But in spite of these interruptions in the latozation process, rainfall in the region is so high that many soils are badly enough leached to qualify as lathosols. Examples are the so-called Baguio Clay Loams, which occur in several places in Mountain Province, occasionally in depths up to 30 feet (Barberra 1963:61). Thus although the region's soils are actually only "intermediate lathosols," or *terra rosa* soils, they are generally not of high quality, and they require conditioning and fertilizing to produce qualities desirable for long-term crop production. Furthermore, the costs of maintaining soils in good condition in this region are somewhat higher than in drier temperate zones, for fertilizers and conditioners tend to be rapidly leached away. Unfortunately, lack of adequate treatment has led to widespread erosion throughout the region, though not on such a grand scale as in some lowland areas. In response to these conditions, terracing again appears advantageous, for terraces are a mechanical means of retarding soil loss, and the irrigation water so frequently used upon them is itself a kind of fertilizer.

A final aspect of the southern Cordilleran landscape is its beauty. Only a complete Philistine could fail to be impressed by such mountains, covered with green vegetation and shrouded in rain clouds and wisps of fog.

POPULATIONS

Mountain Province is one of the least developed areas in the modern Philippines, largely because its difficult approaches and broken terrain have historically presented serious communication problems for the Philippines' succession of national governments—the colonial Spanish and United States, and the Philippine Republic. Nevertheless, this region has long supported moderately dense populations, essentially by means of terrace cultivation and intricate irrigation systems. In 1964, the population of the province was 500,000 persons, who collectively represented several ethnolinguistic categories. Roughly three-quarters of Mountain Province's inhabitants are so-called tribal peoples; they are primarily subsistence-oriented cultivators, culturally different from the people dominant in the lowlands. The remaining inhabitants are predominantly Filipinos of lowland origin (Iloco, Pangasinan, and Tagalog speakers, in that order, are the most numerous), although there are also some Chinese, Americans, Europeans, and Indians in the region.

Somewhat different origins, the communications barriers

41

created by mountainous terrain, and local responses to different environmental conditions have tended to separate the province into a number of areas of aboriginal culture (cf. Dozier 1961, Keesing 1962, Eggan 1963). Because of much social and cultural exchange between these units, none of them stands in splendid isolation. The old administrative boundaries of the subprovinces reflect the most common way of classifying the ethnolinguistic diversity of indigenous upland peoples. The subprovinces of Apayao, Kalinga, Bontoc, and Ifugao were named after the dominant ethnolinguistic group of each region, and Benguet was a place name. The indigenous populations of Benguet are known ethnically as Kankanai and Naibaloi, and are approximately equal in numbers.

Until 1959 Mountain Province was officially a "special" province: its provincial officials were not elected, but appointed by the central government. Since 1959 the inhabitants of the province have, at least in legal terms, full political rights as Philippine citizens. At present, the inhabitants elect their own governor and local officials and participate actively in national elections.

The old subprovincial divisions suggest a kind of unity among tribal peoples which does not, in fact, exist. As is often the case with tribal peoples, no pan-tribal political organization welds all the Kalinga or Ifugao into a single political unit, and considerable cultural diversity exists within each region as one proceeds from place to place. The province's overall ethnic configuration, therefore, is not one of a few large ethnolinguistic groupings, each internally homogenous but different from all others. Rather, it is a sociocultural continuum of locally oriented peoples (Eggan 1960:25). Yet considerable sociocultural diversity exists among the province's peoples, and when persons from different places meet in the marketplace, they often meet as strangers with different sociocultural backgrounds.

The categories employed by the Philippine Bureau of Census and Statistics for reporting census figures render it difficult to obtain precise figures on ethnolinguistic groups, but a population of 180,000 seems a reasonable estimate for the old Benguet subprovince in the 1960 census. Even so, census figures are reported for municipalities, not ethnolinguistic groups, and few communities are ethnically pure. It appears, however, that in 1964 there were, in the old Benguet subprovince, 40,000 native speakers of Kankanai (concentrated in the municipalities of Bakun, Bugias, Kibungan, Mankayan, and part of Kapangan), and 55,000 Naibaloi speakers (the municipalities of Atok, Bokod, Itogon, Kabayan, La Trinidad, Sablan, Tuba, Tublay, a portion of Kapangan, and perhaps 3,000 in Baguio). There were also 2,000 Chinese, 700 Americans and Europeans (largely associated with mines), and the rest mostly Filipinos of lowland origin.

Although Ilocanos dominate the lowland Filipino population statistically, the local population of lowlanders also includes substantial representation from Pangasinan, Pampanga, and the Tagalog-speaking provinces. The category "Chinese" also includes speakers of different dialects, and both Cantonese and Hokkien are spoken locally. Except on issues in which the welfare of the entire Chinese community is at stake, the two tend to go separate ways. Each ethnolinguistic category has its preferred restaurants and places of entertainment, and as much as possible they live in separate residential areas. In effect, then, larger towns are divided into territories as much as the countryside is divided into circles of influence falling under the sway of particular tribal communities (cf. Dozier 1967). During elections, tensions between these groupings can run high, because politicians often exploit differences in order to align ethnic units into voting blocs.

Because Filipinos of lowland origin are numerically dominant in the larger settlements, they also tend to be politically dominant, for to control the towns is to control wealth and power. Lowland Filipinos are generally, therefore, more wealthy and, through their greater abundance of means, better educated, more sophisticated in political and legal matters, and better connected to higher-level officials, including those of the central government. This tendency is especially notable in Baguio City, for in Baguio the lowlanders vastly outnumber the natives and occupy nearly all municipal offices.

SUBSISTENCE AND COMMERCE

The principal means of subsistence among indigenous peoples in the southern Cordillera traditionally has been the cultivation of root crops by means of a swidden (shifting cultivation) technology. Wet rice, grown in terraced hillside fields, has made steady inroads on swidden regimes since its introduction, and appears to be increasing rapidly in popularity. The degree of elaboration of the cultural practices involved makes it appear that this innovation was introduced in the southwestern Ifugao area (Scott 1958), but how long ago is difficult to say because of a complete absence of good archaeological data. Beyer (1953), basing his figure on an estimate of the length of time needed to construct the massive Ifugao terrace system, suggested the first terraces were constructed there 3,000 years ago. However, Scott (1958) has not found this line of reasoning convincing, and Keesing (1962) suggested that the terraces might be of recent origin. At present, the construction of rice terraces is spreading north more deeply into Kalinga and Apayao regions and further south in the old Benguet region (Scott 1958, Keesing 1962, Eggan 1963). Most of the southerly terracing was constructed in the nineteenth and twentieth centuries. At the moment, however, the Benguet area continues to lead all other Mountain Province regions in the production of root crops and in swidden acreage.

Recently, scholars interested in swidden cultivation technology have shown, counter to earlier arguments, that under proper conditions swidden can be a stable and productive system (e.g., Conklin 1954, Freeman 1955, Geertz 1964), and further, that it is a technique well suited to capital-short conditions. Although additional inputs can be used productively, swidden regimes can be productive with little capital outlay and with only small inputs of labor relative to outputs. If efficiency is measured in terms of the ratio between labor inputs and yields, rather than in terms of gross production per land unit, swidden often is a remarkably efficient cultivation system, ingeniously adapted to low-energy technologies in forested regions.

However the critical factor determining the long-term utility and stability of swidden regimes is a population to land ratio adequate to assure a fallow period sufficient to permit the reconstitution of woody plant species in forest growth. As Geertz (1964) so pithily puts the issue, swidden cultivation amounts to cultivating ashes, for the ash cover resulting from burning the cut-over brush provides the nutrients necessary for the successful cropping of the cleared fields. Therefore, once land has been cropped, its fertility decays progressively as the growing food plants utilize these nutrients. Eventually, fertility reaches a point at which returns have been diminished to a degree that renders further cultivation unrewarding, or at which a grass-weed succession becomes unmanageable. At this point, or preferably sooner, the cultivator allows the field to return to forest. When second growth contains a sufficient number of woody plants, the field may again be burned and cropped; but depending upon local conditions of climate and soil, this period of fallowing may require ten years or more before the quantity of woody plants is again adequate to warrant beginning the cycle anew. Obviously, any circumstance which reduces the amount of land available per capita may force cultivators to crop lands too frequently for proper restoration of the forest cover, and therefore to produce a condition of progressive energy loss in the ecosystem.

The southern Cordilleran region is not ideal for the practice of swidden cultivation, and this technique's historical success in the area is undoubtedly attributable to a sparse population relative to the amount of available land. In terms of natural "constraints," the temperature configuration of these highlands does not lead to rapid recovery of second growth. But human intervention factors are even more significant and have progressively reduced the amount of land available for cultivation while at the same time increasing the size of local populations. Immigration, too-frequent burning, lumbering, and mining have all been influential in reducing population-land ratios to levels which, from the perspective of swidden cultivators, are undesirable. At present, in areas near Baguio City and La Trinidad, the period that swidden fields are under intensive cultivation is actually longer than the period during which they are fallowed, thereby reversing the usual relationship between fallow and cultivation in swidden regimes. Gathering plant material (or alternatively rice husks), carrying it to the cultivated fields, burning it, and scattering the ashes compensate in part for the resulting energy loss. This is not, however, a satisfactory adjustment, and the cultivators are well aware that shortened fallow periods are resulting in continuing decrease in yields. Yet no matter how bleak the future of swidden regimes may be in this region, swidden continues to be an important means of subsistence and even commercial production, and swidden fires may be seen somewhere in the distance on virtually any dry day.

The second common mode of subsistence cultivation in the southern Cordillera, irrigated terraces, is much more satisfactory than swidden where population pressure is heavy, for terraces offer the advantage of maintaining fields in permanent production. The liabilities of terrace production are the need for dependable sources of water and for the heavy inputs of labor required to construct relatively small tillable fields. Furthermore, although irrigated terraces will continue to provide some yield almost indefinitely even without the addition of fertilizer, yields on unfertilized terraces are low. According to local agricultural specialists at the La Trinidad Agricultural College, rice yields on local terrace fields have consistently been well under the national average for lowland rice. In brief, the terrace technology of the southern Cordillera is an advance over swidden because it is not so vulnerable to increased population densities, but subsistence production on terraces is less than ideal for a rapidly growing population.

COMMERCIAL INNOVATION IN AGRICULTURE

For at least some of the residents of the southern Cordillera, a new agricultural alternative has been presented: the cultivation of mid-latitude vegetables. These crops, with additional costs and modification of cultural practices involved, can be incorporated into either of the traditional subsistence cultivation technologies. Moreover, these crops have the potential greatly to increase income from local agriculture, for they lend themselves well to the kind of intensive cultivation which can yield high returns from relatively small fields.

Although soils of the Cordilleran region are generally of poor quality in both structure and nutritive content, the valley of the La Trinidad River stands out as an important exception. The Trinidad Valley is a high (4,800 feet) alluvial valley approximately five miles north of Baguio City on the Halsema Road (the "Mountain Trail," see Map 2). The valley itself is small, measuring approximately two by four miles, but it has played a significant historical role in bringing commercially-oriented agriculture to the southern Cordillera Central. Fertile alluvial soils, a temperate climate, and the development of a transport and communication system linking the area to markets have encouraged the development of a commercial agricultural complex which produces market-garden vegetables of a type not grown in large quantities elsewhere in the Philippines. Mid-latitude imports such as head cabbage, pechay, onions, celery, radishes, cauliflower, Irish potatoes, carrots, strawberries, tomatoes, and Kentucky Wonder beans, as well as a large variety of crops of more local origin, are produced here and marketed locally, in the adjacent lowlands, and in Manila.

The pattern of market-garden cultivation which began in the Trinidad region has become much more widely dispersed. In the years since its introduction, many persons who are primarily subsistence cultivators have adopted market-gardening as part of the yearly crop cycle wherever natural and social conditions are favorable. In the Trinidad Valley conditions are most fortuitous, and as one moves in any direction from that area, one encounters progressive production or marketing difficulties. However, though hard figures are not available, the total quantity of market vegetables grown by scattered cultivators outside the valley proper seems many times the production of the valley itself.

The introduction of mid-latitude vegetable gardening was closely linked to the construction of the main artery which connects the southern Cordilleran highlands to Pangasinan, the Kennon Road (1903). Early in the American colonial regime

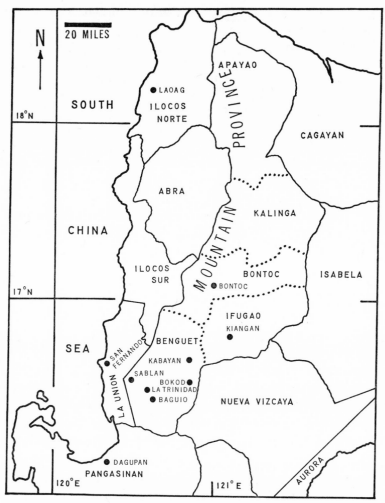

MAP 2: Northwest Luzon

(when it was thought not only fashionable, but necessary, for Westerners in the tropics periodically to retreat to hill stations to protect their health), Baguio City was constructed to serve as a summer capital. The Kennon Road, which is narrow and sinuous, was built to connect the summer capital to Manila via

49

the major road system, which at that time terminated in Pangasinan Province.

Because local indigenous inhabitants were not interested in working for wages, extensive use was made of Japanese labor in this construction. As the story is now told by elderly informants, these men (many of them having agricultural backgrounds) were quick to appreciate the region's agricultural potential, and some of them returned after completion of the construction to become agricultural entrepreneurs (often acquiring land through marriage to local women). Thus, construction of the Kennon Road provided both the necessary technical information and access to markets which made mid-latitude cash crops a real economic alternative. Several informants insisted that vegetable gardens had appeared in La Trinidad by at least 1910, and agreed that such produce was being offered for sale in Baguio City at approximately the same time.

Until the end of World War II market-gardening remained small in scale and dominated by Japanese immigrants. During this period the demand for mid-latitude vegetables in the Philippines was also modest, for produce of this type was not typically a part of daily Filipino diets, and sales were largely limited to foreign—particularly American—elements.

Shortly after World War II, however, a series of events encouraged expansion of market-garden production and participation of native Benguet peoples in that production. First, the Filipino demand for vegetables increased remarkably, partly because of increasing urbanization, but especially because of the growth of the cosmopolitan industrial and commercial area of Greater Manila. Interpretation of figures provided in the 1960 Census indicates that this region had increased in population 8.5 percent since the 1948 Census, while the population of the nation at large increased only 3.2 percent. As Wernstedt and Spencer assume (1967:203), increasing urbanization and the greater levels of educational attainment which accompany it, seem to have resulted in new dietary standards favoring vegetable consumption.

Also important here was the replacement in agricultural entrepreneurial roles of the Japanese by Chinese immigrants. During their military occupation of the Philippines, the Japanese made themselves unpopular, and as a result local Japanese farmers were obliged to leave the Philippines after the defeat of the Japanese military. Chinese (who had hidden from the Japanese by retreating to the mountains, where they lived among native Benguet peoples) then assumed the managerial functions of the larger-scale production and trade operations. This was an important change, for the Chinese increased the scale of operations and hired local tribal peoples for labor, thereby providing them with an opportunity to learn the appropriate technical skills.[1] However, law now forbids ownership of land to noncitizen Chinese, and they have had to look elsewhere to find land to rent or become silent (but domineering) partners with some Philippine citizen in whose name the land is registered.

In spite of prejudicial legislation, the Chinese have not been excluded entirely from the vegetable trade. Chinese who rent

[1] The significance to agricultural innovation of the opportunity to learn technical skills can be demonstrated here by a brief comparison between Bokod and Kabayan, two municipalities near Baguio City, the region's principal market town. Bokod is 30 kilometers closer to the principal market for market-garden produce than Kabayan; yet no market-gardening is done at Bokod, although it is a principal agricultural activity at Kabayan. Because climates, soils, and water sources are essentially similar, the lack of vegetable production at Bokod seems strange indeed. As I interpret these conditions, the explanation is that Kabayan is within walking distance of Chinese holdings where Kabayanos have long worked as laborers. Bokod's inhabitants, however, have not had the same opportunity to learn skills under someone else's supervision, with the latter assuming the financial risks involved.

their land, manage some of the largest operations in the Trinidad Valley, and the largest holdings along the Halsema Road north of La Trinidad are Chinese-operated leaseholds. The vegetable growers' association in this area is an exclusively Chinese cooperative, said to be coordinated by the Chinese Chamber of Commerce in Baguio City.

The Chinese holdings along the Halsema Road show a pattern familiar in Southeast Asia: the Chinese is the entrepreneur who does not, himself, cultivate, preferring instead to hire cheap local labor. Furthermore, these holdings are larger and more heavily capitalized than any of the holdings operated by indigenous peoples. Little of the produce from Chinese holdings is sold in the local markets, and the vegetable growers' cooperative, which owns its own motorized transport for that purpose, markets its produce in Manila. Yet members of the Chinese vegetable growers' cooperative maintain that they realize no financial gain from their operations. Rather, they insist, they provide capital and managerial talent to native owners out of gratitude for the protection the latter provided them during the dark days of the Japanese occupation. Native peoples claim that Chinese control the vegetable trade with Manila entirely and that a non-Chinese local can market his produce in Manila only by selling it wholesale to a Chinese middleman —at the latter's price. Natives also insist that during the early 1950s the Chinese "destroyed" an attempt by local people to form a government-sponsored Farmer's Cooperative Marketing Association (FACOMA). They say the Chinese undersold native produce at a loss until the FACOMA project was bankrupted and had to sell its capital equipment to pay back wages.

Besides trading their own produce, then, the Chinese are active in the first-stage bulking of much native-grown produce, and in the final stages of wholesaling certain categories of capital goods, such as fertilizer, seed, plant cuttings, and insecticides. However one interprets Chinese economic activities, as a blight or a boon, increased demand for vegetables, the displacement of Japanese gardeners, and anti-Chinese legislation together provided the peoples of the southern Cordilleran highlands with a realistic opportunity to produce a cash crop.

At present the technology involved in local market gardening incorporates plants and cultural techniques from several sources: traditional highland techniques, and those borrowed from lowland Filipinos, Japanese, Chinese, and Americans—all have been modified to suit local conditions of climate and relative availability of labor and capital. Considerable interest is expressed in the most modern techniques of cultivation, and literature published by the United States Department of Agriculture is surprisingly widely read, particularly in La Trinidad. But even in the *avant garde* Trinidad Valley, the lack of machine use, the replacement of capital by hand labor, the practice of watering plants by hand from buckets carried on a shoulder pole, the raised crop beds separated by deep drains, the seasonal overlapping of crop beds, and the use of decayed organic matter for fertilizer are collectively reminiscent of Chinese gardening techniques. Such borrowing is hardly surprising, for Chinese gardeners have been successful as local entrepreneurs and therefore are effective role models. Furthermore, with its emphasis on substituting labor for capital, Chinese garden technology is especially adaptable to local conditions of cheap labor and high capital costs. At least for the moment, the American pattern of intensive capital commitment to "neotechnics" (Wolf 1965:35–36)—such things as chemical fertilizers, carefully selected plant varieties, and high energy power sources—is much less practicable for the local farmer.

The increasing unavailability of land pushes the native peoples of the southern Cordillera to adopt cultivation techniques which have higher returns per land unit, and the increasing desire to obtain a wider range of capital and consumers' goods pulls them toward comitting resources to the cultivation of cash crops. The changing nature of consumption patterns is related to the increasing level of literacy, which for the 1960 Census was 52.5 percent of the province as a whole,[2] and to the general "demonstration effects" of modern mass media.

The income necessary to satisfy desires for manufactured goods does not, obviously, have to result from the cultivation of cash crops. Wage labor is an alternate possibility, but in practice it meets immediately with some limitations. In the first place, agricultural labor in Mountain Province generally is poorly paid. The going daily wage in 1964 was two pesos (approximately $.53 US) plus a meal, or a package of locally manufactured cigarettes. On the other hand, the prices of manufactured goods are high relative to American wage-price ratios.

Employment in one of the region's major industries is another possibility, but Filipinos of lowland origin hold nearly all the better paying jobs, with the result that native peoples obtain only lowly paid or seasonal employment. There is, in fact, considerable discrimination in hiring natives even for government jobs. They may, for example, work for one of the local branches of governmental institutions, but they do so in menial capacities. The economically-depressed status of ethnic minorities is a situation familiar to any American reader.

A shift to wet terrace cultivation of rice is an alternative to the decay of swidden regimes resulting from land pressure, and as such is another alternative to growing market crops. However, if one wants additional income, then, all things be-

[2] The presence of so many lowland Filipinos almost certainly inflates this figure, and in some of the rural municipalities of Benguet literacy figures were as low as 20 percent in 1960.

ing equal, there is little comparison between growing wet rice and market-gardening. To compare the income-producing qualities of these two crops precisely is difficult, especially where vegetables are grown only as adjunct crops. Informants estimate that the maximum income one may realize from a single crop of wet rice (few areas will produce a second crop of rice in a given year) on a hectare of land is approximately 800 pesos gross. By comparison, it was estimated that a hectare of irrigated land planted in market vegetables may gross 4,000 pesos, less than half of which would be deferred in production costs. Thus market-gardening seems to be the best income-producing strategy available to local agriculturalists. Unfortunately, market-gardening also involves greater risks, so income is not the only consideration. To cultivate subsistence crops is sometimes safer, particularly when knowledge of the market, and access to it, are poor, or when prices are rising on items which the cultivator would have to purchase if he committed his resources to commercial production.

From this perspective, transportation emerges as a significant element to any cultivator contemplating conversion to market crops. The issue is two-sided. To be able to move vegetables to market quickly is important. Proper handling of most vegetables requires that they be held in the ground until dead ripe, then marketed rapidly before they lose food value and attractive appearance. With few exceptions (e.g., radishes and potatoes), vegetables cannot be stored without impairing their market qualities. And once the cultivator is committed to market vegetable production, reliable access to a market from which subsistence items may be purchased is equally important to him. One cannot subsist upon cabbage or strawberries as upon rice, sweet potatoes, and taro. Thus, in converting to commercial production, the cultivator makes himself dependent upon other producers.

At the time this study was initiated, little specialized transport was available to native producers at costs which they could afford. The Philippine government has little capital to invest in transport systems, and mountain geomorphology presents problems which raise the costs of building roads, especially soil slippage and rock falls along block shoulders (Wernstedt and Spencer 1967:344). Road-building has thus proceeded slowly, and most existing roads still will not support heavily-loaded truck traffic. Local mountain roads are nearly all impassable at various times during the year, especially during the rainy season—unfortunately vegetables are most likely to be brittle and to spoil rapidly during the rainy season, thereby requiring special care in handling and speedy transport to consumers. Most of the vegetables grown in the outlying areas are transported to town in woven bamboo baskets which are lashed to the tops of passenger buses, the latter serving the region as all-purpose vehicles. Moreover, moving vegetables to market often requires the cultivator and his family to carry their vegetables to distant roads where motor transport is available. Because the baskets in which vegetables are packed usually weigh up to 55 kilograms, the willingness of native cultivators to undertake such heavy labor is an indication of powerful commitment to the cultivation of cash crops.

Other factors influencing productive decisions are labor and capital, for unlike traditional crops and cropping techniques, market-gardening requires at least a moderate investment of capital and a heavy investment of labor. Swidden cultivation involves little capital input and can be conducted without heavy labor inputs. Because of these characteristics market vegetables may be grown profitably as a short-term venture in swidden regimes, provided they are planted immediately after the end of the rainy season, when adequate moisture remains. In this latter case short-run profits may be high, for fixed costs and production costs are low. But in the long run, vegetables grown in swiddens deplete the soils, so eventually the swidden cultivator will face the production costs involved in cropping permanent fields, unless the cultivator has access to unusually large quantities of land. Moreover, an additional long-range disadvantage to planting commercial crops in swidden fields is that the cultivator is encouraged to clear and crop more land than he would if merely seeking to support his family, thereby increasing the land shortage. Similarly, market-gardening involves greater investment of labor and capital than does the cultivation of rice on irrigated terraces, at least as the latter is practiced in this region.[3]

THE REQUIREMENTS OF MARKET-GARDEN REGIMES

In direct contrast to the cultivation of traditional crops, cultivators reported that the cultivation of mid-latitude vegetables requires the investment of more labor than the average household can mobilize. In the first place, there are additional watering-labor costs. Vegetables require more precise water control than rice does, for innundation, as rice typically is watered, causes their roots to rot. According to the local ideal, vegetables should be watered, then drained, twice each day. Without constant moisture their growth cycle is interrupted, and they

---

[3] Considerable labor is initially required to construct terraces, but from that point labor demands are light as long as terraces are planted in rice (running approximately 180 man days per year per hectare). Cooperative labor groups (*aduyon*) are often employed in the cultivation and harvesting of terrace rice, but this relates to cultural patterns and not to the work requirements of the technical system. It is believed that the spirit of the rice may escape once harvest is begun if the field is not entirely harvested as soon as possible, and therefore labor pools are desirable. They are also more fun, particularly when they have a heterosexual composition.

57

become tough and fibrous, but they will not tolerate constant flooding. Depending on seasonal costs and prices, and local conditions of water availability, plants may be watered by hand, thus vastly increasing the amount of labor involved in their cultivation.

Second, there are weeding costs, also related to the fact that vegetables require free oxygen and cannot be flooded. The water which covers rice plants in terraces also tends to retard the growth of many common species of weeds. In the case of vegetables the situation is nearly reversed: the constant watering, then draining, of the vegetable field encourages the growth of weeds as it does the growth of vegetables, and weeds must be removed by pulling or hoeing.

Third are additional harvesting costs. Vegetables brought to peak ripeness in the field must be harvested quickly (usually requiring group labor), and then sorted, cleaned, packed, and often carried to a point at which they may be loaded on a rural bus.

With market-gardening labor often accepts only money in payment. Because the cultivator's enterprise is cash-oriented, there is less possibility of obtaining labor through reciprocal labor exchange or by paying for it in kind, as is more customary when the crop is rice. Since the market-garden cultivator's goal is cash income, the laborer feels it is fair to ask for the same thing. For a native entrepreneur to obtain cash for the payment of wages is often difficult, but this inconvenience is counterbalanced by an advantage: hiring persons for wages allows the operator selectively to hire persons who have the necessary knowledge and skills for the tasks at hand. Laborers are not interchangeable where market vegetables are concerned, and hired labor is more efficient than labor obtained through labor exchange.

Informants conceptually distinguish subsistence-oriented

activities from commercially-oriented activities as different spheres of economic action. However, it is evident that self-interest and gain-oriented bargaining occur in each sphere. The difference between them is that different units of measurement are employed—goods-in-kind versus money. Labor may, in traditional practice, be hired for wages-in-kind where subsistence activities are involved, but variations in those wages occur. And each operator must specify ahead of time what he intends to pay, reckoned in bundles of rice, meals, condiments, cigarettes, rice wine, or beer. Furthermore, laborers pick and choose among the various opportunities presented to them just as modern wage laborers do in the United States.

But to return to costs, vegetables require fertilizer and insecticides, unlike rice. Flooding fields of rice tends to fertilize them through the deposits of silt and organic matter in the water and to keep away pests, so additional fertilizer and insecticides are not absolutely necessary for satisfactory yields. Once fields are no longer flooded, however, both must be applied. Fertilizer is a relatively great additional expense. Philippine-produced fertilizers are the cheapest but unfortunately have the reputation of being adulterated. Japanese fertilizers are more popular, but also more expensive.

One does not, therefore, taken up the production of market crops without encountering a need for capital far in excess of the requirements for any of the traditional crops. Unfortunately, capital is in short supply in the rural Philippines. Incomes are generally low, averaging approximately a thousand pesos (about $265 US) per year per rural family in 1960 (1960 Census). As a consequence, capital is not only scarce, but draws a high rate of interest. The legal rate of interest is 12 percent per year, but there is such a demand for capital (for both commercial and noncommercial purposes) that it is extremely difficult to enforce the legal limitation. Lending money (or other forms of capital) at high rates of interest is a thriving and not-too-disreputable activity in the Philippines, even among the mountain peoples. Literature on the Philippines contains many examples of loans of money or goods being made at 50, 100, or even 200 percent interest.

Rural banks have been established in the Philippines, and Philippine administrations have made many serious efforts to put reasonably-priced capital into farmers' hands. But bank reserves in a poor nation are necessarily small, and the practice of using bank credit programs for political purposes, about which Filipinos complain greatly, compounds the problem. Banks also must require security for loans, and in this region few rural people have property which can be used as collateral. Land, the form of potential collateral which comes first to mind in an agrarian society, rarely meets qualification criteria established by banks, because few cultivators have legal title to their holdings. Among the indigenous peoples there are few encumberances on the sale of land, and it may be transferred freely. But the typical land sale is not officially recorded, for to the rural community a transfer of title is legal and binding as long as it has been witnessed by a few of the community's wealthy and prestigous persons (*baknang*). Happily, the lack of land titles has not led, in Mountain Province, to land-grabbing by outsiders, common in many other ethnic areas of the Philippines, possibly as the result of the Mountain Province peoples' reputation for defending their territories tenaciously.

Local moneylenders are another potential source of capital. In local mountain tribal communities this usually means borrowing from a *baknang*, through a transaction known as a *salda*, or land mortgage. A *salda* is somewhat different from the mortgage loans made by Western banks, for the land is more deeply indemnified than is usual in Western societies. In a *salda* loan the debtor must not only repay the principal, but also relinquishes rights to the products of the land to the creditor while the debt is outstanding. The debtor is therefore likely to lose the land, and in the lowlands similar kinds of mortgage arrangements are a major cause of the rising rate of landlessness and share tenancy (e.g., Arnaldo 1955, Hart 1955b, Golay 1956, Wurfel 1958, Anderson 1962). Apparently this has not been a serious problem among the indigenous populations of the southern Cordillera, for the plots of land indemnified are usually small, and there appears to be no time limitation on the subsequent removal of the obligation. All that one requires to regain his *salda* land is the necessary payment, plus the testimony of a person who witnessed the original loan. In the larger settlements, anyone with a little cash on hand is a potential moneylender.

In general the rates of interest at which capital is borrowed are higher than the return one might reasonably anticipate from any legitimate commercial venture the loan might allow one to undertake. Loans, therefore, are much more likely to be obtained for noncommercial, critical events in the debtor's life—a funeral or a wedding, for example. Sources of commercial capital are scarce and tend to be limited to one's relatives. This fact has profound consequences for the local economy and commercial relationships, as we shall see.

BAGUIO CITY

Baguio City, with a 1960[4] population of 50,000 persons, is by far the largest urban area in Mountain Province. In terms of

---

[4] The 1960 census figures are employed throughout the essay unless otherwise indicated. The data in this essay were collected in 1963 and 1964, and I have assumed that the 1960 figures are more representative for the period of time dealt with than the 1970 figures would be.

the size of its urban area, however, this gross figure is misleading. In the Philippines *municipios* are like counties in the United States; each contains a principal urban settlement (the *poblacion* in the Philippines) and a substantial adjacent area which may contain some smaller settlements as well as open countryside. Baguio is a chartered city, different from most other municipalities because of its higher-order political relationships. But because the local tax base and the return of national taxes to the local municipality are both directly linked to population size, it is common in the Philippines to draw city boundaries as broadly as possible. In Baguio only 27,000 persons actually lived in the *poblacion*—the remainder lived in outlying rural areas. In fact, many residents of the city of Baguio are farmers living on their fields. Baguio is several times larger than the second largest community in the province, Itogon, which had a *poblacion* population of 7,400 in 1960 (and which is also in a Naibaloi area).

Baguio City was originally founded as a summer capital for the national administration. Over the years this historical role has been expanded, and many national governmental agencies have established regional offices in Baguio. In 1964, in addition to the public buildings of the summer capital complex itself, there were thirty-seven other national administrative and judicial departments and bureaus represented, as opposed to only twelve such offices for city administration.

However, in the intervening years the city's social functions have increased far beyond those deliberately intended by its creators. As in the fortress and monastery settlements of medieval Europe, the presence of a population center with relatively great powers of consumption has stimulated trade, specialization, and further settlement. For the Philippines (except for a few lowland urban areas), the presence of so many persons who receive regular salaries and wages is unusual and has encouraged merchants to provide a variety of goods and services not usually encountered in Philippine communities of such small size. In commercial terms, Baguio is one of the most progressive communities in the nation, although the commercial district is small in comparison to that typical of an American town of equal population.

Furthermore, the town's own powers of consumption are periodically augmented by the fact that as a hill station—and one which is accessible from the largest urban area in the nation, Manila—it is a popular resort area. Several thousand tourists visit the city each year, with peak seasons occurring during the "dry" months of April and May, and at Christmas. But the owners of the more substantial restaurants, grocery stores, hotels, shops, and motion picture theatres benefit most from tourism, not the petty merchants of the public marketplace.

Because the farmers of Mountain Province produce relatively small quantities of some staples for purchase by city populations, demand exists for the importation of basic foodstuffs from other regions. Thus, substantial quantities of products like rice, fish, cattle, pigs, fowl, processed foods, and lowland fruits must be brought into the Baguio area. The region's relative wealth also produces a demand for manufactured consumers' goods and building materials of kinds not usually demanded in quantities by Philippine towns. The demand for these products, together with the desire to market local produce, produces a need for an extensive distributional system, and this in turn provides opportunities for individuals to make profits.

Baguio City, therefore, fulfills both of the principal functions of a market: it is a center of demand for goods and services produced in other regions and a source of supply for those regions. Its financial institutions, loading and storage facilities, and access to the main system of transport and communication in the adjacent lowlands have combined to establish Baguio as an important center for breaking bulk for distribution to other mountain communities and for collecting mountain products for export to the lowlands. The bus terminals in Baguio City are as conspicuous for the boxes, baskets, crates—and even trussed, live animals—stacked about waiting shipment as they are for their small clusters of human passengers.

Unlike the majority of Philippine provincial towns, which tend to exhibit strong Spanish influence, Baguio City is not constructed around a town square, or *plaza*, which contains all important public buildings (cf. Hart 1955a). It reflects the stronger influence of American planning, and buildings are distributed in a much more random fashion.

The principal section of the town's commercial district is along two main streets which intersect to form a "T." Session Road runs approximately east and west, and is the town's "Main Street." Trinidad Road (which becomes the Halsema Road, or the Mountain Trail, north of La Trinidad) runs roughly north and south (see Map 3). The city hall, which in most Philippine towns is squarely on the plaza, is several hundred feet away from the intersection of these two roads, around the corner to the northwest.

Session Road is lined by the town's more substantial enterprises: Chinese restaurants, Chinese bakeries, some Chinese and Filipino hardware stores, three motion picture theatres (which usually show American movies), and two Philippine-Indian clothing and dry-goods stores. On the south side of Trinidad Road stand several Chinese grocery stores and a few poorer-quality, open-fronted Chinese restaurants. On the north side of Trinidad Road, against a steep hill which seems to stand as an obstacle to further expansion, is the Baguio City Public Market.

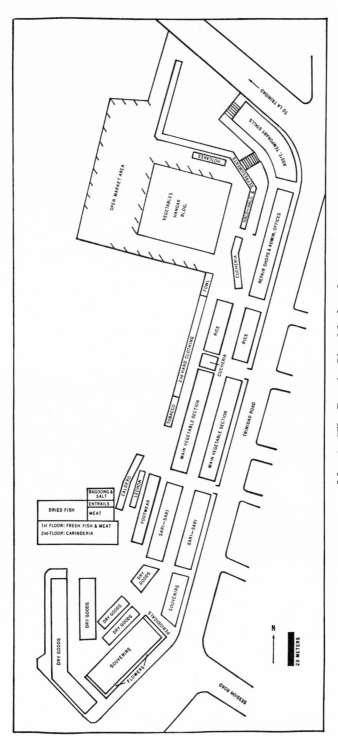

MAP 3: The Baguio City Marketplace

Chapter Three

The Marketplace

MARKETPLACE ECONOMIES

Anthropology has long recognized that in most of the
contemporary nonindustrialized nations of the world
sharp social and cultural differences distinguish elite
and lower-class elements. Elites are essentially urban in orientation; they are better educated and more sophisticated generally
than their lower-class countrymen. They tend to have a near-
monopoly on political power and to draw the bulk of their
income from the nation's extractive, export economy. Furthermore, they are likely to participate in a national, or even international, literate culture. The lower-class segments differ
so much from the elite that they are often thought of as polar
extremes: for example, the "great" and "little" traditions proposed by Professor Redfield (Redfield 1956). The lower-class
elements tend to be rural and agrarian, and to subsist by producing staples for domestic consumption or sale. They are
much less likely to be educated, they tend toward supernatural

66

interpretations of causality, and they are inclined to participate in locally distinctive "traditional" cultures.[1] They generally lack adequate political power to make their own wishes felt at the national level, and some of the most basic decisions—especially production decisions—are made for them by higher levels of authority. Above all, they are poor.

As a result, the lower-class elements are often dependent on the elite and must accomodate themselves to elite cultural and legal domination and economic exploitation. The basic condition in such societies is strongly developed social stratification, and a number of important consequences follow from that fact.

Although the distinction of elites and lower-class elements is commonly made, contemporary agrarian states are complex and may include a number of different lower-class segments. If the local community is not only rural but essentially politically and economically autonomous, the tendency is to refer to it as a tribal unit. If it is linked inextricably to the nation state, it is likely to be classified as peasant (cf. Foster 1967). If the discussion turns to peoples who are similar to peasants culturally, but who constitute the lower class in an urban area or who are plantation workers, they may be classed as a rural proletariat (Mintz 1953).

In nonindustrial societies, a fundamental economic division parallels the basic political divisions of society. In such societies the condition which Boeke (1953) has perhaps overstated as the "dual society, dual economy" condition is common: a capital-intensive economic sector which is essentially international and expansive in outlook exists alongside a small-scale,

[1] If pressed the problem of distinguishing cultural models becomes very complex. Barbara Ward (1965), for example, notes that Chinese peasants distinguish several levels of "conscious" models, toward which behavior is oriented selectively.

labor-intensive economic sector in which the orientation is essentially local and conservative (cf. Higgins 1957, Nash 1964b). A similar, less rigidly drawn distinction appears in Foster's (1948) study of Mexican town communities, in which he notes the existence of "an economy within an economy," a "folk economy" which correlates with a "folk culture" (1948:154). Likewise, Malinowski and de la Fuente (1957) see the commercial shop and the petty vendor existing side by side in Mexico and explain that both remain viable in the same economy because each appeals to a different sector of the market. This allows the "inefficient," small-scale economic sector to persist in the face of what appears to be strong competition from a more efficient economy of scale.

While the labor-intensive economy of the folk sector typically involves transactions of small scale, it is by no means organizationally simple or confined to a single community. It commonly involves a complex framework of economic roles and connects a number of communities or regions. Above all, the institution which symbolizes the folk sector of agrarian states is the marketplace, the site at which persons in any locale may gather at regularly scheduled times to exchange goods and services. The central position of selling sites in the distributional network of such economies does not imply, as Benet (1957) suggested, that "bargained exchange" is limited to such sites. Indeed, bargained exchange is widespread among the tribal peoples of the northern Philippines. The significance of selling sites results from the weak development of supply-and-demand centers in traditional agrarian economies, and the obvious convenience provided when small-scale participants may meet in specified locations where opportunities for exchange are optimized.

Discussion of marketplace economies almost invariably relates them to "peasant" social sectors, and any small-scale

marketing is apt to be termed "peasant marketing" in the literature. However, any attempt to relate marketplaces to particular
social typologies faces some serious difficulties. For example,
although we often think of tribal societies as being autonomous,
in Southeast Asia groups commonly thought of as "hill tribes"
have for centuries maintained systematic, gain-oriented trade
relationships with urban centers and markets (cf. Leach 1954,
Kunstadter 1967). On the other hand, Alice Dewey (1962a)
discusses "peasant marketing" in Java, although most of the
persons involved appear to be townspeople who are professional middlemen and not rural producers.

Although one may question the theoretical significance of
rigorous distinctions between "primitive" and "peasant" societies, perhaps the critical economic difference is one of dependence. Peasants may be conceived as peoples who, like tribes-
men, are essentially concerned with subsistence production,
but, unlike the latter, peasants are *necessarily* dependent upon
the market as a source of cash or for manufactures which they
cannot produce for themselves. This emphasis on the peasant's
inability to avoid the market contrasts with the popular suggestion that peasants market their "surpluses." Peasants are
obliged to sell to the market as the result of pressures rising
from the socioeconomic system of which they are part. Factors
involved include the lack of storage facilities, the need for cash
to pay land rent or taxes (Wolf 1965:9–10), indebtedness to
merchants and elites, or the need to meet ceremonial obligations. Thus, aside from a desire for gain or the calculation that
production exceeds domestic requirements, forces exist which
induce peasants to participate in markets. If we define "peasants" in terms of these political and economic criteria, few of
the marketplace systems described in the literature approach a
pure peasant type.

Several anthropologists recently have attempted to isolate

the diagnostic sociological features of marketplace economies. Mintz, who has probably done more work on such systems than any other anthropologist, refers to them as "internal market systems" (Mintz 1959). He notes that in the contemporary world even these small-scale markets are monetized, a feature which permits much more generalized exchange. Exchange takes place both between groups of the same status ("horizontal exchange") and between those of different status ("vertical exchange"), so internal markets can be thought of as "mechanisms of social articulation." However, the vertical flow is not a balanced one, for relatively few imports pass down the exchange ladder, and the flow of goods (particularly staples) is much heavier in the upward direction as peasant producers provide for elites and nonagricultural specialists. Moreover, the products of the export-oriented, large-scale agricultural sector (e.g., sugar, coconuts, and tobacco in the Philippines) are not accumulated through the marketplaces, but tend to flow through separate channels of collection and distribution.

Because distributional systems of this type tend to be concomitants of peasant societies, the persons who participate in them are commonly part-time marketeers; they produce for consumption as well for sale, but aim merely at maintaining "a culturally-standardized level of life, rather than at continuously expanded production" (Mintz 1959:20). However, although the majority of participants are peasant producers selling their own produce, characteristically marketplaces have in them substantial numbers of persons who are professional sellers and not producers at all. Thus the marketplace may be staffed by a personnel influenced by traditional values, and it may be less capitalistic in orientation than the export sector, but the presence of professional middlemen who depend upon marketing for a living brings into the distributional system a receptivity toward profit and efficiency which encourages innovation. The marketplace, therefore, may become a focus for the development of attitudes much more progressive than those relating to agricultural production.

Finally, Mintz suggests, marketplaces may also be employed as organs of national policy under the control of public officials or influential elites. Thus, whether the market tends to level "class" distinctions or to intensify them depends upon the degree and kind of external controls on it.

Bohannan and Dalton (1962) have attempted a classification of African economies which also merits at least a brief mention here, since it classifies different market relationships. Their economic typology is threefold: economies are classed into "marketless," "peripheral market," and "market" categories. The marketless type is irrelevant to our discussion. In "peripheral" market economies the participants don't depend upon the market as the major source of their income (presumably a statistical determination) and are primarily subsistence cultivators. The market is "peripheral" to the main business at hand, which is subsistence. In these situations the economy is organized in terms of reciprocity and redistribution (Bohannan and Dalton 1962:10). Although the forces of supply and demand operate on the price-formation process in peripheral markets, prices are also strongly influenced by such economically irrational factors as kinship, religion, traditional norms concerning the "justness" of prices, such as Tawney (1926) describes for medieval Europe, or simply "the eagerness of market women not to sell out quickly because the market is a place of entertainment and social intercourse" (Bohannan and Dalton 1962:11). Peripheral market prices fluctuate, affected by supply and demand and by "local institutional peculiarities."

Finally, according to Bohannan and Dalton, peripheral markets don't allocate the basic factors of production among alternative output uses, one usual market function. Because the participant in peripheral markets is essentially a subsistence producer, his interests are more deeply involved in that economic sphere than in the market *per se*. Therefore, changes in prices fail to have a direct effect on how individuals commit their productive factors. The prospect of increased profits in rice production, for example, might not encourage producers to grow more rice, because other social considerations may be more important than increased profits. In consequence, according to Bohannan and Dalton, peripheral markets are not "factor markets." They transact only a limited range of consumers' goods, not basic resources.

In contrast to the "peripheral" condition, participants in a "market" economy depend upon market sales as their major source of income. In the market economy everyone is committed to the market on a full-time basis, and prices are directly determined by supply and demand. In the fully developed market, prices influence production decisions to reallocate resources to alternative uses consistent with the desire to maximize profit. Although both types of market allocate consumers' goods, only the fully-developed market also allocates the factors of production.

But to find any market in which "local institutional peculiarities" did not influence transactions would be difficult. And to the extent that goods are sold on a market, their exchange value is always allocating those factors used in their production. Thus, the distinctions drawn between the types are badly blurred. But for the moment what is most significant is that Bohannan and Dalton place peasant economies in the market category, indicating that at least as far as *organization* is concerned, the peasant economy is fully commercial (Bohannan and Dalton 1962:12, Dalton 1969:65). The difference between modern commercial and peasant systems, therefore, is not economic organization, but the backward technology and traditional culture of the latter. In short, peasant economies are fully modern in organization, but are embedded in traditional social settings. Presumably, therefore, examples of price fluctuations failing to reallocate factors in peasant society are attributable to such things as poorly-developed transport and communication, not to the lack of orientation toward gain on the part of peasants or to frictions in the free mobility of resources.

Finally, Belshaw's (1965) synthesis of the literature on marketplace economies adds dimensions which the discussions previously considered did not pursue. Belshaw's discussion borrows heavily from Mintz' earlier work, as Belshaw specifically declares. Like Mintz, he notes the marginal nature of market commitment among a large proportion of the participants, and draws attention to the small scale of the transactions, the large number of sellers relative to the number of buyers, and the multisectorial nature of the peasant economy. However, rather than emphasizing the separation of the several sectors of the nonindustrial economy, Belshaw stresses their interpenetration. The "sophisticated commercial sector" and the "prestational" exchange sector of the folk economy are more or less bounded and discrete, but each exerts pressures on the marketplace sector by competing with it for resources. By extension, therefore, the marketplace sector cannot be understood solely in terms of its own internal dynamic. Rather, it can only be understood (e.g., the source of its "underdevelopment") in terms of its competitive relationships with other sectors.

The significance of Belshaw's work results from his attempt to consider the dynamics of such systems through isolating the factors operating to restrict their growth. An appreciation of these "constraints" is particularly useful to an understanding of social relationships in the marketplace. However, "economic growth" does not mean merely an increase in the size of the marketplace sector or in the number of persons participating but refers to the *per capita* accumulation of capital. Marketplace systems are expanding rapidly in terms of the numbers of participants. The degree to which capital is being accumulated is much more problematic.

Some of the factors which inhibit the growth of marketplace economies are apparent and have already been mentioned as elements influencing decisions to convert to cash-cropping among southern Cordilleran peoples. The risks involved in growing market crops when capital reserves are small and difficult to obtain and the lack of technical knowledge are as constraining on the expansion of commercial exchange as they are on production. Likewise, poor transport and communication inhibit growth in distributional systems. Poor development of the latter renders supply flows irregular, increases marketing costs, and retards the possibility of appealing to new markets. As Belshaw indicates (1965:83), undeveloped transport systems may oblige the seller physically to accompany all the goods he wishes to move. Poor quality transport and communications are likely the essential reasons for the "regional" emphasis in marketplace economies.

In theory, where capital supplies are short and highly priced, the extension of credit is one of the principal means of expanding commercial operations and increasing the opportunities for profit. However the Philippines lacks a system of contract law effective or cheap enough at the lower levels of the social order to constitute an efficient means of sanctioning loans. When a Filipino petty merchant speaks of a contract, he is almost certainly referring to a verbal agreement, not to a signed and witnessed legal document. Furthermore, although the Philippine system of public administration includes the establishment of courts at the *municipio* level, courts in general are greatly mistrusted. Filipinos view their courts as slow and expensive far beyond their means; and more important, courts commonly are roundly criticized for a purported tendency to render arbitrary decisions based on political or financial considerations rather than upon the specific legal points at issue. Whether these charges are accurate is largely irrelevant. Filipinos appear to believe them, and this belief influences their behavior. Accordingly, local merchants are anxious to avoid situations in which resort to legal action may be necessary.

From the perspective of a poorer-class Filipino, therefore, there are no practical, official means of enforcing credit agreements, and lending risks are reduced to acceptable levels only when effective nonofficial sanctions may be brought to bear. Public opinion, economic sanctions, or the obligations of kinship or other valued social relations are the factors which carry credit in this economy, not contract law. To increase the scale of commercial relations is also to require dealing with strangers. Commercial investments, therefore, commonly involve high risks, and persons with capital are inclined to prefer safe investments such as the purchase of land.

But above all, Belshaw argues, competition tends most to limit the accumulation of capital. On this point much of the literature on marketplace economies supports Belshaw. A number of writers have argued that the large numbers of buyers and sellers who participate, the small scale of transactions, and the nearly perfect resource mobility which characterizes such economies result in an empirical condition closely approximating the theoretical model of pure competition.[2] Foster, for

---

[2] But not a model of *perfect* competition. The difference is the amount of information participants are assumed to have. Because poorly developed communication networks are characteristic of the societies in which marketplace systems are likely to be found, it is safe to assume that information is far less than perfect.

example, remarks that in the Mexican "folk economy" with which he is concerned, "supply and demand function in almost classic textbook form" (Foster 1948:160). Mintz similarly suggests that the "internal marketing systems" which he has done much to define, "are typified by competition which is nearly perfect" (1959:24). However, he also cautions that because market activity tends to follow a regular yearly round, it is apt to result in social relations of a personal kind which may, in turn, influence competition. Yet in spite of Mintz' caution, Belshaw summarizes the literature as suggesting that "monetized peasant markets" represent "a close approximation to the economists' model of pure competition" (1965:57). They present "conditions which as closely approximate pure competition as any institution other than some of the stock and commodity markets of the sophisticated financial world" (1965:77). Belshaw freely admits that although we have many studies of the transformation of primitive societies to peasant states, there has been "almost no study of the sociology of marketing in such [peasant] societies" (1965:54). In short, We have few data on which to base generalizations.

Belshaw argues that fierce competition tends to keep profits low and to retard the accumulation of capital reserves necessary for reinvestment and for undertaking large-scale enterprises.[3] In what amounts to an extension of Schumpeter's

[3] To readers familiar with descriptions of the behavior of peasants, the assumption that peasant marketeers would reinvest increased savings in yet other income-producing ventures, rather than, say, in obligations (cf. Nash 1966, and his discussion of "leveling mechanisms"; or Wolf 1965, and his discussion of the "funds" which compete for peasant incomes), may seem questionable. However, as Mintz (1964b) has indicated, marketplace vendors often use capital more expansively than do elites in the same population. It is perhaps unfortunate that elite patterns of consumption so often provide the model toward which peasants orient their actions as they become more wealthy.

theoretical defense of monopolistic practices in downward-trending business cycles (Schumpeter 1950:91 ff.), Belshaw holds that, "profit taking would not be possible *at all* if it were not for frictions in the system of free competition" (Belshaw 1965:77, emphasis added). He argues that *gross* market income may grow, but if there are no restrictions on the entry or exit of participants, the entry of ever more sellers into the market tends to absorb income growth. One might conclude that unusual competition is one important reason why per capita incomes remain low in peasant societies. From this perspective, the accumulation of capital depends upon some means of limiting the number of sellers, whether by providing potential additional participants with more attractive economic alternatives (as is more common in developed economies), or by more arbitrary means of exclusion.

Belshaw's propositions draw attention to the importance of "frictions" in the marketplace system, but to test these ideas is difficult because we have no empirical examples of "frictionless" markets. Yet there seems to be, in existing literature on marketplace systems, a strong correlation between small-scale transactions and vigorous competition. Mintz noted that "the movement of human beings, by weight, may exceed the movement of produce itself in these systems" (1959:24). In the case of the Javanese marketplace, both Dewey (1962a, 1962b, 1964) and Geertz (1962a, 1963) note the large number of middleman roles which intervene between production and the ultimate consumption of goods. As Geertz says: "One piece of cloth often has ten or a dozen owners between the time it leaves the Chinese-owned factory in a nearby city and the time it is finally sold to someone in a Modjokuto village who seems likely to use it" (Geertz 1963:31). He also notes that in the case of agricultural produce, which must first be transported from the countryside and then distributed, the number of trader roles is even greater. Accordingly, competition is keen and actions are economically rational to the extreme. In the Javanese marketplace: "... the aim is always to get as much out of the deal immediately at hand as possible, and the bazaar trader is perpetually looking for a chance to make a smaller or larger killing, not attempting to build up a steady clientele or a steadily growing business" (Geertz 1962a: 391). Thus income is divided into a large number of small portions, and few individual traders are able to accumulate appreciable amounts of capital. In the Javanese marketplace, both risks and profits are thinly, if equitably, distributed, and it is significant, as Belshaw shows (1965:82), that in accounting for Javanese economic growth Geertz ignores the marketplace, turning instead to the entrepreneurial role of the traditional elite for his explanation.

Two particularly significant problematic themes emerge from discussions of marketplace systems. First, if one is interested in examining an empirical example of rational, self-interested, economic relationships, he could do no better than to consider a marketplace system. Second, given the constraints which limit profit-taking in marketplace systems, an understanding of the strategies employed by participants as they attempt to overcome those constraints is crucial to an understanding of marketplace sociology.

LOCAL ECONOMIC SECTORS

The public market in Baguio City is the central institution in the distributional system of a regionally-oriented, small-scale economy. As such it contrasts sharply with the other sector of the city's economy, the capital-intensive, large-scale commercial economy represented by the Chinese and lowland-Filipino-owned shops of Session Road.

The contrast between the two sectors is expressed in several ways. The most obvious difference is the size and appointment of places of business. The downtown shops are relatively large (though perhaps small by American standards), they are usually enclosed by glass show windows, and they are typically finished well in dressed lumber and plaster. By comparison (although there is great variation in this regard), market stalls are generally small, open, and usually made of rough lumber. In some areas of the market, sellers don't have stalls at all and are obliged to sit on the ground in the open.

Second, the kinds of goods offered for sale are different. The downtown shops stock more expensive manufactures and imports than do the traders in the public marketplace. One goes to the downtown merchants to purchase any kind of hardware (other than agricultural implements and *bolos*, the large work knife which is commonly carried), good quality kitchen utensils, radios, phonographs, books, imported foods, or a high quality meal. The marketplace specializes in agricultural produce, craft goods, common household utensils (particularly pottery ones), staple processed foods, and the cheaper manufactures. One goes to the marketplace to find such things as fresh meat, fowl, rice, vegetables, special foods common to peasant diets, coils of rattan (for lashing), cheaper patent medicines, or the kinds of charms and religious relics which appeal more to the less educated. However, in terms of the goods distributed, the two sectors are not absolutely discrete. Duplication occurs especially in the case of manufactured goods; however, when similar items are offered for sale in both sectors, the quality of goods offered in the downtown shops is generally superior (and the prices higher). For example, one can buy clothing in both places, but clothing sold in the marketplace is poorly sewn (deliberately so in order to reduce its price) and is made of poorer-quality cloth. Furthermore, there is typically a vast difference in the quantities available of manufactures or processed wares. In general, each marketplace seller has a limited range of goods and a small inventory, a fact which —as we shall see—encourages considerable cooperative borrowing of goods among marketplace sellers. To the degree that wares are packaged, the marketplace tends to carry the smaller, more uneconomically-sized packages.

In keeping with the basic distinctions between kinds and qualities of goods, a third point of contrast is that the two sectors appeal to different clienteles. The downtown shops appeal to the more well-to-do: wage-earning and professional lowland Filipinos, Chinese businessmen, the foreign technician element (particularly mining company personnel), and tourists. The clientele attracted to the public marketplace tends to be from the poorer classes: the lower-ranking employees of local businesses, wage laborers from the mines and lumbering companies, and peasant farmers.

However, again the distinction is not absolute. Some staple foods are available only in the marketplace, so regardless of one's position in society, one must consume something from the marketplace. Depending upon the social image he wishes to maintain, or his position in the local hierarchy, an individual member of the elite may find the prospect of shopping in the marketplace distasteful and may prefer to send a domestic servant to do his marketplace shopping. Yet, many wealthy persons view shopping in the public market as an amusing game, an opportunity to see the lengths to which the lower orders will go to make a profit. Politicians, however, generally take care to be seen in the market as a demonstration of their democratic dispositions. Similarly, to the extent that poorer-class persons wish to purchase more expensive items, they may be obliged to turn to the larger downtown shops. In the latter case, the lower-class buyer may approach the shopkeeper with considerable deference.

Sellers in the two sectors differ just as buyers do. The merchants who operate the larger shops are among the community's more influential members and often occupy leadership roles in local service organizations—the Lions Club, the Knights of Columbus, the Chamber of Commerce, and so on. By local standards, the larger shopkeepers are wealthy and well educated, and they tend to live in the better sections of town. Although marketplace sellers are not an homogeneous collectivity, they tend to have originated in, and to continue to belong to, lower-class elements. Their incomes are typically low, they are less likely to be educated, and those who live in town live in less desirable areas. Some of the marketplace sellers, particularly those from native ethnolinguistic groups, are squatters: they reside in shacks hastily constructed on public, or unused private, lands. Squatters pay no rent or taxes, are generally held in contempt by all other elements of the city's population, and can maintain their positions only because they receive paternalistic attention from politicians. Some vendors who regularly sell in the local marketplace live outside town on farmsteads, and others live completely outside the limits of Baguio City. A few reside as far away as Pangasinan and La Union and make the trip to Baguio and return several times each week.

The presence of peasant producers selling in the marketplace and the strong countryside orientation of many of the town-dwelling merchants and laborers lend a strong flavor of rural culture to the marketplace. Yet in spite of this orientation, all marketeers seem to share one goal in common with substantial shopkeepers: to see that their children receive an education.

Surprisingly, this desire is evident even among the poorest traders, who often deprive themselves in order to keep their children in school.

The fourth point of difference is business techniques and strategies. The downtown merchants typically have attractive window displays, they usually advertise, they occasionally have "sales" in which bargains are featured on lead items, and in general indicate some familiarity with modern merchandizing principles. This is particularly noticeable in the manner in which items are priced and sales conducted. In the larger shops items are tagged and priced. Moreover, these prices are often noted in odd cents and are not "rounded off." This price is the actual selling price, not the opening bid in what buyer and seller assume is a bargaining situation. Haggling is not characteristic of transactions in downtown shops. Yet shopkeepers will sell at prices less than those indicated on the price tag. For example, after I became known as a person who would be in the community for some time, I received some "discounts."

A few of the larger stalls in the marketplace show attractively arranged displays, but more commonly goods are simply stacked in ways calculated to save space, or arranged in terms of the lot sizes (often simply piles of things) customers are likely to buy. In the marketplace prices are almost never marked on goods. The usual mode of transaction in the marketplace is overt bargaining: bid is matched with counterbid until an agreement is reached on the selling price, or until it is obvious that agreement cannot be reached. For a seller to mark the minimum price at which he was actually willing to sell would be ruinous, for most buyers would assume that price to be the seller's opening bid and would be insulted by his refusal to adjust that price to a counteroffer. In this process prices are never bargained in terms of odd cents, but always in multiples of five. The reasons for this, I was assured, are two: first, it is easier for poorly educated people ("like the natives") to calculate prices in terms of fives and tens; and second, this facilitates exchanging money, since the seller needn't have a large supply of small coins on hand.

An important difference is in the organization of enterprises in the two sectors. Both are "family" enterprises, not owned by stock corporations and conducted by managers. But the downtown shops are managed in accord with commercial accounting techniques which produce a conceptual distinction between the "family" and the "firm." In the management of the larger shops there exists a notion of "capital" distinct from the resources of the family, and there is concern for capital gains, losses, and rates of turnover.

The ability of marketplace sellers to manage their businesses efficiently varies considerably. Some are spectacularly clever and approach a condition of optimal use of their capital, while others seem to have little business skill or knowledge of the market. Many market stalls are, in effect, managed from outside the market by suppliers. However, a marketplace seller who employs a system of record keeping is unusual, so there is little evidence that market vendors in general think about capital the way shopkeepers do. In the marketplace the household and the firm share the same resources because the conceptual means rarely exist to distinguish them. The result is that the goals of the household often compete with those of the family's business in a direct way, thereby encouraging the "irrational" use of capital. Although the orientation of marketplace sellers is thoroughly and undeniably commercial, many of them have only the grossest measures of gains and losses. A frequent answer to the question "How do you determine financial success?" is, "As long as there is something on the shelves." As long as they can both sell and eat from the same stock, the business is a success.

THE BAGUIO CITY MARKETPLACE

The public marketplace at Baguio City is similar to Mintz' "internal markets" or to Belshaw's "monetized peasant markets" in its organization. In terms of the "central place" typology utilized by Skinner in describing the situation in traditional south China, it is a "central market" (Skinner 1964). That is, the Baguio marketplace is a daily affair situated in a strategic position in the transportation and communication network, and it is a source of supply for many lesser markets which do not meet daily. It has wholesaling functions, it receives imports and distributes them to the hinterlands, and it collects local products for shipment to other areas.

The Baguio market, however, is not a "true" peasant market, if that term means that the participants are essentially subsistence producers who market on a part-time basis. In this sense, the Baguio marketplace leans heavily toward the "fully commercial" end of the continuum (the "market" type suggested by Bohannan and Dalton), for only about a third of the sellers participating on any given day are not full-time traders. The majority of sellers, therefore, are dependent upon the market for their major source of income and pursue the ancient practice of attempting to buy cheaply and sell dearly. Thus, whether the Baguio City market is a "peasant marketplace" depends largely on the typology one has in mind, and the problem is not significant enough to detain us. Certainly it shares many features with other markets which have been described as such.

By Philippine provincial standards, the marketplace in Baguio City is large and complex (includes many roles). Many provincial town markets are cyclical, with markets "rotating" among several towns; the Baguio market—or some portions of it—is in operation every day of the year. The municipal government officially sets marketing hours to provide a twelve-hour day (7 A.M. to 7 P.M.). However, the hours of daily activity normally are much longer, for although the police oblige everyone to close his shop in the evening, sales are often transacted earlier than 7 in the morning. Sellers—particularly those who deal in perishables, such as meat or vegetables—are often on hand before daylight to buy their stocks from wholesalers, or to receive them from deals previously arranged.

The time individual sellers spend in the market varies considerably with such attributes as the seller's economic role, the product or service offered, the season of the year, and personal initiative. Meat vendors, as an example, must be on hand early to have their animals inspected, to butcher them, and to have them prepared for sale before the moisture and heat of the day can spoil the meat. Customers are aware that unless they make prior arrangements the best meat will be sold by eight or nine o'clock in the morning. Souvenir sellers keep different hours. They open late (often after 10), and tend to remain open late, for their most important customers are tourists, who are likely to be late risers. During slow seasons, such as during the rains, nearly everyone is more inclined to be sluggish, and many sellers don't bother to conduct their businesses at all; some even seek other means of temporary employment. For most sellers, however, marketplace selling implies a routine of long, slow days in which the tedium is only infrequently broken by the appearance of a customer. Among professional sellers the work day is likely to be so long that the market stall becomes, in effect, a second household. The family may, as a unit, open the stall in the morning and close it at night. Meals may be prepared and eaten on the spot. Children may be cared for in the stall, or if they are of school age, they may leave for school from the stall and return to it after school hours. In many respects, therefore, the marketplace is a community, and one which operates according to norms and sanctions appropriate to the circumstances. In a real way these sellers are often neighbors and not merely competitors. For example, patterns of food sharing common among friendly neighbors in rural Philippine villages (cf. Lewis 1971:103–105) are not unusual in the marketplace, though this practice is not nearly so well developed as in the village community.

Though some activity may always be observed in the marketplace, there are decided fluctuations in its intensity which are both daily and seasonal in nature. The busiest daily period is from 7 until roughly 10 in the morning. The marketplace lacks refrigeration, and unless perishables are moved during the early morning the buyer is likely to pay a penalty in the loss of quality and the seller in a loss of income—a fact which organizes shopping habits. A second, though minor, peak occurs toward the end of the market day, roughly between 3 P.M. and 6 P.M. as customers stop on the way home from places of employment. Many "country" sellers (i.e., those who don't live in the city) don't stay beyond the morning rush, for they have long distances to travel. Weekends and holidays are always much busier than weekdays, for at these times persons from outlying areas are most likely to use city facilities and to increase local demand in the market.

The seasonal fluctuation in market activity is in some ways more dramatic. The peak season occurs during the relatively dry months of March, April, and May. At this time hot, unpleasant weather occurs in most lowland areas, while the weather in the mountains remains fairly dry and relatively cool. Also at this time the public schools traditionally take their "summer" recess, so these months are a popular vacation period. Accordingly there is a marked increase in tourism during the dry season. These are also peak months for the harvesting of local vegetable crops and for lumbering activity, so at this time of year greater quantities of money are likely to be in circulation. The doldrums in the marketplace occur immediately after the dry-season peak, for by mid-June the rains have usually begun in earnest, and by July they have reached such intensity that commerce is difficult to conduct. The rain is often so intense that people dislike leaving shelter, and on some days the town streets are almost deserted at midday. This is a difficult time for sellers, not only because the number of potential buyers is much smaller, but also because flows of supplies become irregular and losses from spoilage and damage are increased. Locally-grown produce is much less plentiful during the wet season, because few farmers wish to risk cultivating during the heavy rains. Livestock and fowl are more susceptible to diseases at this time, and sellers don't like to have large quantities of them on hand. Marine fishing, which provides many of the fish sold locally, becomes much more dangerous and less productive during the rains. The mines and lumber companies curtail operations, and all transportation becomes more difficult and more expensive. And because buyers' incomes are reduced at this time, they tend to restrict their purchases to necessities. Vendors may have so little to sell that they are obliged to ration their goods among their best customers. During the wet season many sellers deliberately reduce inventories to the bare minimum. The magnitude of difference between the seasonal low and the seasonal peak is difficult to determine objectively, for statistical reports on marketplace activity are lacking, but a sample of experienced sellers suggested that July and August sales levels are only 20 percent of the dry-season peak.

These seasonal variations have additional implications for the sellers of some goods, for the changes in climatic conditions not only produce fluctuating demand, but also bring changes in the kinds of products demanded. For example, dry-goods sellers may find that during the wet season customers want sweaters, sweatshirts, and waterproof jackets, rather than the loosely-fitted short-sleeved shirts typically worn during drier weather. Or footwear sellers find that their leather shoes are not moving well because the market now demands rubber or canvas boots and shoes. These seasonal variations require sellers of affected products to liquidate their inventories periodically in order to provide themselves with working capital and with salable goods; and at each liquidation they are in danger of suffering substantial losses. This is all the more inducement to operate with minimal inventories, and it has some important implications for the nature of competition in the marketplace. But sellers are aware of these seasonal changes, and keep them in mind as they plan their respective commercial strategies.

The physical structure of the Baguio marketplace is an agglomeration, the result of planning and construction which has taken place at different times, and which has been suited to different resources and needs. However, none of the buildings in the marketplace is very old, for the market suffered heavy damage during World War II, and all the buildings in current use have been built or substantially rebuilt since that time. They clearly were not all constructed with a single architectural style in mind. Each building is divided into a number of small, open stalls, *puestos* (selling locations), which are allotted to individual sellers.

The area of the marketplace referred to by residents as the "main" section (see Map 3) houses nearly a third of the sellers and consists of substantial buildings constructed at city expense. These buildings are made of stone and wood and have tin roofs. The area of the market which fronts on Trinidad Road, and which is most visible to, say, tourists just entering town, contains some sizable stalls enclosed by glass. However, these are souvenir sellers' stalls in which are sold locally-produced silverwork, weaving, and wood carving, and except for their location these businesses have little in common with the remainder of the marketplace. Their business methods and incomes and the personal attributes of their operators have much more in common with the substantial merchants of Session Road. A few sellers have operations in both places.

Stalls in this main area are subjected to relatively heavy taxes but are nevertheless cheaper to rent than downtown locations. The stalls of the main market are well located and large by marketplace standards, and are therefore likely to be operated by the more affluent professional sellers. Yet under some circumstances the size and location of these stalls do not compensate for their additional fixed costs, for at times the sellers in the less substantial "open market" may attract customers from this main area.

Owners have modified many stalls in the main market area from the original construction to suit particular requirements, often at their own expense. A large number of the meat and fish sellers have display counters made of tile-covered wood, so that—lacking refrigeration—stalls may be washed down periodically to reduce odor and spoilage (and also, some of their more cynical neighbors suggest, to add weight to their wares).

The remainder of the marketplace is not so adequately housed and consists largely of unpainted wooden structures and temporary tar-papered, or awning-covered, pavilions, which can be erected at much less cost. As one moves away from the more immediately visible and accessible main section and toward the rear of the marketplace, accomodations in general become less spacious and durable. In these other areas the entire stall structure has often been erected at the owner's expense. The quality of sellers' accomodations decreases until in the north corner of the marketplace there is nothing more than an asphalt-surfaced yard. That area happens to be least accessible from the town side, but most accessible to the area in town in which the buses from outlying regions unload passengers. This is the "open market" in which "*puesto*" means nothing more than a space large enough to accomodate a few woven fibre mats upon which goods may be arranged for display. In many respects this is the most colorful area of the marketplace, for here one is most likely to encounter peasants and tribal peoples from many other areas, each selling the products of his own labor.

In addition to the sellers who operate from these fixed locations, a considerable number of "mobile firms," or roving sellers, are scattered about the marketplace. They move through the crowd, occasionally pausing where there is space enough, though each has a favorite territory. There usually are ice cream, *halo halo* (an ice, vegetable, and fruit drink), and soft-drink sellers congregating wherever pathways intersect, wheeled *lechon* (roast pork) carts near the meat sellers' area, *chucheria* (nicknacks, such as pocketknives, costume jewelry, key chains, and other trinkets) sellers sandwiched between buildings, and *curanderos* (folk healers) offering medicine shows and selling charms in the walkways. Weaving through the crowd and adding to the general impression of confusion are the *kombois*, men who sell their labor as porters and "Man Fridays" to vendors and their customers. One must often be alert to avoid being injured by some *komboi* moving a heavy load of goods on a two-wheeled hand cart. A busy day in the marketplace conveys the impression that market behavior is random and not at all amenable to systematic investigation.

REGIONAL FUNCTIONS OF THE MARKETPLACE

Like other social institutions, marketplaces have "functions," or operations, which they perform within the social contexts in which they are embedded. The term "function," however, does not imply that the marketplace contributes to the continuity of a given set of social and cultural arrangements. In fact, as we have seen, Polanyi (1947, 1957) and Dalton (1961), among others, have argued that markets are sources of social conflict and disruption. "Function" here implies any latent or manifest social or economic operation which the marketplace performs.

In the first place, the Baguio marketplace provides the opportunity—the place, time, personnel, and social understandings —for exchanging goods and services on a scale which greatly transcends the limits of the local community. It offers local peoples access to goods not otherwise available to them and in turn provides them with the possibility of selling local products to a much greater population than that of the immediate region. And by increasing the scale of exchange, the market also provides a means for connecting the national economy with the local economy. Through the marketplace, manufactures and imports are made available to rural cultivators, while rural produce flows "up" the distributional apparatus.

Second, the network of market relationships constitutes a system of communication. The most obvious kind of information which flows along this network concerns prices and other marketing conditions. This information influences not only market traders, but also the production decisions made by rural cultivators, whom it provides information about the marketability of specific crops. Furthermore, because the market is monetized and money-prices make price information transferable, marketplace prices influence rural behavior by establishing standards of value around which rural exchanges may be organized. Accordingly, though barter-in-kind is not unusual in rural areas, these exchanges take place in terms of the monetary value of the items transacted. In this respect it is unfortunate that local communication networks are not better developed, for lack of information about prices and possible sales outlets undoubtedly reduces commitment to commercial activities in rural areas. However, not all the information transmitted along the network of market relations is economic information. Local social events, gossip about common acquaintances, and perhaps above all, information about local, provincial, national, or even international politics are all discussed in the marketplace, particularly when mobile middlemen "pass by."

Third, sellers in the marketplace provide the services of collecting and bulk-breaking. In the course of their operations market vendors provide savings for local consumers by purchasing goods in relatively large quantities, then breaking these quantities into units small enough for modest local purchasing power. One can hardly overstress the small scale of market transactions. In the Baguio marketplace, for example, one may purchase a tin-can scoop of lard, salt, or sugar, a soft-drink-bottle measure of cooking oil or kerosene, a single slice of melon or squash, bananas by the individual fruit, cough medicine by the spoonful, a thimble-sized container of Metholatum, a two-ounce enevelope of some popular American detergent, a single cigarette and a match; or one may rent a pulp magazine by the hour. By reducing quantities to this minute scale, marketplace sellers also serve the manufacturer, for if quantities were not reduced to tiny portions they probably would not be salable at all. This function best answers the question, "Why the public market?" Transactions may be on a small and uneconomic scale, but given the level of local personal income, the marketplace is an efficient system of distribution. Representatives of industrial and commercial firms who wish to sell their products at the local level are also obliged to work through the marketplace and its intermediaries.

In the course of their collection function, marketplace sellers also obtain, from innumerable sources, rural products which are bulked for wholesale. The goods usually collected are agricultural and forest products (e.g., vines, woods, bamboo, and broomstraw) and cottage manufactures (e.g., woodcarvings, textiles, silverwork, and some furniture). In some cases these are sold locally to city dwellers, but much rural production is also bulked in this way and sold wholesale to higher-level merchants for resale in more distant markets.

Fourth, the marketplace functions as a source of capital and credit. This complex topic is the subject of further discussion (Chapter VI), but a few preliminary remarks are in order. The need for capital, together with accumulated years of commercial experience with money, has stimulated the development of some sophisticated capital-provision institutions. The most important are cooperative credit associations, but under certain circumstances professional intermediaries will also make small loans to producers, and suppliers will lend money or goods to retailers. Credit is widely used in the Baguio marketplace, and to understand the operation of the marketplace without considering credit relationships would be impossible.

The fifth function of the marketplace is as an instrument of economic nationalism. It is quite apparent, given recent Philippine economic history, that Filipinos are willing to forego a measure of economic efficiency in order to gain citizen control of all sectors of the economy. Accordingly, much economic legislation is intended not so much to improve economic performance of Filipinos as it is to restrict competition from alien operations. To the present the main economic objects of nationalistic attention have been the alien Chinese, although more selective pressure has also been applied to American, European, and Indian interests. The Chinese are obvious targets for several reasons. They are the most numerous of any alien minority group, comprising perhaps 2 percent of the total population,[4] as opposed to roughly 30,000 (.1 percent of the population) alien Americans and Europeans resident in the Philippines (1960 Census). Second, Chinese are greatly disliked, a dislike frequently expressed in public news media and private conversation. Chinese irritate Filipinos because of their apparent lack of interest in being assimilated more thoroughly into Philippine society and culture. They seem to adjust only to the minimal degree necessary to get on, and are inclined to take considerable interest and pride in preserving Chinese cultural integrity and social forms. They are an embattled ethnic group and commonly express the belief that their coherence can be maintained only through the maintenance of economic cooperation throughout the Chinese community. Finally, and perhaps most important, among Philippine foreign minorities, the Chinese are especially likely to compete directly with Filipino businesses. Americans and Europeans are inclined to specialize in providing goods and services which Filipinos cannot yet provide for themselves: for example, heavy industry. Chinese, however, are more apt to be middlemen and wholesalers, or restaurant or hotel keepers, things which Filipinos can do very well. As the Philippine industrial sector grows and the level of technical skill increases, American and European interests will probably also come more under attack. In fact, the process seems well under way.

Beginning with the establishment of the Philippine Republic, selling in public marketplaces legally has been restricted to Philippine citizens (Republic Act 1292, 1946). Furthermore, unlike much national legislation, this is a popular law and is vigorously enforced at the local level. Chinese are influential

---

[4] According to Wurfel (1964:710), who argues that the official 1960 census figure is too low because of the large number of illegal immigrants not counted.

in the local economy, but they are excluded from the marketplace. In 1964, for example, there were no noncitizen Chinese operating in the Baguio City marketplace, though there were many rumors that some of the more successful marketplace vendors were cooperating with the Chinese (i.e., were Chinese "dummies"). There was also a considerable scandal in 1964 and 1965 when a group of local Filipino politicians leased public lands adjacent to the public market to some Chinese developers who intended to build a competing marketplace for Chinese. This would have posed a serious threat to the Filipino market, but the plan was exposed and blocked by a lawsuit brought, initially, by the officers of the local market sellers' association.

In itself the nationalization of public marketplaces would have had little competitive significance aside from enabling Filipino petty merchants to obtain cheaper selling locations. But economic nationalization efforts were considerably strengthened in 1954 by the Retail Trade Nationalization Act (Republic Act 1180, 1954). This legislation made it illegal for any enterprise valued in excess of (approximately) $1200 US, and not wholly owned by Philippine citizens, to participate in retail trade (the only exceptions are aliens who sell their own agricultural produce—from land they can't own). Noncitizens can engage in retail trade, but the law limits them to approximately the same level of capitalization as the Filipino firms with which they compete. Because aliens are typically subjected to special fees and taxes, including local city assessments, and are prevented from enjoying the cheap rents of public marketplaces, the alien restriction laws provided some *de facto* advantages: they reduced the level of capitalization of alien retail enterprises, while at the same time increasing their fixed costs.

For years Chinese have also been deeply involved in the

wholesale trade of processed foods. In Baguio, for example, although they operate from locations outside the marketplace, they often have virtual control of the sale of such commodities in the public market itself. In an effort to deal with this "problem," the national government established the National Marketing Corporation (NAMARCO, created by Administrative Order No. 44, 1955, and now defunct). The NAMARCO organization imported processed foods and some novelty "lead" items (e.g., apples, grapes, and oranges from the United States) in large quantities and released them tax free and at cost to Filipino merchants. The intent was to subsidize the Filipino merchant until Chinese control was weakened.

Unfortunately for the Filipino merchant, the net effect of the NAMARCO program was much less than it should have been, largely because of the possibilities for graft and profiteering inherent in its organization. The NAMARCO distributional system consisted of a series of private distributors who were classified according to the size of their capital assets and then given franchises to distribute goods in territories sized accordingly. Each distributor was allowed to keep a part of the goods he distributed to retail through his own firm, but each was also required to send the remainder down the scale to lesser-order distributors until the ultimate small retailer had his share. The profit margin was fixed by law for both the retail and wholesale prices of these goods so that they became slightly more expensive as they changed hands, usually at the rate of 5 percent at each level. But the potential for chicanery is obvious. High-level dealers could make many times more profit by keeping NAMARCO stocks to sell at retail prices rather than passing them down the chain for wholesale prices. The temptation was too great for many dealers to resist, and lower-level NAMARCO sellers complained bitterly that they did not get their quotas of NAMARCO goods or that they got the less desirable commodities. Moreover, there was little consistency or continuity in the commodities provided, so it was difficult for the seller to anticipate what goods he would receive and to build a steady demand for them among his clients. But in spite of its shortcomings, NAMARCO delivered some relatively cheap goods into the hands of Filipino retailers and seemed to be making inroads on the Chinese wholesale grocery trade. Chinese sellers admitted that they did not like to stock items in which there was NAMARCO competition, and the NAMARCO program was one reason that some of the small grocery (*sari sari*) stalls in the marketplace were able to survive.

A sixth function of the local marketplace is the provision of adjunct economic opportunities for low-income families. The small scale of marketing operations and the low initial capital investment relative to other alternatives make marketing practical as a supplemental source of income. In local Philippine economies individuals tend to spread risks broadly by distributing resources among a number of enterprises, rather than investing everything in one. This basic strategy leads to a more or less constant search for investment opportunities, or alternative production strategies, and results in the utilization of almost every conceivable economic niche.[5] Often a man operates one business and his wife operates another, and even professional people are apt to have two or three sidelines supplemental to their professional activities.

On any given day roughly 70 percent of the sellers in the marketplace are women, most of whom are married, and whose husbands have nonmarket sources of income. Thus to a consid-

---

[5] The strategy of utilizing all available opportunities even induces women and children to go about the streets collecting animal manure, which is then sold as fertilizer to vegetable farmers. It is also common knowledge that the wives of many local professional people and city officials operate some of the larger stalls in the marketplace.

erable extent, the market represents not only an adjunct activity, but also a sexual division of labor. However, men tend to operate the larger businesses: there is a direct relationship between male management and the size of the operation. A woman often starts a commercial operation, but if it promises to produce more income than other occupations in which the couple may be involved, the husband is apt to assume management (or at least to assume the appearance of managing the business, as some women say). Otherwise, husbands tend to stay in the background, though many assist their wives' commercial ventures when not otherwise occupied: for example, by taking short trips to the countryside to obtain supplies.

The high percentage of female sellers is also understandable considering the relative value of unskilled labor in various sectors of the economy. The common wage for agricultural labor in Mountain Province in 1964 was two pesos per day. Even the small-scale operators in the open market anticipate a profit of at least three pesos per day, and it is not particularly uncommon for them to net ten. Thus the potential value of female labor is much greater in the marketplace than on the rural labor market. A reasonably alert market seller can produce as much income on the average as some semiskilled female occupations: for example, seamstresses usually make about four pesos per day. But market selling also involves greater risks than wage labor.

Although evidence is inconclusive and largely impressionistic, the "adjunct" nature of much female market participation also appears to affect prices. Because women's labor would otherwise go unused in many cases, they are inclined to view any income as pure profit, and seem consistently to accept profit margins which would not satisfy more professional sellers. Objective measure of this proposition is difficult because profit margins and degree of dependence on the market for income are difficult to assess in each case.

The seventh function provided by the Baguio marketplace— although one usually thinks of marketplaces in terms of their distributional functions—is small-scale production, for this, too, produces income from otherwise unproductive labor. For example, fresh fruit which remains unsold at the end of the market day is sometimes taken home and converted into preserves which are then retailed. On many days in the marketplace there are long pauses between customers, and much of the seller's time could be used more profitably. Vendors therefore often seek additional ways of using their time productively. They do such things as split bamboo (or some other fibrous material) to weave into baskets or bags for carrying or shipping produce and then sell or loan them to favorite customers. Coconuts are sometimes husked during slack periods so that they may be sold for a few additional centavos. Or those who have the skill may purchase dried flowers and make wreaths, which are popular as gifts. Many women spend otherwise idle hours sewing new clothes or mending old ones, either for their own families or for sale—often by agreement with some dry-goods seller or one of the local tailors. But in all cases this production is of the "cottage" type: it does not involve a complex technology, many productive steps, or large-scale capital commitment. For production of this kind, one needs only a certain amount of skill and plenty of time.

Finally, the marketplace functions as a source of revenue for the local city administration. Market sellers are charged a variety of rents and fees (see Table 2) which collectively amount to a substantial part of the city's revenues. Because market vendors occupy city property, they are much more exposed to the collection of all taxes, including national income

Table 2

Weekly Stall Rental Fees

Area	No. of Stalls	Average Fee (pesos)	Average Fee (dollars)[a]
Bagoong	19	2.86	.76
Caldero	13	10.30	2.79
Carinderia	31	11.15	3.07
Cucheria	35	2.42	.65
Curio & Souvenir	16	24.10	6.43
Dry Goods	180	7.37	1.97
Second-Hand Clothes	25	3.29	.88
Entrails	36	1.78	.47
Fish	150	2.26	.60
Flowers	32	3.77	1.01
Footwear	36	8.71	2.32
Fowls	18	2.47	.66
Halo-halo	8	2.50	.67
Hotcake	20	5.45	1.48
Lechon	11	2.59	.69
Meat	36	7.80	2.08
Periodicals	7	4.85	1.29
Rice	48	7.00	1.86
Sari-sari	131	5.02	1.34
Tobacco	17	1.35	.36
Vegetables (Main)	188	3.59	.96
Vegetables (Hangar)	452	2.77	.74
Refreshments	12	8.94	2.38

[a]Conversion to US dollars at the ratio 3.75:1.

taxes, than most other merchants. There is a local office of the National Bureau of Internal Revenue in Baguio City, of which the "permanent" sellers in the marketplace are very aware. The BIR has been criticized for not having adequate knowledge concerning from whom taxes should be collected in any region, but prosperous marketplace sellers are visible.

Chapter Four

The Marketplace and Political Process

MARKETPLACE ADMINISTRATION

Although many scholars consider marketplace economies likely to feature free and intense competition (Foster 1948, Mintz 1959, Belshaw 1965, all discussed in Chapter III), this is by no means a universal condition of marketplace organization. Among the many forces that modify market competition, it seems to be especially common to find that public authority has manipulated marketplaces to further its own ends. Marketplaces are important centers of communication and income, convenient for authority to use to disseminate information about laws and ordinances, or to hold court, or for taxation, or to channel market activities in particular desired directions. Depending on the nature and degree of this intervention, the formally rational operation attributed to markets may be considerably modified. For this reason a

101

market can manifest all the visible attributes of free market systems (e.g., money, profits, professional intermediaries, etc.) without the forces of supply and demand being given free rein in price formation. For example, in a posthumously published work Polanyi (1966) has shown that prices in the historic marketplaces of Dahomey were set by public authority, although Dahomey at that time had a fully monetized economy oriented toward commercial gain. These politically-induced modifications do not rule out choice; they only constrain and channel it.

In the Philippines local bureaucracy has the right to intervene broadly in market relationships. "A set of rules of social organization" (Dalton 1969:66) governing market activity are set forth explicitly in laws and ordinances and in the local ideal culture, and can be elicited in detail from any competent informant. We will see how much knowledge of these rules assists us in understanding the "real world processes and institutions" of the marketplace.

All Philippine public markets are legally under the control of "a relevant public authority" (Republic Act 1292, 1946), although this does not imply a uniform set of ordinances which govern all markets. In most provincial towns "relevant public authority" means administrative control by the provincial governor and the provincial board. But in chartered cities, such as Baguio, control over the marketplace is given to the city government itself.

There are three principal reasons for public control of marketplaces. First, local authorities maintain order in the marketplace. As in any large congregation, there must exist ways of preventing and resolving conflict. Accordingly, the authorities have established a set of rules to maintain order and to protect individual interests (and also to look after the interests of authority itself). Second, as we have seen, marketplaces are organs of economic nationalism, and public authority has the obligation of excluding aliens from the public market. Finally, public control of exchange centers affords local government the opportunity to use these as sources of revenue. In Baguio, total city revenues from market tax sources exceed $2,000 US per week (see Table 3). Neither of the latter purposes is ef-

TABLE 3

Expected Weekly Collections of
Market Stall Rental Fees

Area	Expected Weekly Collection (pesos)	Expected Weekly Collections (dollars)[a]
Bagoong	25.75	6.87
Caldero	133.96	35.72
Carinderia	367.85	98.09
Chucheria	77.58	20.69
Curio & Souvenir	385.62	102.83
Dry Goods	1333.12	355.50
Second-Hand Clothes	82.34	21.96
Entrails	67.50	18.00
Fish	386.50	130.67
Flowers	48.95	13.05
Footwear	287.52	76.67
Fowls	44.50	11.87
Halo-halo	29.94	7.98
Hotcake	113.40	30.24
Lechon	28.50	7.60
Meat	280.72	74.86
Periodicals	33.96	9.06
Rice	336.00	89.60
Sari-sari	522.07	139.41
Tobacco	23.00	6.13
Vegetables	1930.44	514.79
Refreshments	80.50	21.47
Total	6639.72	1771.06

[a]Conversion to US dollars at the ratio 3.75:1.

fectively served in Baguio but they remain aspects of the ideal structure of the marketplace to which, at the least, lip service must be paid, and they are necessary and sufficient justification for bureaucratic intervention in the marketplace.

One of the basic interests which the local city government has in the marketplace is the rental of *puestos*. The "rule" is that each *puesto* in the marketplace is owned by the city and rented to an occupant on a weekly basis, or on a daily basis in the open market. This rental fee varies with the area of the market in which the stall is situated, its size, and the principal commodity to be sold. In the Baguio marketplace rentals range from (with all variables averaged) approximately $.20 US per meter per week for *carinderia* (cooked food) *puestos*, to approximately $1.85 per square meter per week for sellers who deal in cleaned rice (see Table 3, p. 103). A stallholder may be charged additionally for every container of goods which cannot be accomodated within his allotted space. Moreover, a number of special fees are levied on particular services and commodities. For example, the *kombois* who load, unload, and move goods about the marketplace must pay a fee to sell their services in the marketplace. Meat sellers must have city licenses, and they must pay stable fees, slaughter fees, inspection fees, and city transport charges on every animal killed. The city's general attitude toward fees may be, perhaps, best symbolized by its treatment of the sale of dogs for food. Dogs are a popular source of protein among native mountain peoples, and eating them is considered masculine among some of the lowland groups. However, to sell a dog for food is illegal in Baguio. But there is a separate market for dog selling, and every sale is taxed.

Nonstallholding sellers who trade in the marketplace are taxed a charge (*corteis*) of approximately $.10 US per container of goods (which usually means per woven bamboo basket). The city employs six persons full time to collect market fees. However, the coming and going of so many sellers, plus the great variety of charges, makes fee collection difficult. Not surprisingly, sellers claim that the fee collectors show favoritism to their friends, and that they accept bribes.

In any chartered Philippine city the operation of the public marketplace is the responsibility of an administrative body, the market committee. This committee is composed of the city treasurer, a representative each from the offices of the mayor and city council, and a representative of the market sellers themselves. In Baguio some of the marketplace sellers have formed a legally-chartered organization, the Baguio City Market Vendors' Association (BAMARVA), and the president of that association is the vendors' representative on the committee.

The committee is expressly empowered to conduct the drawing of lots for use-rights to market stalls and to settle any civil disputes which arise. However, the market committee does not have the right to draft laws and ordinances governing the operation of the market. The mayor and city council retain these powers. Furthermore, no organ of the city government has the legal right to regulate prices directly. In the past, however, mayors have often attempted such interference. For example, a past mayor deliberately attempted to force marketplace sellers to establish fixed prices on goods so that bargaining could be avoided. He failed utterly. Furthermore, several sellers reported that past mayors frequently exerted pressure on vendors to lower prices so that Baguio would not establish a reputation for cheating tourists. These last efforts also ended in failure, for marketplace sellers noted that prices in the downtown shops weren't reduced, and they tended to see the whole thing as yet another attempt to exploit them.

The day-to-day supervision of the market is delegated to an official appointed by the mayor, the market superintendent.

He, in turn, has a staff of secretaries, clerks, collectors, market sweepers, and an assistant superintendent.

By city law, the right to occupy a market stall may be obtained in only one way: drawing the stall by lot and then signing a lease-rental agreement. The occupant must agree to keep the stall clean, pay all rents and fees on a weekly basis, conduct his business in person (to prevent a few individuals from monopolizing stalls and then subletting them), and to refrain from selling stall occupation rights to another person. The seller may be expelled from the stall for violating any of these stipulations.

When a stall becomes available through vacancy or new construction, anyone desiring to lease it may file an application with the market superintendent. All applications are placed in a container, and at a publicly announced time an application is drawn at random from the container. Any citizen may apply for a stall, but no "family" (this unit is not defined) may hold more than two stalls simultaneously. There are no other legal means to obtain a market stall.

In addition to the stallholding sellers, the number of sellers in the marketplace lawfully may be increased by so-called open-market vendors. These are sellers who occupy the "open market area" (see Map 3, p. 65) in which there are no stalls. Legally, however, open-market sellers are allowed to sell in the marketplace only on weekends and holidays, at which times there is also an influx of additional buyers from outside the city. On those occasions, there is no legal restriction upon sellers' participation except that they must pay *corteis* charges.

Another rule set out by municipal authority requires that the marketplace be "zoned" by product. The marketplace is divided into administrative sections, in each of which the sale of goods is limited to a particular class of commodities. Fresh fruit and vegetables may only be sold in the vegetable section, processed food in the grocery section, and so on. The market superintendent's records show twenty-one such zones (see Appendix I, p. 289, for the content of market zones), but there is not complete agreement about the number and boundaries of these among city officials. One of the duties of the market superintendent is to see that the zoning ordinance is enforced, and any seller found violating the restriction loses all rights to hold a stall in the marketplace.

Although there is an historical explanation for the zoning restriction, its continuation into the present appears to be an expression of a misunderstanding by local officials about the nature of the marketplace economy. The present justification for the ordinance is that it facilitates the collection of rentals and fees. But the consequence of the ordinance is an arbitrary restriction on the number of sellers of particular goods—a case of the bureaucratic tail wagging the economic dog. The obvious result is an infringement upon the free exercise of supply and demand: the number of sellers of particular products is fixed by administrative decision, not by the interplay of economic forces. As matters stand, these arbitrary limitations imply high prices in those areas of the market in which the number of sellers is kept low relative to demand, and lower prices and an increased number of business failures in those areas in which mobility is more nearly perfect.

The zoning ordinance is unpopular among marketplace sellers, although at the level of "real world processes" matters are not so desperate as they might seem. In the first place, not all sellers are affected, and the more substantial stallholders are most likely to feel any constraint. Open-market sellers aren't stallholders and are therefore not subject to zoning restrictions. They may sell anything legally salable as long as they first pay the necessary fees. Yet as much as possible open-market sellers "zone" themselves: vendors of the same principal products tend to congregate in the same area of the open market. Thus we have an apparent oddity: the more substantial, stallholding sellers oppose the zoning ordinance, while the open-market vendors deliberately zone themselves.

Resolution of this contradiction involves the different commercial strategies pursued by sellers in the two locations. The stallholder is likely to emphasize development of regular relationships with customers who trade with him habitually, so he will try to expand his enterprise by servicing the entire range of his customers' demands—selling more and more to the same people. In contrast, the open-market seller has relatively few regular customers and in addition has some special problems in communication. He is likely also to be a middleman, or collector, making wholesale purchases in rural areas until he accumulates enough goods to make a trip to Baguio worthwhile. Because this kind of trading requires precise knowledge about sources of supply, the middleman-seller is encouraged to deal in a narrow range of goods. He (or just as likely, she) is, therefore, largely unconcerned with zoning restrictions, having already decided upon a specialized line of products. Also, conveying to potential customers information concerning where, in a large and crowded market, sellers of particular goods are to be found is difficult. It is useful, therefore, for sellers of the same commodities to cluster together and to return to the same location repeatedly. Finally, there is the matter of price information. By clustering with other sellers of the same product, one may participate in the same price structure.[1]

The present zoning ordinance, which applies only to stallholders, is understandable as a vestigial remnant of earlier market organization. It was formulated in the days when all local

[1] Once again I am indebted to Sidney Mintz (personal communication) for suggesting to me some of the problems of communicating price information in developing areas.

marketplace sellers were of the "open-market" type. That is, they were free to sell different goods on different days, as the market dictated opportunities, and to move about accordingly. They were, therefore, much less affected by attempts to zone them than sellers are today.

In summary, one would anticipate that the rules of social organization imposed on the marketplace by duly-elected officials would seriously qualify some of the fundamental requirements of the ideal-type market. For example, legal restrictions limit competition by restricting the number of sellers who may participate: aliens can't participate at all, open-market sellers can sell only on specified days, and only limited numbers of persons can sell some products. Moreover, public officials attempt to influence prices, and the limitation on the number of *puestos* which each family may occupy implies arbitrary limitations on the growth of family enterprises.

However, a considerable gulf exists between the *de jure* regulations and the *de facto* behavior of "real world processes." Everyone in the local community is thoroughly familiar with all the rules of organization enumerated, and many informants explicitly affirm the principal that some regulation of the market is appropriate. Moreover, sellers know that authorities enforce the rules from time to time. Consequently, vendors know that they must keep the rules in mind, and, above all, that they must avoid drawing attention to breaches of them through obvious violations. But behavior deviates so widely from the rules that no public official is likely to make a sustained effort to enforce them. Furthermore, the nature of the local political process virtually eliminates any possibility of conscientious enforcement. The Baguio marketplace falls short of the ideal-type competitive market, but that fact has little to do with "the rules of social organization," as I hope now to demonstrate.

THE LOCAL-LEVEL POLITICAL PROCESS[2]

In general, the organization of the Philippine political system is, at least at the legal level, much like that of the United States, after which it was patterned. A constitution establishes the legal basis for government, and against it specific laws are tested for legality. Powers are separated American-style among executive, legislative, and judicial branches, and order depends upon the "checks and balances" of countervailing forces. The principal officials of the executive and legislative branches are elected by popular vote, and the legislature is bicameral, consisting of a senate and house of representatives. There also exists an hierarchical arrangement of administrative units governed by a combination of elected and appointed officials: provinces, municipalities, chartered cities, and barrios.

The two governments are also similar at the unofficial level, for the political process in each case involves two major parties (Liberals and Nacionalistas in the Philippines) and several minor ones. The chief distinction between American and Philippine governmental organization is that the latter leans more toward a "unitary" system, with power in the hands of national officials, and culminates in a presidency which has, legally, more power than its American counterpart. The often-observed tendency of lower levels of officialdom to turn to higher levels for decisions is not merely a Filipino cultural phenomenon but reflects the legal structure of government.

However, the two systems differ most sharply in their *de facto* political processes—reflections of the different cultural systems which influence them. The first important distinction at this level rises from the fact that, as many commentators have mentioned (e.g., Wurfel 1964, Grossholtz 1964, Lande

[2] This account has been rendered somewhat obsolete; circumstances changed considerably after the declaration of martial law on September 25, 1972.

1964, Corpus 1965, Agpalo 1965), Philippine political parties are not groups which enjoy stable memberships over time, which express strong doctrinaire orientations that carry over into different stances on issues, or which involve strict party discipline. Rather, they are coalitions, often short-term ones, of interest groups and personal factions which are associated for the collective purpose of furthering common goals. The ends of the nation, or of particular regions, are not necessarily ignored, but such organization tends to depress political altruism. At any given moment political parties represent real, if nondoctrinaire, divisions, but party membership is fluid and tends to change rapidly. Considerable shifting of loyalties to parties is usual, rather than the exception, as individuals work out more suitable arrangements. In both local and national elections fence-jumping is common. Loyalty to *persons*, however, is another matter.

A second significant difference is that some high-level Filipino legislators are elected at large, rather than upon a specified territorial basis. Thus, although members of the lower house represent districts, senators (and the members of city councils of chartered cities) are elected at large. The rationale for at-large elections is apparent: it is an attempt to create a set of officials who will represent the entire body politic rather than simply special interests. In such elections each party nominates a full slate of candidates; winners are selected according to the number of votes they receive, regardless of party affiliation. Because each candidate knows that some candidates from the opposing parties will almost certainly be elected, members of the same party compete not only with the opposition, but also with each other. Such an arrangement strains party discipline and encourages voters to support people, not parties. It strengthens an already powerful tendency toward personalism in Philippine politics.

111

In structural terms both American and Philippine political parties are corporate groups in the sense in which Weber (1947:145–146) used that term,[3] yet at the processual level their fundamental nature is different. American parties tend to advocate different principles of government and take different stands consistent with them on particular issues. Voters customarily align themselves in accord with a party's principles (or their perception of these), and they tend to vote for candidates on the basis of party affiliation. In the Philippines, however, important interparty distinctions on principles of government, or even upon specific issues, are rare. Party effort is more likely to be directed to pragmatic interest, and philosophy rarely enters the campaign (Grossholtz 1964:239). The poorer-class Filipino, in particular, is much more likely to vote for a candidate because of some interest-serving arrangement agreed upon with a candidate or one of his representatives, or because his personal social attachments are stronger with one candidate than with others.

Lynch (1959) and Hollnsteiner (1963) have referred to these associations of office seekers and their personal clienteles as alliance systems, and Hollnsteiner summarizes their organization in the following terms: "Where power is concerned a network of supporters is crucial to the person interested in gaining and maintaining power. These followers are provided through the alliance system, a network of reciprocal relationships whose members extend to one another and expect mutual assistance and loyalty" (1963:63). The patron-client dyads between political figures and voters have a large number of

[3] For Weber the corporate group has the following characteristics: it consists of a plurality of individuals; membership is limited by specific rules of admission; and internal power is differentially distributed among goal-oriented offices, usually a leader and an administrative staff (Weber 1947).

possible bases for existence. Kinship or ritual kinship (god-parenthood or co-godparenthood) are common reciprocal relationships which politicians seek to exploit. Or the relationship may involve some favor done for the voter in the past, or one anticipated in the future. But the general principle is interpersonal mutuality, or reciprocity. This personalistic political association is most practicable at the local level, where direct contact between candidate and follower makes specific agreements more practical, and where strong social bonds strengthen the sanctions which maintain the relationship. Because political relations involve not only power, but also bonds of sentiment and economic interest, local elections are likely to be spirited and often result in injured feelings, recrimination, and violence.

Higher-level elections have essentially the same structure as local elections, but as one goes up the scale there is more necessity to find allies who are not only voters, but who themselves are the leaders of coalitions and control blocs of votes. Also, there is greater use of mass communications media to gain support from voters unattached to candidates by the bonds of personalism. Thus, a political party, even at the national level, is an hierarchy of interlocking coalitions, each of which focuses on a power seeker (or a few of them). These organizational features become apparent when individual politicians shift party affiliations and take their personal followings with them.

Furthermore, parties often become symbols for divisions which are only locally significant. For example, in Baguio City the 1963 elections for mayor and city council were ostensibly a contest between candidates representing the two major national parties. The most significant division, however, had little to do with either platforms or personalities. Rather, the majority of the members of one party were Ilocano emigrants from Ilocos Sur, and the majority of the other consisted of Ilocanos from nearby La Union.

The arrangements made by individual politicians with potential supporters are the most important consideration in an actual election. This process is not simple, primarily because rival claims are typically made on the loyalties of both politician and supporter, while the means to satisfy these claims are limited. For example, voters anticipate that in exchange for their support in the election politicians will provide such services as legal counsel, mediation with courts and administrators, assistance in obtaining jobs, or perhaps money-lending. As long as a politician can meet these demands his alliance relationships tend to be durable, but the demand usually exceeds the personal resources of the office-seeker. Therefore, unless a politician is successful in gaining access to additional means, such as the public funds and opportunities to dispense largesse that holding an office usually conveys, he will ultimately fail to hold his supporters. The alliance is, therefore, inherently unstable, and this instability is expressed in the so-called *ningas kugon* (grass fire) phenomenon, in which leaders rise and decline rapidly.

Similarly, individual voters may be subject to several claims on their votes through a multiplicity of the kinds of relationships from which politicians seek to draw support. One may, for example, have two or more kinsmen or ritual kinsmen who are politicians, or have obligations (for services rendered) to more than one political figure. Under these circumstances, the individual must calculate carefully how to vote in order to obtain his goals while attempting to avoiding conflict. To cite Hollnsteiner again:

The voter is thus required to weigh all the relevant circumstances and to place all claimants for his vote in a hierarchy of *utang na loob* ["special obligation"] creditors. The values of his society dictate that the one highest on the list should gain his support. Behaviorally, however, expediency often supplants utang na loob as the decisive factor (1963:80).

One is not likely to find a clearer statement of economizing behavior than Hollnsteiner's description of the process through which Filipinos choose their political allegiances.

Politics in Baguio City

The political process in chartered Philippine cities, such as Baguio, differs in no significant way from the general model just described. Structurally, however, the administration of chartered cities is "missing" one level, for provincial governments have no official jurisdiction over chartered cities within their boundaries. Politicians in chartered cities, therefore, relate more directly to national party and administrative figures, and are likely to enjoy prestige and access to pork-barrel funds out of proportion to the number of votes they actually control.

In Baguio City the offices of mayor, vice mayor, and the six city councilmen are all elective, all for four-year terms. Each of the incumbent city officials in 1964 was affiliated with one of the two major national parties, but it is not uncommon for "independents" to stand for office. In the city elections of 1963, for example, an independent candidate for vice mayor made an excellent showing. However, independents in the Philippines, as in the United States, are less likely to be elected because they are apt to lack the resources necessary to wage extensive campaigns.

City councilmen are elected at large, not from municipal districts (although each candidate has his strongholds), and each major party nominates a full slate of six candidates for the six offices. (In the city elections of 1963 nine independent candidates also ran for city council, bringing the total to twenty-one.) Each voter then chooses six of these candidates, and the six top vote-getters win. The at-large election encourages candidates to campaign in other candidates' strongholds (including those of one's fellow party members), which ensures a lively election.

In the city election of 1963, approximately 25,000 voters were registered in the municipal district, 17,500 of whom voted for at least one candidate. The winning mayoral candidate received 10,500 votes, and the most popular candidate for city council received 12,500 votes. The least-popular winning city-council candidate received 8,900. The number of votes obtained by the most popular city councilman was said to be unusually large, and greatly enhanced his personal prestige and power, because it showed that he would be a strong contender for higher office in the future. But the point to be made is that about 9,000 votes would elect a candidate for city council, and a few more votes can get one elected mayor.

Local *liders* (non-office-holding "whips" or "ward bosses" who represent particular candidates) estimate that the 1200-odd stallholders in the marketplace, together with their immediate families and employees, represent at least 3,000 votes. Because about 9,000 votes will normally assure election to city office, the presence of so many voters with high-priority interests in common attracts considerable attention among local politicians. That market vendors have never felt the commonality of their interests strongly enough to vote as a bloc does not dim their potential in the eyes of local office seekers, and the two most prominent areas of concentrated political activity in town are the city hall and the marketplace. Vendors are becoming sophisticated in dealing with officials and office seekers, at least in knowing how to use the political threat their numbers constitute.

The campaign for local offices may be viewed at two levels. At one level it is public and general, or "diffuse" in Adrian Mayer's terms (1966); at the other it is private and "specific." At the diffuse level there is little difference between candidates' offerings, unless the opposition has been guilty of some notorious offense of which one side may take advantage. All candidates claim to possess essentially the same qualities. Each presents himself as "approachable," and not aloof from the common man. He is "sympathetic" and amenable to pleas for "consideration," or in other words, will seriously entertain supplicants' requests for special treatment and favors. The candidates stand solidly in favor of clean government: government free of bribery, favoritism, or conflict of interest. The candidate is always pledged to root out the rascals responsible for the sorry state of affairs alleged to exist at the moment. And finally, the candidate is strongly nationalistic, particularly in regard to economic affairs. The candidates and their active supporters stress these lofty qualities at both formal and informal gatherings, and in mimeographed literature. At this level the strategy is to make out that one is the sympathetic, patronly, honest, champion of the common man, while portraying opponents as ruthless, corrupt, high-handed, aristocratic, and violent enemies of the average person. Much preelection campaign oratory and literature is thoroughly scurrilous, and charges of blackmail and violence flow back and forth. In the following political broadside, widely distributed in the 1963 election, only the names of persons, places, and political parties have been altered:

SPECIAL INTELLIGENCE REPORT TO OUR PEOPLE
Confidential reports have been received that Mayor Luz's camp has issued secret orders to imported goons to liquidate rival Mayorality candidate Teofilo. This desperate measure is being resorted to, to ensure perpetuation of Luz in power.

Luz's group has been resorting to terrorism since the start of the campaign. Several Y Party supporters have been beaten up mercilessly by armed bodyguards in separate incidents at Kapan, Apang, and elsewhere. Juan D., our Y Party leader at Agno, was kidnapped from his house at 10:00 in the evening by armed men and brought to Mayor Luz's house. He was released only at 3:00 in the morning after being threatened with death and the demolition of his house if he continued supporting the Y Party. During the last registration days, armed goons intimidated Y Party precinct workers as they opposed the goons' attempt to register flying hostesses as illegal female voters. Luz's men have been having a field day hauling down our streamers and posters in the city. Luz yesterday afternoon also issued an illegal order impounding and confiscating all La Union vehicles sporting stickers to demobilize his opponents.

These events are a continuation of Luz's liking for the use of force. In 1961 he forcibly entered Councilor Nevada's office and threatened to kill the latter for investigating anomalies in the Mayor's office. The Mayor even slapped a woman who went to seek his assistance. Not long after, in the presence of market vendors, he called for Engineer Dolor, then after ordering his bodyguards to hold his arms, he slapped and mauled Dolor. Engineer Cruz of the City Engineer's Office, who issued a certification on anomalous purchases of machinery, is being hounded by armed goons of the Mayor to withdraw the certification. The Mayor personally supervised the demolition of a poor man's hut at Apusan, only to give the same lot to a close relative of his. In 1960, in a fit of anger, he ousted a government employee's family from their home at the height of the rainy season and compelled the poor wife and her numberous brood to spend the cold rainy night under the pine trees. The husband, a teacher, was then in the interior along the Mountain Trail.

The Mayor's suit against the 300 squatters in Ligon, considering them as public NUISANCES, and threatening their demolition and removal, is more of a veiled coercive measure intended to put our poor people under his power. The evil desire of the Mayor to intimidate our squatters, however, has been forestalled by our party, who secured an injunction from the court prohibiting all officials from further harassing in any manner, actual occupants of so-called squatter buildings during the pendency of the litigation.

The Mayor likewise has started to resort to his usual vote buying spree. No less than 70,000 pesos "tong" money will be used to flood the entire city particularly the squatter areas, to bolster his candidacy. They have already started the past two nights.

To prevent the Mayor from further resorting to violence, terrorism, intimidation, and vote-buying, and to ensure free, orderly expression of the popular will, the local party has requested the intervention of the Commission on Elections to STOP Luz from trampling upon the rights and liberties of our people!!!

At the specific level candidates seek to appeal directly to sentimental relationships, to special interests that groups may have, and to narrowly personal, pragmatic interests of the kind already mentioned. Informants repeatedly stressed the venal, unethical, and sometimes illegal nature of these arrangements—but participated in them nevertheless. In fact, one anecdote repeated by several informants had it that in the city elections of 1959 several candidates from one party not only bought votes outright (a common charge), but paid for them with counterfeit money! If the story is accurate, then it must surely be the limit on a continuum of political subterfuge. But whether true or not, that the story was so widely retold and believed says much about the nature of "specific level" political transactions in this region.

One offer to marketplace sellers during the 1963 election was that all market fees would be reduced 20 percent, provided that certain candidates were elected. (See Appendix II, p. 291, for other kinds of offers.) Furthermore, appeal was also commonly made to ethnolinguistic groups. For example, a number of families of marketplace sellers immigrated from

Batangas Province (south of Manila). These persons are not only active marketeers, but some are also involved in the local variant of the "numbers racket," *jueding*. According to informants, an attractive, and apparently largely successful, appeal was made to them on the basis of their being a small minority "in an Ilocano town." Specifically, it was pointed out to them that Batangueños were far from home and badly needed a "voice for protection," that is, they needed to align themselves with an Ilocano faction in order to have access to meaningful political influence.

RULES AND PROCESS IN THE MARKETPLACE

From its founding in 1903 until 1959, Baguio City (and Mountain Province) was governed by officials appointed by the national government, rather than locally elected. The entire province was considered a "special" region because of the high proportion of aboriginal peoples in its population. Until 1959 both the mayor and vice mayor, and four of the six city councilmen, were appointed by the national government. All the restrictive measures relating to stallholding, zoning, open-market participation, etc., were passed prior to the transition from appointed to elected officials. The institution of local elections was a turning point in local politics and local marketplace activities: it is a critical time boundary to informants, who refer to the period prior to 1959 as "before."

As long as the city was governed by appointees of the national government, laws were likely to be enforced rigorously, for central bureaucratic authority, and not an electorate, judged incumbents' performances. As long as the popularity of the official's local performance had little to do with his welfare, there were no means for appealing to him for "considera-tion." The official who properly performed his role was the one who conscientiously implemented instructions and regu-lations from higher levels of authority, not the man who was "approachable" and "reasonable."

Sellers who operated in the marketplace prior to the insti-tution of electoral government are unanimous in their ap-proval of marketplace conditions during that time. It is widely claimed that "before" market stalls and walkways were kept clean and unobstructed, that stalls and sellers were orderly, that market fees were collected fairly, and above all that the restriction of use of the marketplace to legal, rent-paying, stall-holders was enforced. This, it is alleged, was the time when stall shelves were well stocked and business brisk, so that no one had any quarrel with the zoning ordinance. For those who were there, it seems, the late 1940s and the 1950s were a golden age of marketing in the city marketplace. Participation was limited, but those who had stalls managed to prosper, largely as the result of "frictions" in the competitive process which were introduced by political authority.

Instituting electoral forms of authority changed this situ-ation dramatically, for these have tended to clear away the uni-versalism of an appointed bureaucracy, substituting for it a form much more prone to the personalism characteristic of Filipino patterns of interaction. If *elected* officials aren't "ap-proachable," they will not remain long in office.

In the marketplace the payoffs that potential supporters seek from politicians are typically intercession with market authorities to prevent the enforcement of marketplace regula-tions. Because sellers can now approach local authorities with some expectation of acquiring their patronage, the market sup-erintendent and his staff have, in effect, become powerless to enforce ordinances. The result is that official marketplace administrative roles have become almost entirely clerical in nature, rather than directive.

The neutralization of marketplace authority by self-interested politicians has resulted in a number of significant behavioral departures from the "rules of social organization." Perhaps the most obvious change is the steady decline in enforcement of the zoning ordinance. Violation of the ordinance has become routine. One may, for example, buy souvenir woodcarvings in the clothing sections, woven fabric in the vegetable section, and vegetables in the fish section. As the number of outside sellers has increased, so has competition, and few sellers have resisted the temptation to spread risks and widen the range of demand met for individual customers by extending the variety of their stocks. A tendency toward zoning remains, as the result of history and the nature of "supply" relationships (a point to be clarified below), but there is little fear among sellers that violations of the ordinance will be prosecuted.

The institution of elected officials has also affected stall tenure rights in the marketplace, and the mode of transferring them. The only way to obtain stalls legally is through drawing lots, and the stallholder must also pay weekly rent and operate the stall himself in order to meet legal tenure requirements. In practice, however, things work out differently, as individual sellers strive to take advantage of economic opportunities, and to reduce risk.

In many cases during the time that they operate businesses from a stall, sellers acquire fixed capital and other assets, some of which are potentially transferable. For example, often a stallholder cultivates a clientele which comes to depend upon him as the sole supplier of a given class of goods. Furthermore, vendors often add improvements to their stalls at their own expense. Many have added display counters, carefully constructed siding and flooring, storage cabinets, shelves, or perhaps a better roof. These tangible and intangible assets may be transferred on the occasion of an exchange of use rights in a stall, just as they are at sales of businesses at more sophisticated economic levels. If stalls were, in fact, transferred in the legal manner (by lot), previous occupants would lose all opportunity to be compensated for their proprietary rights. Transfers of stalls are now accomplished, therefore, rather more simply than the public officials who established the rules had in mind: they are bought, sold, and subleased. But selling rights in stalls cannot take place unless the participants are assured immunity from legal prosecution, and that is precisely one of the benefits afforded by the character of the local political process.

Not that stalls are never obtained legally. Newly-constructed stall facilities are rented according to the rules (except for some political favoritism), but drawing lots is clearly not *typical*, and the more desirable stalls are never obtained according to the rules.

The sale price of a stall is calculated largely on the basis of the same factors employed by the city in computing market fees—size, location, and the nature of the goods sold. A stall's value, however, also includes the value of any customers the new operator is likely to obtain (upon recommendation of the previous stallholder and suitable credit arrangements), the value of the inventory, and the value of improvements made by the previous stallholder. The cost of assuming a stall varies from approximately $20 US to several hundred dollars. The most expensive stall on which it was possible to obtain reliable information was approximately $500 US, but it was said that some stalls have sold for twice that amount. Because stalls in good locations are likely to continue to appreciate in value, tenure rights to market stalls are considered good speculative investments, even by persons who have no intention of occupying them, including—it is said—some substantial downtown businessmen. Now and then stalls remain unoccupied for weeks, as their "owners" wait for the right opportunity to dispose of them. Rights to well-situated stalls are also considered adequate collateral by some of the marketplace's moneylenders. Moreover, there also exist in the marketplace "landlords" who hold rights to several stalls which they, in turn, lease to others. This situation usually comes about when moneylenders foreclose on bad debts in which stalls have served as security. One middle-aged lady who could occasionally be seen sitting, quietly sewing, in any of several stalls about the marketplace, was such a moneylender-landlady; she sought to minimize her risks by visiting and spending some time observing the businesses indebted to her.

One of the most important legal restrictions which has been effectively neutralized is the limitation on "outside" competition, or open-market selling. Any seller who is a qualified voter has a good possibility of finding one or another politically influential person who, in exchange for his support, will intercede with authorities on his behalf. In fact, as an election approaches, political aspirants themselves commonly take an active role in searching out such opportunities. One common occurrence is for the political figure to intercede with the market superintendent to obtain permission for nonstallholders to sell in the marketplace. These sellers usually carry notes bearing the signature of some important man as protection from the marketplace administration. To their stallholding colleagues, such sellers are known accordingly and, somewhat derisively, as card carriers.

The continuous participation of open-market sellers had become so commonplace that before the 1963 election authorities rarely bothered to clarify the legal statuses involved. The result was an increasingly large number of open-market participants, some not even registered voters in Baguio City. Stallholders often expressed righteous anger over these conditions, complaining that many sellers who had no right to legal circumvention were nevertheless practicing it!

One serious municipal problem which has emerged from political patronage in the marketplace is that it has become increasingly difficult for the city treasurer's office to collect rentals and fees from marketplace sellers.[4] Because sellers so frequently carry their appeals to higher official levels, for the market superintendent to evict stallholders for nonpayment of fees is difficult, and marketplace revenue collections are substantially in arrears (see Table 4). Figures on market fee delinquency show a considerable delinquency rate in 19 of the 21 administrative sections of the marketplace. As far as one may determine objectively, the extent of this delinquency does not necessarily reflect an *inability* to pay fees, and is therefore no index of business success. In fact, a list of principal delinquents revealed the names of—to judge by appearance and reputation —some of the most successful sellers in the marketplace. The problem is that market fee delinquency is as much a measure of a man's political influence as of his economic prosperity (or lack of it). Some indication of the magnitude of the problem is that in 1963 market fee delinquency totalled over 26,000 pesos (about \$7,000 US), which *averages* more than three weeks' delinquency per market stall—the legal period of eviction for nonpayment of rents and fees (see Table 4).

Finally, political patronage has removed direct legal limitations on the expansion of individual enterprises in the market-

---

[4] This problem, by no means limited to the collection of market fees, is general throughout municipal revenue collection. A feature of municipal life—certainly not unique to the Philippines—is that those most capable of paying taxes are the persons with enough influence to avoid them. The result is that revenues on all city services are greatly in arrears.

TABLE 4

Market Fee Delinquency[a]

Area	Total Delinquency	Average per Stall	Average Weeks per Stall[b]
Bagoong	365.14	40.57	14.2
Caldero	222.50	17.11	1.7
Carinderia	4506.50	145.37	6.1
Chucheria	3035.53	86.71	35.8
Curio & Souvenir	1047.28	65.45	4.1
Dry Goods	4271.51	23.73	3.2
Second-Hand Clothes	622.91	24.52	7.5
Entrails	159.01	4.42	2.4
Fish	4998.25	33.32	14.7
Flowers	1034.60	32.33	8.6
Fowls	289.50	16.09	6.5
Halo-halo	185.84	23.23	9.3
Vegetables (Hangar)	1975.99	163.75	35.8
Hotcake	1046.91	52.35	9.6
Meat	435.06	12.08	1.5
Periodicals	4.51	.64	.1
Rice[c]	–	–	–
Sari-sari	1255.16	9.58	1.9
Tobacco	248.43	14.61	10.8
Vegetables (Main)	210.19	1.10	.3
Vegetables (Hangar)	520.20	1.15	.4
Refreshments	1975.99	163.75	18.2

[a]In Philippine pesos.

[b]According to the "rules" stallholders are supposed to be evicted from the marketplace after three consecutive weeks of delinquency.

[c]Rice sellers' market fees are paid by the rice millers who supply the rice sold in the marketplace.

place. It is possible to obtain initial entry to the market by purchasing tenure rights to a stall and to avoid the two-stall limit legally imposed upon families. However, because the rules against these activities are specific and detailed, and because expansion is undertaken at the expense of other stallholders' interests, the stall operator must move forward carefully. A sudden change in stall operators could attract considerable attention from neighbors, and public attention could oblige authorities either to take action or lose esteem. Accordingly, the acquisition of additional stalls is a gradual process and one which the entrepreneur attempts to accomplish with considerable *delicadeza* (finesse), even though both the authorities and the operators of adjacent stalls are aware of the transaction.

After the rights to a stall have been purchased, or an agreement for transfer is struck, the new operator begins to make visits to the stall. As the visits of the new operator increase in frequency, the old operator's appearances diminish in inverse proportion until the new operator assumes complete control (in a few cases, the old operator lingered about the premises until he had been paid in full). If the new operator has several stalls and can not operate them all personally (unless they are contiguous), he may wish to bring employees into the operation. In this case, the employee is usually incorporated through the same gradual process. Ordinarily, as long as both partners in the transfer are satisfied, and as long as there are no delinquent fees owed on the stall (a token payment seems sufficient in any event), stalls change hands smoothly without official interference. Occasionally, however, one of the partners to the agreement feels that he has been cheated and decides to renege on his agreement and contest the transfer. Such cases are then referred to the market committee, and if their solution is not acceptable, to court. Not surprisingly, the market committee is likely to support the *de facto* situation, not the legal rule. But the one case which, in 1964, went both to the market committee and to court provides another impression. In that case the court reversed the decision of the market committee and found in favor of the legal holder. The knowledge that the court upheld the rule and not the behavioral practice, and that courts are likely to continue to do so, both enhances the value of political patronage and encourages some attention to the rules.

Because of the technical illegality of selling stallholding rights, to distinguish operators who are the "owners" of the stall from those who are merely employees of some stall-owning entrepreneur is often difficult. To determine accurately the number of persons holding more stalls than the legal limit is not possible. To my knowledge, however, at least forty persons in the marketplace have rights to three or more stalls. Even more revealing, most of these multiple-stall operations involve *contiguous* stalls. The statistical odds against obtaining three or more contiguous stalls by drawing lots are staggering and clearly demonstrate the actual nature of stall acquisition. By using political patronage, and by the purchase of facilities, a few marketplace sellers have been able to consolidate substantial holdings—amounting to small shops—in the marketplace.

MARKETPLACE ORGANIZATIONS AND POLITICAL ACTION

Although I have so far treated the dyadic relations of the alliance system as if their inevitable outcome were mutually advantageous, this is clearly not always the case. Either partner in the dyad can exploit the other. Since the mutualistic advantages in the relationship are rarely manifested simultaneously, one partner can obtain his own satisfactions and then default on his obligations. Such behavior usually terminates the relationship, but it is common in the Philippines, as elsewhere, for politicians to renege on campaign promises, or for voters to find that the costs of voting for particular politicians are, after all, too high to pay. Because of the multiplex nature (political, economic, sentimental, etc.) of the relationships, defaults on such agreements are often accompanied by hard feelings, but such lapses happen frequently in spite of rules and norms. Inducement to default commonly occurs, because individuals have many dyadic relationships, some of which compete for the same resources. Inevitably individuals find themselves caught between social obligation and self-interest. Hollnsteiner referred to this situation when she spoke of ranking obligations and interests in a hierarchy of preferences (Hollnsteiner 1963:80).

Because they imply a bloc of votes and have the durable organization to call politicians to account, groups are better capable of wresting concessions from politicians than individuals are. For example, in 1959, at the time of the first general elections held in Baguio City, plans were underway for the construction of new, more modern *carinderia* (cooked food) facilities in the marketplace. These plans called for the use of public money in the proposed construction, and had been suggested, and lobbied for, by the *carinderia* sellers, who promised to support certain candidates in return for the new facilities. However, in spite of their common interests, the *carinderia* sellers did not form an organization to attain their goals, and no leader was chosen to represent them.

Informants alleged that at the time these negotiations were in progress, the operators of several Chinese restaurants adjacent to the marketplace became concerned about the competition which a new *carinderia* area would impose. It is said that a counteroffer was made to the same candidates through the Chinese Chamber of Commerce, an offer designed to block the new *carinderia* construction. Few Chinese could vote, but being relatively wealthy they could make substantial contributions to party war chests. Some candidates supported by both the Chinese and the Filipino *carinderia* sellers were elected and faced a dilemma: how to implement the terms of one agreement without violating the terms of the other. The choice involved considering the loss of a few individual *carinderia* sellers' votes in the next election, as opposed to forfeiting important potential financial backing in many successive elections if they defaulted on their agreement with a strong and durable Chinese association. The resolution they formulated was a masterstroke of local-level political diplomacy. New *carinderia* facilities were constructed according to agreement, but they were placed well back from the main thoroughfare, and on the second floor of the main market building. They are directly over the fish market, where the odor is ferocious even for the initiated. Accordingly, the *carinderia* sellers' business is generally poor. The market fee delinquency table is not a good indicator of business success or failure, but it is interesting to note that the delinquency rate in the *carinderia* section is among the highest.

Some of the more politically aware sellers have long recognized the potential benefits of forming a market vendors' association, and efforts in that direction began as early as 1953. Membership was initially small, goals were modest, and the functions of the organization were officially limited to informing city officials of grievances. The major impetus to form the organization at that point, apparently, was overzealous enforcement of minor market regulations by the local police. Interest in the organization grew when its representative was included on the market committee, and in 1955 articles of incorporation were filed for the Baguio City Market Vendors' Association (BAMARVA). A slate of officials has been elected every year since 1955.

The BAMARVA articles of incorporation list the primary functions of the organization to be advancement of a number of goals so general and commendable they could offend no one: the maintenance of order and cleanliness in the marketplace,

the improvement of economic prosperity, economic nationalism, and charitable mutual aid. In practice, however, little is
done to promote these goals, and the chief group activity to
which members will admit is the provision of burial expenses
for the deceased indigent.

During city elections the main function of BAMARVA
emerges: BAMARVA is first and foremost a political pressure
group. However, its officials are anxious not to impart the impression that BAMARVA is a political unit because of their fear
of political reprisals if their candidates lose. BAMARVA's main
objective is to secure the election of officials—regardless of
party affiliation—who are pledged to policies favorable to marketplace interests. Politicians are aware of BAMARVA's role, and
are careful to seek out BAMARVA officers and policy makers, to
entertain them, to solicit their opinions, and to assure them that
they support policies which advance BAMARVA interests. At
times all the candidates of both political parties have claimed
to support BAMARVA demands, and one of the *ex officio* duties
of BAMARVA officials is to meet with candidates in order to assess
their "sensitivity," to evaluate their acceptability for other
sellers. The election of BAMARVA officials themselves is typically
undertaken in consideration of city-level politics, and the president is always a man known to "have the ear" of either incumbent city officials or powerful challengers. In recent years
several BAMARVA officials have also been *liders* for major party
candidates. Interestingly enough, supporting candidates favorable to marketplace interests may well oblige these *liders* to
support some candidates from a party in opposition to their
own, clear evidence of the priority of interest over party discipline. Additional evidence of BAMARVA's role as a political
action group is that since the institution of electoral government, membership has grown approximately 300 percent faster
than the marketplace seller population (see Table 5). In 1964

131

TABLE 5

Marketplace Growth 1953–1963[a]

Section	No. Stalls 1953	No. Stalls 1963	% of growth
Bagoong	6	10	67
Caldero	8	13	63
Carinderia	22	31	40
Chucheria	13	35	169
Curio	10	16	60
Dry Goods	170	180	6
Entrails	6	36	500
Fish	130	150	15
Flowers	10	32	220
Footwear	30	36	20
Fowls	18	18	0
Halo-halo	5	8	60
Meat	25	36	44
Periodicals	5	7	40
Rice	30	48	60
Sari-sari	105	131	25
Tobacco	14	17	21
Vegetables (Main)	188	188	0
Vegetables (Hangar)	112	452	303
Refreshments	8	12	50

[a]1953 is the earliest year for which figures were available. These figures represent the number of administrative stall units recognized by the city treasurer's office. They do not necessarily represent an increase in the number of vendors, for many vendors incorporate several stalls into a single operation. Thus on any given day the number of enterprises can only be determined by a cautious headcount. Moreover, many stalls classed in a given category are, in practice, likely to be involved in the sale of some other commodity, because, as explained in the text, "zoning" has broken down badly. For example, some of the stalls in the "vegetable" section are, in fact, involved in the sale of *sari-sari* items, and not in the sale of vegetables.

the association's officials claimed that 60 percent of all market sellers were members.

Because BAMARVA has such a large membership, and no other interest group in the city approaches it in size, it might logically attempt to elect some of its own members to office. This has never happened, and the two marketplace sellers who ran in local elections were badly beaten at the polls and got little solid support from the marketplace. Marketplace sellers suffer from a shortage of personal finances for conducting campaigns and lack the status expected of a serious contender for local office. Moreover, vendor-candidates are looked upon as having overstepped the limits of propriety.

BAMARVA, therefore, doesn't present a solid front. Members are united on only the most general issues, and there is no feeling that they should close ranks to protect the interests of a minority of members—no realization that if they protect the fish sellers today, their entire association may profit tomorrow. For example, BAMARVA officials generated widespread support for candidates pledged to a reduction in market fees, but there was no interest at all in marshalling a common effort to prevent the market superintendent from moving some *chucheria* sellers to poorer locations. However, the threat that BAMARVA members might vote as a bloc gives its officials considerable bargaining power.

Other associations have also been formed, largely as responses to conflicts of interest which occurred in the past. However, these others tend to concentrate on a narrower range of interests than BAMARVA does. For example, the fish sellers formed an association in an effort to obtain better facilities from the city, and to establish a supply of low-priced capital. The lowland-Filipino sellers of the main vegetable section organized in an effort to get their rents reduced to the level of the other—much poorer—vegetable-selling areas. And the vegetable sellers of aboriginal origin were, in 1964, in the midst of an effort to organize in order to lobby for legislation protecting them from the alleged excesses of Chinese middlemen. None of these latter organizations, however, had become active politically, and a strong suspicion expressed by many nonmember sellers was that some of them were dummy organizations for moneylenders. Thus BAMARVA remains the principal organ for political expression in the marketplace, and its importance is reflected in its own elections. These are vigorously contested and involve the same kind of alliance politics, patronage campaigning, vote-buying, charges of violence, distribution of libelous literature, and so on, that characterize higher-level election campaigns.

In sum, the legal statutes which gave Baguio City citizens the right to elect their own officials simultaneously provided the social mechanism for neutralizing restrictive legislation, thereby providing the marketplace with great potential for the exercise of free competition. But to understand marketplace behavior one must proceed beyond the "rules of social organization" to consider the individual interests expressed in interpersonal action. We obtain different views of "the reality of society" by emphasizing one or the other of these different levels of analysis.

Chapter Five

Marketplace Roles

Marketplaces are primarily distributional organizations. However, "distributional" activities may be separated only analytically from those of production and consumption. Production has already been discussed, but before a discussion of distributional roles *per se*, it is useful to consider some aspects of local consumption roles and behavior patterns.

Consumption Patterns

"Buyer" roles consist of two basic activities distinguished by the ends to which transacted goods are directed. In the first place, there are "wholesaling" activities, large quantity purchases for intended resale at a profit. Wholesaling activities are basic to the distributional process, and will be considered below. The immediate concern is with the second kind of buyer activity, purchase for consumption.

The great majority of transactions in the Baguio market-place are purchases made by buyers for household use, not for bulking and resale. Furthermore, with the exception of a few nonperishable staples (e.g., rice, salt, sugar, cooking oil, and kerosene), Filipinos characteristically purchase supplies on a daily or near-daily basis. These consumption patterns relate to the generally low family incomes and the lack of preservation technology, which make budgeting and saving through quantity purchases unfeasible for most lower-class persons. Frequent purchasing is time-consuming and is generally perceived as an inconvenience (and not as a form of recreation, as is sometimes alleged to occur among marketeers elsewhere, cf. Bohannan and Dalton 1962), but it is a pattern of behavior well adjusted to local incomes. For persons accustomed to Western shopping habits, the distances which Filipinos frequently travel to make small purchases are surprising.

As noted, the marketplace is essentially a lower-class institution. Local professionals and elites do not enter the marketplace frequently, although the fresh agricultural produce which they consume they obtain in the marketplace. Some sellers, accordingly, reckon important persons among their customers (though they may deal through a servant), and often point with pride to the distinguished households they serve. But the great majority of marketplace purchases are made by low-income households.

The consumption habits of indigenous peoples help to explain the treatment often given them by stallholders. Cordilleran peoples in general have fewer opportunities to earn cash incomes than lowland Filipinos have, and as a result they are not as highly valued as potential steady customers. The indifferent treatment they so often receive from lowland Filipinos, and their low incomes, incline natives to distribute purchases among many sellers, rather than to return to the same seller repeatedly. They are also apt to bargain forcefully before making a purchase. When seller and buyer are not acquainted, sellers offer the highest opening bids to natives, Spaniards, Euroamericans, and Filipinos, in that order. Natives head the list because they bargain with such enthusiasm, followed by Spaniards, who are more wealthy but who are thought to be such clever traders that the seller is again likely to have to retreat from his opening bid. Euroamericans rank third because they are thought to be wealthy but poor traders (Peace Corps volunteers have had considerable impact on altering that general assumption). Filipinos are fourth because they are more apt to share the same perception of value and to come rapidly to agreement on prices.

DISTRIBUTIONAL ROLES

Local persons may earn profits in trading in a seemingly infinite number of ways, and an exhaustive description of all these would be a monumental task. To enumerate the main role patterns is necessary, however, to facilitate the principal theme of the discussion: the nature of social relations in the marketplace economy. But the descriptive categories employed—economic roles—are not persons. Persons are apt to combine two or more of these roles in order to increase their own savings. In fact, high mobility between specialized trading roles appears to be an important feature of marketplace systems.

At a high level of generalization, marketplace operations vary in their emphasis upon transport and stockpiling, or "storage-accumulation" (Belshaw 1965:66). At a more specific level (and for practical reasons), economic roles in the Baguio marketplace system are highly differentiated and specialized. There are several reasons for local role differentiation.

First, the unusually high level of local demand encourages the accumulation of a wide variety of goods. At the same time, however, supply centers tend to be erratic in production and widely diffused geographically, so that successful trading involves such detailed information about supply sources that a given trader is unlikely to have adequate knowledge for more than a few classes of products. For example, large-scale producers of cattle, poultry, pigs, or goats are few. Those who wish to deal in these items must seek them out in small lots from dispersed individual producers, so traders need specific information about producers. This encourages traders to specialize in a narrow range of distributional functions and to deal in a narrow range of goods in order to reduce risks. The ideal is to diversify activities to spread risks, but this ideal strategy is limited by the practical demand for information. Such conditions encourage maintenance of a large number of specialists, each dealing in a few classes of goods. And sellers lend or trade goods with one another in order to acquire greater variety.

Second, the problem of transportation makes it impractical for a seller both to operate a stall in the marketplace and to function as a middleman by going out to collect supplies in the countryside. Transport is too slow and unreliable for individuals to do both on a consistent basis. Yet success in the market requires an assured supply of goods and a daily selling operation. Therefore, some sellers attempt to increase savings by keeping both supply and trading roles in the same family (typically, the wife stays in the market, the husband collects in the countryside), but the arrangement is not a popular one. Thus, severe limitations on time and space limit the number of distributional roles an individual can perform.

Third, is the complex problem of "personalism" in economic role articulation. One prominent characteristic of social relationships in the market system, to be developed further in subsequent sections of this essay, is that one's trading alters are not usually interchangeable. Alters possess certain qualities which set them apart, in the eyes of actors, from other persons who would otherwise be available for recruitment to a given alter role. Or put slightly differently, "noneconomic" factors recruit persons to economic roles.

The basis for this is again the necessity to reduce risks in rural-based enterprises, and this involves two considerations. First, it is to the rural producers' advantage to develop routine market outlets so that they may depend upon having their products collected and taken to market—and even more, so that they may depend upon the fairness of the prices offered. Second, credit is usually an aspect of the relationship, because the rural producer doesn't expect payment from the middleman until after the goods have been collected, taken to market, and sold. Some basis of trust is important, therefore, in order to secure these arrangements. There is almost invariably a strong prestational element in such relationships.

Because of the highly personalized nature of many producer-distributor relationships, it is difficult for a large-scale operator to interpose himself between rural producers and collectors in order to assume collection functions. These personal associations resemble petty-scale cartels, a condition which encourages a proliferation of specialized roles rather than a combination of them.

Again an example illustrates the point. Among the eighteen stallholders in the Baguio marketplace who specialize in selling live fowl were two sisters who had immigrated from neighboring Pangasinan. Their usual sources of supply were several "carriers," that is, persons who travel about the countryside collecting fowl until they have accumulated enough to make a trip to the market worthwhile. In this case the fowl were crated, taken to Baguio on the top of a passenger bus, and then sold wholesale to the market retailers. Carriers usually sell to persons with whom they habitually deal.

In 1963 our two fowl sellers decided that they could increase their profits substantially by dividing the work involved in their business, sending one sister to the lowlands to obtain the stocks of fowl which were to be sold in Baguio. This attempt, however, ended in failure precisely because producers refused to sell birds to anyone other than the carriers with whom they usually dealt. The carriers had proved they could be trusted, and represented secure, well-tried outlets. Producers were reluctant to try untested intermediaries, even though the latter offered slightly higher prices. According to the sellers, in order to obtain stocks they would have to offer such high price inducements that profits would be too little to make the venture worthwhile.

Some rural producers who might otherwise prefer to sell directly to retailers are afraid to do so because Baguio market-sellers have a reputation for shrewd trading. They find it preferable to sell their products to professional carriers, who are more familiar with marketing procedures and conditions, and can deal more successfully with sophisticated city traders.

Role specialization in the local marketplace system may be classified on the basis of the point in the distributional process at which the role intervenes. Using the marketplace in Baguio as a point of reference, it is possible to distinguish classes of roles in terms of one of three stages of the circulation of goods: collection and transport of goods to the marketplace ("internal transport roles"), storage-accumulation and bulk breaking for buyers in the marketplace ("vending roles"), and collection and transport of goods from the marketplace ("external transport roles"). The number of roles specifically enumerated below could be doubled by drawing a further distinction between wholesale and retail selling. But this conceptual distinction involves few behavioral differences, and they will be noted only where they appear particularly significant.

The Peasant-Producer. The peasant-producer, as the term suggests, himself markets some portion of a self-produced product. In this particular locale, however, the peasant is more likely to sell to a retailer or a carrier than to market his own product. Indeed, as we have seen, producers tend to deal habitually with the same retailers and intermediaries, and thus tend to have long-standing relationships with them. Producers are likely to become retailers only when conditions result in a strong sellers' market. However, some producers are only "target marketeers": they participate in the market only to the extent necessary to attain some specific goal which requires cash.

Because by definition peasant-producers are rural producers, the majority of them live well outside the city limits, and some actually live in lowland provinces, coming to Baguio City in search of higher prices. Yet because of the geographic limits of the "city," some peasant-producers live in the city and can vote in city elections.

A variation on this general role pattern sometimes occurs when the producer is a member of one of the indigenous ethno-linguistic groups. It is not uncommon for natives to deliver agricultural produce, cottage manufactures, or forest products which they have gathered to a stallholder in the marketplace. These products are exchanged for credit in the stallholder's goods equal to the monetary value of the native's products. This is technically a form of barter, because goods are exchanged for other goods, but it takes place in terms of the money value of the goods on the market. Murphy (1955) terms this barter credit. This barter-credit relationship tends to bind the stallholder and the native together, for credit in stock, unlike cash, has low liquidity and cannot be easily transferred. The relationship tends to be all the more self-perpetuating because natives tend to obtain credit first and then to provide products to remove the obligations which they have incurred. This situation can be easily manipulated by the stallholder and may result in the native becoming increasingly indebted to him.

Producer and retailer, then, are commonly joined through a multidimensional relationship which goes beyond the element of material self-interest. Of necessity there are also elements of social obligation, value, and trust, or the relationship could not endure.

Carriers. The second category of internal transport roles consists of "carrier roles." Carriers are intermediaries who may produce a small proportion of the goods which they sell, but who are primarily concerned with collecting small quantities of goods produced by others and transporting these to market, where they are resold. In most cases these "surplus" quantities of goods are obtained from primary producers, but there are also carriers who accumulate stocks by purchasing them in lower-order marketplaces for resale in Baguio City. Carriers usually prefer to dispose of the goods they have collected by selling them wholesale to professional retailers (often on credit), thus placing the burden of risk on the retailer. But again, if prices are relatively high and demand brisk, carriers often attempt to earn additional savings by retailing.

Carriers who have been long involved with trade tend to have personalized, long-standing relationships at both ends of the distributional network, with rural producers in the countryside and sellers in the marketplace. These relationships reduce risks in ways already demonstrated and also reduce the quantity of operating capital required to be a carrier.

Because of the connection between carrier roles and information about the countryside, most carriers are themselves rural people, and their prime sources of supply are relatives and neighbors. Because they are rural residents, their work often involves traveling long distances. As a result, for them to get to market on a daily basis is difficult. But their persistence and endurance are remarkable. For example, one middle-aged lady averaged five weekly trips to Baguio from points in Pangasinan Province which were 60 kilometers and more distant, and had done so for five consecutive months until the rainy season forced her to slow down.

Not all carriers are rural residents, however, and some of them occupy dual roles: they are both carriers and "peddlers" (see below). They have been lured to Baguio City not only by the hope of additional profit to be made selling there, but also by the opportunity to carry small quantities of manufactured items from Baguio to the countryside. These goods are then sold in lesser-order marketplaces, or in the *sari-sari* stores which are sometimes maintained in private residences, or from door to door in small communities.

Most carriers are small-scale operators, and have an operating capital of less than 100 pesos (roughly $25 US). The small scale of this trade is due both to low income and to the credit function which these roles involve, but it is aggravated by the weak development of available transport. Carriers must use unspecialized public transport (usually passenger buses and jeepneys), and often they simply walk. Passenger buses in the Philippines are usually constructed with their bodies raised well above their frames in order to provide storage space between the frame and body. In addition, they have racks on top to accomodate small quantities of freight, usually contained in baskets which are tied in place. Jeepneys are old military vehicles whose frames and canopies have been extended in order to accommodate more passengers and baggage. They usually operate on more or less regular schedules between specific points, like short-haul public carriers. However, they often may be hired for special trips, at additional cost to the customer. It is not possible to say what part of the commodities moved through the Philippine internal distributional system is transported at some point in these two kinds of conveyances, but the percentage must be high.

Practically speaking, therefore, adequate commercial transport is not available, and carriers must usually accompany their own stocks in transit, a necessity which establishes a low limit on the quantities which can be handled on a given occasion. There is obviously a quantum jump from the amount of capital needed in using public transport and the quantity necessary for obtaining one's own transportation.

Agents. The final category of "internal transport roles" is the class to which local marketplace participants apply the term "agent." An agent is a representative of a large jobbing, wholesaling, importing, manufacturing, or rice-milling firm. When we consider agent roles, we are investigating the ways by which manufactures, processed foods, etc., are conveyed to the local marketplace. These roles form the connecting link in the downward flow of goods from the capital-intensive sector of the national-international economy to the localized marketplaces of the "peasant" economic sector.

Agents provide important distributional functions. In the first place, few marketplace sellers could afford to make the trips to the central plains and to the Manila-Makati area which would be necessary if local sellers had to initiate the distribution of manufactured goods. To make arrangements with local agents is far more convenient. Second, agents are principal sources of capital, and many of the goods stocked on local sellers' shelves actually belong to some large Manila-based firm. While extending credit at the local level is a high-risk undertaking, it is essential that agents' firms do so. In effect, the seller who stocks the manufacturer's products becomes a kind of regional wholesale outlet, for the seller will, in turn, extend credit both to lesser-order sellers and to his own retail customers. For the agent's firm to be able to work through the local seller is a great convenience, for the firm is, in effect, using the seller's knowledge of local market conditions and local people. A firm would require a huge sales force to carry out the functions supplied by local marketplace sellers. The firm not only makes a profit on selling to the marketplace seller but also from interest on credit extended to him.

Collectively through these internal transport roles nearly all goods are supplied to the local marketplace. There are some additional channels, but they are either government-sponsored, such as those already discussed (e.g., NAMARCO), or else they are grossly illegal and account for only a small part of the total quantities of goods moved (e.g., stolen, smuggled, and black-market goods).

VENDOR ROLES

Many minor distinctions could be made between the several varieties of accumulation, storage, and bulk-breaking ("vendor") roles: principle product traded, whether strategies emphasize short or long-term gain, mode of appealing to customers, or even the vendor's ethnic identity. However, the most general critical distinction to be made is between the "main" and "open" market areas. This is, essentially, a distinction between stallholding and nonstallholding sellers respectively.

Stallholders. Stallholders, as the term suggests, are marketplace vendors who rent selling facilities from the city on a continuing weekly basis. They are treated here as a category in opposition to the vendors of the open-market area, locally referred to as transients, or those who merely occupy space in the market upon daily payment of market fees. Most stallholders are professional sellers: they are deeply committed to buy and sell in the market as an important, if not the principal, source of income. Occupying a stall involves certain fixed costs, and the willingness to pay these amounts to a powerful professional commitment. It is not, however, uncommon for stallholders to take recesses from their marketplace operations, especially during slow seasonal periods, or even to use their liquid capital in some short-term venture other than selling in the market. The less prosperous fish vendors who have no access to fishponds, for example, often suspend market operations during the rainy season, when the sources of marine fish are few. Furthermore, most stallholders live in the city, not simply because it is more convenient, but because there is a high correlation between being able to vote in the city and the ability to obtain rights to a stall.

As might be anticipated, the amount of capital one has or can borrow in large part determines the product one chooses to sell. At the "low investment" pole of the continuum of capital availability stand produce sellers who may have literally none of their own capital invested (and who have nothing to sell but their labor expended in collecting goods, and their knowledge of the marketplace). At the "high investment" pole we find sellers who deal principally in manufactured goods. Meat selling also demands relatively heavy capital inputs, for cattle are expensive (about $120 to $150 US per head for an animal old enough to slaughter) and cannot be subdivided into lower-priced units. Moreover, selling meat in the marketplace involves many special taxes and high risks (cattle die easily in wet climates). However, the class of commodities in which a trader deals is not always a good index of the level of capital investment. For example, some of the poorest sellers in the marketplace are some women who sell canned goods, because they may obtain these on credit from local Chinese wholesalers. In effect, then, these women are selling their labor, their ability to attract customers on social-relational grounds, and their rights of access to a selling location in the marketplace.

The size of the seller's operating capital leads to further role specialization among stallholders, for few can afford operations requiring heavy capital investment. Those who can, therefore, have the opportunity to function as wholesalers, providing stocks to other sellers. Moreover, because there are but a few principal sources of supply for many classes of goods, further opportunities for income exist through manipulation of these sources. "Shortages" in particular classes of goods artificially produced by monopolistic (or monopsonistic) practices are not unusual, as we shall see.

Information is not easily obtained about such things as income and capital investment levels, or credit relationships. Attempts to obtain data of these kinds early in the investigation were nearly disastrous, for they led to the widespread rumor that the investigator and his assistants were special agents of the Philippine Bureau of Internal Revenue. This led to the suspension of data-gathering operations for more than a week, until satisfactory assurances could be given. Furthermore, even when such data are collected there are no practical means of verifying the responses which were offered by informants, and some very high or low figures which were elicited lead one to suspect they were capriciously offered. Specific financial information proved to be obtainable only after long personal association had established a basis for trust, and the number of such relationships an investigator may establish is low. Although assessment of the value of inventories on hand would seem a possible method for objective assessment of investment levels, this too proved fruitless. There is no way to determine objectively whether the seller owns his stock or is merely selling goods owned by someone else. Finally, in occasional cases it is futile to ask informants about their investments because they simply don't know how much capital they have invested, or if they are gaining or losing capital. Also, the notion of "capital" was not always an easy one to relate to local ways of thinking about conducting business. For instance, some vendors had to purchase rights to their *puestos*, and therefore included that purchase price as an "investment." Others, however, had obtained their *puestos* through political patronage or by drawing lots and therefore did not think of their stalls as capital. As a consequence of these operational difficulties, figures reported here are estimates made by officials of the Baguio City Market Vendors' Association, or by sellers who seemed especially experienced and knowledgeable.

Levels of investment in marketplace operations are generally low. Not only do all the hard data obtained support that generalization, but so do the life styles of the marketplace sellers. Their consumption patterns and residences, and the nature of the educational opportunities they seek for their children, all suggest that a modest appraisal of their incomes is realistic.

Some surprisingly high investment figures were nevertheless reported in certain areas of the marketplace: footwear, souvenirs, clothing, meat, rice, kitchenware, and the larger marketplace grocery stores and *carinderias*. The highest investment figures reported were from footwear and clothing sellers. One footwear seller reported an investment of $11,200 US, and the four lowest estimates were approximately $5,000. For clothing sellers, the reported high was $9,800, and the low was $1,875. It is to be anticipated that sellers of these more expensive commodities would have relatively higher investments and also use more modern techniques of accounting and merchandising. However, given the responses obtained from sellers of other products, those obtained from footwear and clothing sellers were outstanding. The resolution of this anomaly is that most of the value of these enterprises is in inventory, and although some of these vendors represent the inventory to be their property, that any stallholder owns his entire stock is unlikely. Indeed, when the footwear and clothing figures collected from operators were shown to BAMARVA officials, they promptly laughed. Yet they acknowledged that one or two footwear sellers might well have as much as $5,000 invested in their operations, and that a few clothing sellers probably had $3,000 invested. Speaking more generally, they thought marketplace sellers who had more than $500 operating capital unusual. As far as general income levels are concerned, the same body of experts suggested that, "Most of us don't make what the sweepers make," in reference to the four pesos per day (approximately $1 US) paid to the marketplace sweepers.

The number of *enterprises* is substantially less than the number of *stalls*, for several stalls may be combined into a single enterprise. But Table 3 (p. 103) shows that agricultural produce vendors operate the greatest percentage of stalls. Persons whose specialty is selling vegetables and fruits operate 640 stalls. If we consider that vegetable sellers are those least likely to have multiple-stall enterprises, and that nearly all the open-market sellers are also selling these commodities, it's apparent that agricultural products are by far the most frequently sold goods in the marketplace. On any given occasion, up to three quarters of the persons selling in the marketplace are offering vegetables as at least one of the commodities which they sell.

A distinct ethnic division among vegetable sellers finds expression in both spatial and functional terms. With only eight exceptions, the 188 stalls in the vegetable-selling area of the main market are operated by Filipinos of lowland origin. Stalls housed in the "Hangar Building" are held by native mountain peoples or, in the few cases in which they are held by lowland Filipinos, they are nevertheless operated by native employees.

This "native" section (officially known as the vegetable extension area) consists of an old "government issue" aircraft hangar which was moved into the marketplace in 1955. The inside of the building has been divided into 452 stalls each of which is only one and a half meters square. These vegetable sellers' stalls are flanked on both ends of the building by some small *sari-sari* and dried-fish sellers' stalls, also operated by natives. There are but two entrances to the building, but neither is on the more convenient town side. Aisles between stalls are exceedingly narrow (usually about two feet wide, considering the space occupied by baskets of goods protruding from stalls), and difficult to negotiate. The minute size of the stalls allows little space for storage or for display, and there is little of the rich variety of vegetables and fruits common in the main vegetable section. It is apparent from observation that retail trade in this section is lethargic, and the overall impression is one of gloom and poverty. Sellers in this area reported an average investment of only $40 in their retail businesses, a figure which—at least on the surface—seems to support the general impression of poverty which the scene conveys.

The difficulties involved in displaying and storing goods, together with the problem of access to their selling locations,

would seem adequate explanation for the low rate of investment in retail operations in the native area of the market. There
is, however, a better one: native sellers are more interested in
wholesaling than in retailing, and the abject poverty of the
Hangar Building is largely an illusion.

According to local informants, few native sellers held stalls
in the marketplace prior to the acquisition of the Hangar
Building. Prior to that time native retail sellers operated along
the streets near the marketplace. However, two events helped
to change those conditions. First, city officials came to the con-
clusion that it was not fitting for a town of Baguio's stature to
have G-strung and *tapi*-skirted natives selling wares along the
city's busy streets. Second, at this time in recent Philippine history there was an awakening of concern for ethnic minorities
which sprang largely from the unusual sensitivity of the late
President Magsaysay's regime to social problems. Local native
sellers also insisted there was a third factor: selling along the
streets gave the native seller some locational advantages over
the marketplace-bound lowland stallholders, and the latter
complained loudly.

The opening of the Hangar Building, and the subsequent
concentration of native produce sellers in that area, were therefore part of a general "ethnic uplift" program (of which the
attempt to organize a local marketing cooperative mentioned
above was also part). The local programs are said to be largely
the result of lobbying by a Baguio businessman and politician
who had a special interest in native peoples as a result of being
"half Naibaloi." Moreover, this gentleman is also said to have
"had the ear" of President Magsaysay and to have obtained the
latter's personal endorsement for these local projects.

Thus, only a temporary enhancement of their power position enabled native peoples to obtain even their present facilities in the marketplace. They do, however, have an economic

specialization—wholesaling—which they manage to maintain, and that ability is related to yet another set of "subjective" factors, as we shall see.

Open-Market Vendors. The "open-market" area of the marketplace is the area not enclosed by roofing and in which there are no stalls. Open-market sellers, therefore, are non-stallholding sellers who operate their enterprises by displaying wares on woven mats, behind which they squat or stand. The number of such sellers varies considerably from time to time during the day, from day to day during the week, and from season to season, as the marketplace economy itself ebbs and flows. In spite of laws restricting open-market selling to weekends and holidays, there is always some activity in the area. However, open-market sellers are most numerous on weekends, especially during the tourist season, when the level of local demand is increased. Not surprisingly, they tend to disappear during the peak of the rainy season, when travel is difficult and incomes are low. On several occasions I counted more than 300 open-market sellers, and on weekends they are so numerous that they tend to overflow to other areas of the market, where they obstruct all the aisles and passageways in the marketplace.

The degree of market involvement among open-market sellers varies considerably. Stallholders often allude to open-market sellers as "transients," and in a sense they are correct. But what the stallholders mean—that they are irregular visitors to the marketplace and follow no planned routine—is often not the case. Many open-market vendors are regular participants in the Baguio marketplace, and visit it as part of a carefully planned cycle of economic events. Many open-market sellers are "transient" only because they don't rent stalls. A large (and variable) proportion of open-market sellers combine those roles with peasant-producer or carrier roles, or both.

While roughly half of the main-market stallholders are men, the proportion of females among open-market sellers is much greater. Men are often evident in any group of open-market sellers, but they usually turn out to be the husbands of female vendors, and play a minor part in actual selling operations. The typical open-market seller is a woman who is a member of a farm family and depends upon marketplace selling for at least a quarter of her income. Only a small percentage of her stock is the result of her own production, and most of it is collected in the area adjacent to her home. Most open-market sellers are local people who attend this particular market because of its proximity, but nearly a third travel from La Union and Pangasinan provinces. The latter are characteristically "buy and sell" ladies (carriers) who have come to Baguio partly because of the probability of higher prices, and partly because they hope to obtain stocks in Baguio to resell elsewhere.

Neither the quantity nor the variety of goods offered for sale in the open market is as great as is typical among the stallholders of the main market. Yet the range of products is impressive, and some items available in the open market cannot normally be obtained from stallholders at all. These latter products are "specialty" items associated with lower-class dietary preferences in other regions, which emigrants from those areas may desire. One may, for example, purchase from open-market sellers the tiny, poor-quality fish and shrimp which are not sold by stallholding fish sellers, and which are suitable for the manufacture of certain kinds of *bagoong* (fermented fish sauce). Interested buyers may also purchase here a kind of marine gastropod highly valued in areas of the northwest coast, or the kind of fresh-water eels which no reputable fish vendor would handle. Similarly, the open-market area is the only place in the city to purchase the varieties of red mountain rices used for producing the ritual wine which local mountain people consume in ceremonies. Surprisingly, cottage industries are poorly represented among open-market sellers, but fibre mats, baskets, and carrying bags are usually available, and small quantities of homespun cotton cloth are often sold. However, with the exception of an occasional wandering peddler's wares, machine manufactures are almost never offered for sale in the open market.

In spite of open-market specializations, many commodities sold in the open market are also sold by stallholders. This is especially true of agricultural products. To a large extent, therefore, the sellers in the two areas see themselves as competitors, and considerable friction and ill will exists between them. Most of the advantage in this competition lies with the stallholders, for they have more operating capital and better commercial and political connections. Nevertheless, open-market sellers have some elements in their favor. In the first place, the poorer, less-sophisticated buyers feel more comfortable dealing with open-market sellers and using trading "styles" (see below) to which they are better accustomed. Rural buyers are more reluctant to approach the urbane, sophisticated (and often indifferent) stallholder, especially when the buyer is a native mountaineer.

There is also a widespread belief—apparently present at all levels of the local social order—that produce is fresher and prices lower in the open market. As a result, particularly on weekends, even relatively well-off shoppers buying in the open market are not unusual. Because this notion is easily subjected to empirical testing, I made an attempt to verify it. Several buyers (members of different local ethnolinguistic groups) were given funds and asked on repeated occasions to make comparable purchases in both the open and main market areas with as little time intervening between the two purchases as possible. In an effort to assure conscientious bargaining, assistants were given fixed sums and told that they could keep all their purchases. The commodities purchased under these conditions were then weighed and measured and assessed for quality by a panel of "experts," a number of long-time marketeers who were not informed of the intent of the investigation.

The resulting data showed that price differences between the two areas were insignificant, but very slightly higher in the main market (though either section might express higher prices on a given day). However, what did vary noticeably was the quality of the merchandise, invariably in favor of the stall-holding sellers. This, of course, is also an element of "price." For instance, milkfish (*bangus*) were on the whole approximately five centavos per kilogram cheaper in the open market, but were not so fat or so fresh as fish bought from sellers in the main market. Vegetables and fruits were no fresher and were also generally smaller than those for sale in the main area, although prices per weight unit were almost identical. In short, one may pay slightly less for commodities in the open market, but not for precisely the same quality commodities. Yet for anyone whose primary concern is saving a few centavos, the open market affords a slight advantage, though the buyer must be willing to forego some desirable attributes of the product.

Furthermore, open-market sellers have fewer fixed costs than stallholders, so the former are not inevitably bound to producing income in order to meet those costs. Open-market sellers can therefore "disengage" from marketing more easily and invest their time and capital in other economic sectors or in other marketplaces. The moment that market conditions shift to the buyers' advantage, the open-market seller may take her stocks and leave, or trade them for commodities she feels she can sell elsewhere to recoup losses sustained locally.

Finally, open-market sellers tend to be conservative in their estimation of the quantity of goods which they can sell, and therefore minimize the risks involved in oversupply. They express fear that they will end the day with an unsold supply of perishable commodities—fear which is a reflection of real conditions, for one such day could obliterate a small operating capital. As one elderly lady expressed the matter, "I bring but a little, I make but a little, but I never lose." Activity in the open-market area reflects this conservatism and mobility, for the open market is often nearly deserted by early afternoon.

The capital invested by open-market sellers is characteristically small, overlapping in its upper limits only the lowest figures in the stallholder range (positions which, again, tend to be occupied by indigenous mountain people). The average figure offered in a sample of fifty randomly drawn informants was only 40 pesos (just over $10 US). But the startling aspect of open-market operations was the large number of vendors who offered, as an aside, the comment that they could operate with no capital of their own. As long as the carrier-seller proved his reliability, rural producers were willing to send produce on consignment, receiving payment for it on the carrier's return trip, or at least at some specified future time. This may be done on the basis of a price established at the time, or on a profit-sharing basis, so that if he wishes the producer has an opportunity to share the risks and benefits involved.

If the 40-peso figure supplied is, indeed, accurate, the returns realized by the sellers in turning over their capital are respectable, for they claim to make a minimum daily profit of four pesos, and have expectations of making as much as ten.

Of course to determine objectively and accurately profit per-centages is difficult, because much of the stock carried belongs to producers with whom profits are divided. Moreover, even if these figures are approximately correct, accumulation would nevertheless occur slowly, for there are always some costs. Subsistence costs necessitate an outlay of at least one and a half pesos per day, and transportation is likely to cost another peso. Thus profit margins are almost certainly small, and if the value of the sellers' labor were to be discounted, profits would tend to disappear. But it is precisely the surplus of available labor in the rural economy that provides one of the primary incentives to "buy and sell," and labor is ordinarily not given value unless one is actually employed for wages. In the eyes of the sellers the only relevant issue is the difference between what they pay for their goods, plus out-of-pocket expenses, and the price they receive for those goods in the marketplace.

Given these conditions, open-market selling seems to be a generally sound means of supplementing farm income, and is probably—as we have seen—consistently more rewarding than selling labor on the unskilled labor market. Yet it is still not likely to be the pathway to significant capital accumulation, nor does it bring about, in itself, the transition to large-scale enterprise. Those interested in the latter must make every effort to obtain a stall in the main market and to develop a clientele of steady customers. Unfortunately, success at the latter requires a larger body of operating capital than is necessary for partici-pation in the open market.

Vendor Roles and Transactional Styles. In addition to the diagnostic features so far enumerated which distinguish stall-holder and open-market seller roles, these roles also differ in the ways in which they relate to buyer roles—the "styles" of interaction through which market transactions are accomplished. These differences illuminate the subjective elements of marketplace behavior.

Many of the distinctions between commercial practices in the two main divisions of the marketplace emerge from three fundamental aspects of buy-and-sell activity. The first is the information about the different classes of products on which price formation is based. In this regard, a common set of principles operates in both marketplace areas, but the tendency to emphasize commodities with slightly different characteristics leads to rather different behavior. The second major difference pertains to the frequency of interaction between sellers and specific individual buyers. Stallholders are likely to conduct business from the same location year after year; open-market sellers—often by necessity—most typically do not conduct trade on a daily basis. The former, therefore, tend to develop more long-standing relationships with particular customers, that is, to form clienteles. Obviously, such long-standing associations have much to do with the way in which buyer and sellers interact. The third difference emerges from the more frequent use of standardized measures of quantity and quality in the main market. These measures tend to increase the amount of information about a product which is available to both buyer and seller and thus provide a basis for general agreement about the relevant characteristics of the commodity.

In both the main and open-market areas of the marketplace price formation is established by acts of transaction themselves, and these are, of course, subject to information about previous transactions involving the same products. Yet this is much less true of manufactures, for their prices are little affected by demand for them in the local market. Because prices on manufactures and imports are, at this level, "givens," it is useful here to distinguish them from locally-produced commodities.

Bidding on locally-produced goods is opened by first-stage collectors (carriers) based on opening prices which were acceptable to buyers on the previous day, or on the most recent occasion for which price information is known. Informants specified that except under unusual conditions negotiations are based on "opening" prices for the previous occasion rather than "closing" prices. Prices fluctuate during the day, reflecting supply and demand and especially the sellers' fear that they may be caught at the end of the day's trading with unsold perishable commodities. Thus "closing" prices on perishables are almost always falling, but reflect temporary market conditions. Opening prices are therefore assumed more accurately to reflect longer-term market trends, although they are accepted only as rough standards from which bidding commences.

Manufactures present quite different conditions. The minimum selling price for manufactures (or anything else produced in the capital-intensive economic sector) is determined by production costs and interest rates on potentially competing output uses of capital. Production, transport, and other fixed costs are not negotiable, and come to the local marketplace as if from another world. Local sellers can't obtain these commodities for less whether or not they can be sold locally, and, given existing conditions, the prices of manufactures are inevitably relatively dear in terms of rural incomes.

Prices in the marketplace are reckoned in terms of minimum increments of five centavos and not in odd cents, in spite of a nationwide "Respect the Centavo" campaign which was formulated under the auspices of (then) President Macapagal. However, when dealing with manufacturing firms or wholesale houses or their agents, local sellers bid in odd cents. The selling prices of commodities must, therefore, be translated into local terms. Most commonly this is done by adjustment to

159

the lowest multiple of five which will yet yield a minimum of two centavos per-unit profit to the seller. For example, if the per-unit wholesale price of a can of milk is 42 centavos, the vendor's minimum selling price is 45 centavos. But if the wholesale price is 44 centavos per unit, the lowest retail price the seller will accept is 50 centavos. Otherwise, odd centavos are reckoned only in large quantity purchases in which the total price of the lot is figured closely and then rounded to a five-centavo multiple. Ideally, of course, the seller attempts to obtain as many price increments as he can, consistent with other considerations—such as securing a clientele through demonstrations of largesse.

Because their commercial strategies must take into account that they are habitual marketeers, most stallholders make an effort to provide as attractive displays of goods as possible given the space available. They do so both to catch the eye of the passer-by and to demonstrate that the seller is an able and dependable supplier with whom a customer would do well to trade on an enduring basis.

The majority of transactions in either area of the marketplace involve bargaining, or haggling, over price. However, "haggling" suggests rather more aggressive negotiation than often occurs. Assuming that the buyer is not a steady customer, he typically (somewhat casually) inquires about the price of an item, and the seller responds by offering a bid above the price at which he will actually sell. If he is interested, the customer offers a lower counterbid, and the process continues until a mutually acceptable price is reached, or until it becomes apparent it will not be possible to reach agreement. Prices fluctuate rapidly, but most buyers do enough casual shopping to have acquired quite accurate information about current prices. Both buyer and seller are therefore informed, and opening bid and counterbid typically reflect this information by closely approximating the eventual selling price. A bid well outside the range of realistic selling prices usually draws a laugh from the seller, calculated to show the buyer that his bid was accepted as an attempt at humor, but occasionally such a bid stimulates some sarcasm. But considerable agreement on price usually exists, and only the superficial or unknowledgeable buyer is taken advantage of in the haggling process. In transactions with stallholders this process of bidding and counterbidding is typically quite restrained, and most stallholders have some customers with whom they do not haggle at all. The reasons for the latter will become apparent in subsequent discussion.

Yet etiquette among stallholders allows the customer enough latitude to shop foolishly if he is bent upon doing so. Vendors in this marketplace rarely "cry their wares," so that a buyer is forced to inquire actively about prices. Furthermore, for a seller to break into another seller's negotiations with a customer is considered rude; the cultural view of proper behavior does not allow for directly competitive bidding between sellers. An incautious buyer, therefore, could well be duped, and competing sellers would not interfere.

But in spite of the rules of local bargaining etiquette, there are sellers in the marketplace who make a practice of attempting to entice customers from their colleagues. This is said to be especially true of the members of one particular regional group, the lowland Filipinos from Batangas Province, collectively considered by their fellows to be absolute pirates because of their frequent violations of marketplace ethics. Interestingly enough, local police reported that Batangueños were involved in arguments and fights with other sellers in a frequency greatly disproportionate to their numbers.

Although haggling is the transactional norm in the marketplace, it does not emerge from any necessary animosity and only rarely involves a capricious play factor. Rather, it reflects uncertainty concerning quantity, quality, or the stability of the supply of items transacted. When commodities are standardized, when there is no reason to assume that there will be a dramatic change in their availability (the reader will recall that shortages are occasionally induced artificially), and when the commodities are familiar to local buyers and sellers, there may be no haggling involved at all. But to the extent that knowledge about commodities is lacking, haggling is certain to occur, and the range of bids reflects the degree of uncertainty.[1]

In the local economy standardized items are almost exclusively those obtained from the capital-intensive economic sector: imports, manufactures, etc. Everyone knows that one package of Lucky Strike cigarettes is similar to another, or that all cans of Darigold recombined milk are very much alike. They likewise know that a package of Lucky Strikes is one peso everywhere, and that an eight-ounce can of Darigold milk costs 45 centavos (unless one buys these items in large quantities). These are standardized, familiar items, and unless a shortage of them is anticipated, there is little possibility that any seller will succeed in raising the price, or the buyer in lowering it. Qualities, quantities, and prices are too well known in these cases to allow for the magnitude of disagreement or ignorance which is reflected in bargaining behavior.

The wholesale prices on some standard items are so widely known that sellers are unable to adjust selling prices upward more than one profit increment over cost. Within a limited range of common purchases this leads to a peculiar result: the

---

[1] These data support Alice Dewey's analysis of bargaining in the Javanese peasant marketplace. Dewey remarks that, "In general, the greater the fluctuation in quality and supply, the wider the range within which bids will be made by both buyer and seller, since market conditions are harder to judge and testing must allow for this" (Dewey 1962a:73).

percent of profit realized is much greater when one sells cheaper items than when he sells more expensive ones. For example, a 5-centavo profit on a 15-centavo item is 33 percent gross profit, but the same profit margin on a one-peso item is only 5 percent gross. Theoretically, therefore, if one were to trade in such items, he would do best to concentrate on the cheaper ones. Unfortunately, attempts to test this proposition yielded inconclusive results, for few sellers reckon matters so closely, or are in a position to exercise free choice concerning the kinds of stocks they will sell.

"Nonstandard" items in the marketplace economy include nearly all agricultural products, and the sale of such products characteristically involves haggling. Products in this class come from many sources and are not graded by established standards of quality or quantity prior to being offered for sale. It is therefore in the sale of these commodities especially that uncertainty is likely to be most extreme and bargaining most intense.

Yet the correlations between haggling and agricultural products and its absence in the case of machine manufactures are not absolute. Some manufactured items by their nature lead to ambiguities and uncertainties regarding their value. Footwear and clothing are examples. In these cases the products may be manufactured from several kinds of materials, and the element of design or "style" becomes significant. Accordingly, purchases of footgear and clothing are usually bargained, although rubber and canvas shoes and denim trousers are such common items that their sale rarely involves haggling. Also, some kinds of agricultural products are usually sold without bargaining, because they are so frequently purchased that everyone knows the going price and the features to consider in establishing quality. Rice and bananas are such items, for they are staples available the year round. The usual ways in which meat animals and fowl are sold offer an interesting case in point. If these are purchased live, quantity (dressed weight) and quality are both difficult to determine. Haggling is invariably involved in such sales. But if they are slaughtered and dressed prior to sale, they are purchased by scale weight and no haggling takes place. The "nonstandard" living creatures are "standardized" by converting them to commodities.

The sale of nonstandard items offers the seller the best opportunity to take advantage of the buyer, for it is less likely that the buyer's information is as good as the seller's. Correspondingly, because profit margins are likely to be greater on these goods than on standard items, in transacting these goods sellers are in the best position to grant price concessions to preferred customers.

But in one situation haggling always seems to occur, regardless of the class of product—quantity purchases. It is foolish for a buyer to haggle over the price of a *ganta* (the commonly used measure, about 4.5 lbs.) of rice unless he feels that the quality is grossly misrepresented, but it is reasonable for him to haggle over an entire sack. The principle of economy-of-scale is widely appreciated, and when a large purchase is made the buyer expects a reduction in the seller's per-unit profit.

Stallholders are much more likely to use generally-accepted, standardized measures than open-market sellers, a fact which tends to explain the greater intensity and frequency of bargaining in the open-market area. Some of the measures employed are internationally standard, or nearly so (e.g., kilograms, yards, and gallons), but others are a much more local phenomenon (e.g., beer bottles, Coca-Cola bottles, and empty tin cans). Moreover, many stallholders use fulcrum scales for weighing appropriate commodities.

The open market presents a different set of conditions in several ways. In the first place, while bargaining tends to be restrained and occasionally absent in stallholder-buyer transactions, haggling is the only mode of purchase observable in the open market. The greater tendency to bargain appears to be the result of the factors already distinguished: uncertainty about the properties of the products, more sporadic market participation, ephemeral seller-buyer contacts, and the infrequent use of standard measures. In the open market one finds few commodities of the standardized types which are so significant in the main-market area. Thus the degree to which bargaining is stressed in the open market results largely from the lack of information buyers have about the commodities sold there. Second, in contrast to the majority of stallholder transactions, those in the open market do not typically bring together buyers and sellers who have long-standing commercial associations. They therefore lack the social basis characteristic of main-market relationships. The temporary nature of the majority of buyer-seller relations does little to further the development of mutual trust, and bargaining is accordingly more necessary. Open-market sellers, too, may have a few steady customers who wait for them to appear, but even in those instances bargaining typically occurs. However, in the latter case it is bargaining with a different spirit, much closer to the transactional style of the main market. The difference is one of degree, but the degree of difference is marked.

A third important difference is the infrequent use of standard measures by open-market sellers. In the main-market area, where goods are much more frequently weighed and measured, the fundamental issue involved in bargaining is one of quality. Most stallholding sellers, at any given moment, are asking similar prices per unit of measure, so that only quality remains as a point to contest. A stallholder usually justifies a higher opening bid than his neighbors', when this is pointed out to him, by claiming that his stock is of higher quality than that of his competitors.

Instead of being measured precisely, open-market goods are apt to be divided into *atados*, little heaps or bundles which buyers are likely to find of convenient size. These piles are arranged in two ways. Some are organized so that they contain a variety of quality, while others are arranged so that their contents are of uniform quality. Bidding on these may take two forms. The buyer may haggle the price of a specific pile (or piles), or he may offer a sum of money, after which bargaining determines what that money will buy—a local variation of "packaging to price."

But *atado* selling also tends to encourage haggling as a style of transaction, for it adds a variable not so apparently present in stallholder transactions. In buying by the pile the buyer is contesting not only quality, as he does when he deals with stallholders, but quantity as well. In effect, when he chooses to buy by *atado* measures he is putting his own ability to estimate quality and quantity into direct competition with the seller's, and *caveat emptor* takes on special meaning. However, because the *atado* mode of purchase also appears to offer additional latitude for savings, and because of the belief that prices are cheaper in the open market anyway, buyers are often attracted to the open market in preference to the main area. There is little doubt that some of the more well-to-do shoppers enjoy matching skill with open-market sellers. However, the activity is not so diverting for the seller, and his interest is only in selling his stock as quickly as possible for as high a price as possible, consistent with a general desire to keep customers coming back.

Whenever there is a large influx of buyers into the marketplace, the appeal of the open market may be so strong that stallholders whose *puestos* are in especially poor locations leave their stalls and take up spaces in the open-market section. They run the risk of having to pay additional fees in doing so, but the opportunity to contact a larger number of possible buyers makes the potential rewards worth the increased risks. Interestingly, when stallholders become open-market vendors their behavior undergoes a marked change. They leave behind their scales and measures, arrange their wares in *atado* displays, and bargain with vigor—clear indication that the differences between the two areas are incorporated into the cultural expectations of local buyers.

EXTERNAL TRANSPORT ROLES

"External transport roles," the final category of economic roles in the local internal distributional system, for the most part distribute Mountain Province products to other markets. Specifically, persons occupying such roles use the accumulation function of the Baguio marketplace for the collection of goods which are then transported and resold. These roles differ from the carrier roles described earlier, for their function is taking goods from the local marketplace to other markets. But from the perspective of another market these same roles are carrier roles. Yet external transport roles differ from carrier roles in ways other than the direction in which they move goods. Many also differ widely in the scale of activities and the quantities of capital involved. Some external transport roles are aspects of sizable enterprises.

By employing such criteria as whether they move goods to lower-order or higher-order markets, the scale of operations, and the kind of transport employed, it is possible to distinguish two major varieties of external transport roles, "peddler" and "middleman" roles. The latter, as we shall see, are also important in establishing connections between the local-regional economy (the "internal marketing system") and the national economy.

Peddlers. Peddler roles, which involve purchasing small quantities of goods from stallholders in the marketplace and transporting them to rural areas for resale, are directed to lesser-order markets. The peddler is another kind of mobile firm, a traveling merchant who seeks to increase the scale of demand for his products by covering a wider range (cf. Stine 1962). His income is derived from two kinds of opportunities: first, the opportunity to use his labor to increase the market value of his stock; and second, the opportunity to isolate buyers from other sellers of the same commodities, thereby capitalizing on their lack of information.

Transportation, which is of obvious importance to peddlers, typically consists of public conveyance or foot travel. Inadequate transport again places limitations on the quantities of goods which the peddler may carry on particular occasions. These are limitations shared by carriers, but dealing in relatively high-value, low-bulk commodities, rather than agricultural products, allows the peddler to move more capital than carriers typically do. Cheap ready-to-wear clothing and knick-nacks are the most common items handled, but peddlers also trade in rubber and canvas footgear, ornaments, charms, and patent medicines.

Peddlers perform several operations which make them important to the marketplace economy. First, in transporting goods to rural areas they expand the size of the region served by goods moving through the Baguio marketplace. Baguio stallholders may not appreciate the long-term economic implications of these activities, but they are certainly aware that peddlers are good customers and value them accordingly. Second, peddlers are involved in breaking bulk. Their stock is purchased in wholesale quantities in Baguio City and then sold piecemeal in the small-scale transactions appropriate to rural-village incomes. Finally, they perform a credit function. Most peddlers have more or less fixed territories in which they operate and routes which they habitually follow. It is common practice to provide goods on credit on one trip, then to collect for them on the next—or perhaps after harvest. In fact, peddlers characteristically have credit relationships at both ends of the distributional network, just as carriers do. They usually obtain their stock on credit from Baguio stallholders and in turn sell it on credit to their own customers. Thus, to a considerable extent peddlers, too, operate on borrowed capital. The commodities in which each peddler deals are in large part determined by the goods he can obtain on credit by taking advantage of personalistic relationships which he has with stallholders in the marketplace.

In addition to the peddler role just described, there exists another, far less consequential role of this general type which demonstrates the extent of interest in the most minuscule profits. Selling of this kind is similar to peddlers' activities, except that it is confined to the immediate area of the marketplace. It might be termed "micropeddling." Micropeddlers are not deeply committed trading intermediaries at all but are merely persons seeking a small profit for the satisfaction of some minor goal. They characteristically utilize some special relationship with a larger-scale seller to obtain a small quantity of goods at a price below the current market value. They then attempt to sell these goods at the normal market price. Such peddlers commonly stand in front of the marketplace, sometimes calling out to passers-by. On busy days micropeddlers tend to cluster around entrances to the marketplace, making entry to it rather difficult. For this reason they are often harassed by the police and are unpopular with other sellers.

Data collected on micropeddlers indicate that the size of their stock is so small that even under the most ideal conditions the return from their sales would rarely exceed 50 centavos (less than $.15 US). This is the kind of trade in which a woman might participate in order to buy a few leaves of tobacco, or a package of locally-produced cigarettes, or which a child might undertake in order to buy some candy.

Middlemen. Middleman roles, like peddler roles, also involve the use of the marketplace as a source of supply, and the transport of commodities obtained there for resale in other markets. The important differences between these two kinds of external distributional roles are: first, middleman roles involve much larger capital investments; second, middlemen have access to privately-owned transport; and third, middlemen move goods primarily to higher-order markets. Peddler roles, on the other hand, involve a maximum substitution of labor for capital, the use of public transport, and "trading down" to lower-order markets. Moreover, while peddler roles may be filled by women, middleman roles were found to be filled exclusively by males.

The greater quantities of investment capital controlled by middlemen enhance their opportunities for profit, for they can undertake ventures on a scale not possible for marketplace sellers. The greatest part of produce shipped from Baguio goes to public markets in the greater Manila area and is distributed on consignment. That is, payment is not received until the produce is sold. Marketplace sellers lack the capital (and apparently the organizational skill) to organize this transport or to finance the seller in more distant markets, precisely the operations carried out by middlemen. As a result of their advantages, middlemen have been able to exert rigorous monopsonistic control over the external marketing of the mid-latitude vegetables produced in the Baguio area.

It would, however, be misleading to suggest that middlemen obtain their supplies of produce exclusively in the marketplace.

Most of them also purchase vegetables directly from rural producers, and some even buy the produce of whole fields prior to harvest. Nevertheless, the marketplace remains an important source of supply for middlemen, because it provides certain advantages. First, by purchasing produce in the marketplace the middleman can obtain large quantities without having to visit dispersed farmsteads. This increases the purchase price slightly, but it also reduces transport costs and avoids some risks of spoilage. Second, because rural producers tend to look upon middlemen as sources of production capital, by purchasing in the marketplace the middleman can limit his involvement in extending credit and other favors to rural producers. Third, operating from the marketplace assures the middleman of the easy availability of the widest possible variety of fruits and vegetables, for the market makes available variety not found in specific regions. In sum, to purchase stocks in the marketplace is far more convenient and less risky. But middlemen do not distribute their purchasing evenly throughout the marketplace. They prefer to deal with the native vendors in the Hangar Building because the "natives" are the marketplace's vegetable wholesalers, and their prices are lower.

Yet another distinctive aspect of middlemen roles is that, with the exception of a few lowland Filipinos from the Manila area, the persons who perform these roles are Chinese. Furthermore, local Filipinos adamantly insist that these men are not individual operators at all, but "agents" for a Chinese organization which they refer to as "The Syndicate." The latter term faithfully reflects the general opinion of local traders that there is something sinister about the organization of the entire external vegetable trade. These middlemen are further alleged to obtain unusually cheap transportation by using trucks which belong to the Mountain Province Cooperative Marketing Association, the Chinese organization involved in the commercial development of agriculture along the Halsema Road.[2]

Although the accuracy of these charges was not verified (for obvious reasons), a communication network links local Chinese with associates in Manila, and along it information about Manila market conditions is relayed twice each week via radio-telephone. This information alone provides Chinese vegetable buyers with a considerable advantage over local sellers, for no one else has such current facts. Chinese can take advantage of the market, for they have considerable control over external marketing outlets and can—by their own admission—either withhold or dump produce on the Manila market. They can also have considerable impact on vegetable prices in the public markets of Manila. No local Filipino is happy to deal with Chinese, but if one hopes to market his agricultural produce "externally," there are no more acceptable alternatives.

[2] Some informants, including a few local Chinese farmers, insisted that the Mountain Province Cooperative Marketing Association and "The Syndicate" were the same organization. Others claimed they were not the same organization, but that the two were careful not to compete with one another and offered one another substantial assistance. Clarifying the circumstances was not worth the risk of alienating Chinese informants, and the matter was not pursued.

Chapter Six

Capital and Credit

t the most general and objective (etic) level of consideration the commercial problems faced by sellers in
the Baguio City marketplace are those faced by traders the world over: they must somehow acquire a body of capital, turn it over in such a way that profit is realized, and
hopefully accumulate additional capital. Not all sellers express
awareness of a conceptual category, "capital," although a surprising number of them use the term in describing their operations. However, the term is used here in a critical and objective
sense. As an effort to avoid the extensive arguments about the
most useful way to think about capital (cf. Knight 1956:77–
88), the definition offered here is an elementary one. Capital is
any quantity of goods, services, or resources (or disposal rights
over these which are symbolized in exchange media, such as
money) which is withheld from consumption with the intent
of increasing future income. In this treatment, therefore, the
quality which distinguishes the "capital" qualities of resource
elements is the use to which they are put, not some inherent,

purely "capital" quality they possess. However, at the subjective (emic) level, for capital "to exist," the conceptual means must exist to set aside a portion of one's resources and designate it as capital. This requires particular technical-symbolic accounting skills, and by no means do all sellers possess these. The reckoning of success by the ability to "live off the shelves" (i.e., off one's trading stock), which was alluded to earlier, is symptomatic of the fact that inexperienced sellers tend to lack these skills. But in spite of these limitations on local sellers' knowledge of market theory, they are all aware that in trading income is obtained by turning over stocks at a profit. Sellers are all interested in profits, but the less sophisticated have more difficulty determining profits and losses and retreat to the "as long as there is something on the shelves" measure of success.

Similarly, at the objective (etic) level, "credit" refers to the lending of goods and services (or money) without immediate return against the promise of future repayment (cf. Firth 1964a:29). Credit involves both the debtor's obligation to repay and the lender's expectation that the repayment will be forthcoming.

More specifically, sellers in the Baguio marketplace are confronted with a special set of problems which limit commercial activities, the growth-inhibiting factors enumerated in Chapter II. Summarized, these amounted to: low income, the lack of institutionalized sources of reasonably-priced credit, poor transport facilities, the physical environment and climate, and the lack of contractual legal sanctions at the local level. Sellers in the marketplace economy have sought to reduce the risks resulting from these factors primarily through subjectively-valued social relationships which involve credit and which sanction its use. In fact, credit is so widely used in the local marketplace economy that the articulation of virtually all roles in the marketplace involves credit as one dimension. In this section the economic aspects of capital acquisition will be discussed; in the next chapter, the social relations themselves.

BANKS

The low level of incomes among marketplace participants produces conditions in which sellers are more or less constantly searching for capital in the form of cash or goods, or both. Considering only marketplace outlays for the moment, sellers need capital to acquire trading stocks and because the extensive use of credit—and its role in competition with other sellers —often creates runs on liquid assets. In the frantic, rob-Peter-to-pay-Paul atmosphere of marketplace credit relationships, an individual's credit rating among his colleagues—or even the life of the enterprise itself—may depend on the seller's ability to produce small sums on a few hours' notice. Accordingly, great value is placed on sources of capital, and repayment of loans has high priority because participants seek to maintain good credit ratings.[1]

In theory marketplace sellers can obtain small loans from the local branch of the Philippine National Bank. Under a government-sponsored "Retailer's Loan Plan," a retailer can supposedly borrow a total of 60 percent of the value of his inventory for eighteen months at 4 percent per annum interest. If this plan were put into practice, it would undoubtedly have a profound effect on the nature of local commerce. In fact, however, some stipulations make it difficult for marketplace

---

[1] This statement is generally true although it is necessary to distinguish loans obtained from government sources from those obtained from private sources. Government funds tend to be considered "just due," and obligations to repay them are not so strongly felt.

175

sellers to qualify for these loans and render attempts to obtain them unattractive.

In the first place, to obtain a bank loan the seller must offer collateral valued in excess of the value of the loan and be able to demonstrate that this collateral is unencumbered by other outstanding obligations. As noted earlier, few sellers have any property of consequence (including, often, their stock itself), and more than half of them deal in perishable commodities which are not acceptable as security anyway. In practice, the only sellers who can qualify for bank loans are already large-scale operators and trade in durable goods.

Second, applicants are required to submit to an investigation of their businesses. Because few sellers keep any written records, they rarely are able to provide the kind of information demanded by the investigating official. Furthermore, even if they keep such records, sellers fear investigation because of possible ultimate involvement with the Bureau of Internal Revenue. Although many sellers pay taxes, the usual modes of operation in the marketplace—unposted bargained prices, *atado* selling, etc.—render estimating business volume or profit difficult and, therefore, tend to keep tax assessments low. The investigation also cripples the program in another way. The needs of market sellers tend to be immediate, so that to be useful capital must be forthcoming on short notice. Sellers complain that even if they qualified for bank loans, these loans would have little benefit, for the crisis would have come and gone, or the speculative opportunity have slipped away, before the capital could be made available.

Finally, a "moral character" provision attached to retailers' loans takes into account such matters as the applicant's reputation for drinking, gambling, and womanizing. Like any moral stipulation in law, it can be applied carte blanche, and the personal whims of the bank officials are thereby allowed full rein.

Feelings against the local branch of the national bank among marketplace sellers accordingly ran high, and charges of political manipulation with national bank money were common. Though objectivity obliges skepticism about these charges, some events suggest some reason for them. During the election campaigns waged before the general election of 1963, one candidate for national office who spoke in the city promised that bank loans would be awarded those who supported him if he won. Several local businessmen informed me that they had been told that if they continued to support certain candidates, their bank loans would be recalled prematurely. Finally, a number of informants insisted that bank money was financing usurers in the marketplace, a percentage of the profit being returned to bank officials. In brief, the national bank had a poor reputation locally, and may well have been awarding loans on grounds other than the applicants' qualifications.

CREDIT ASSOCIATIONS

The need for credit and the opportunity to earn savings by extending credit have given rise to several kinds of moneylending institutions in the marketplace itself. Among these have been attempts (but only occasionally successful ones) to organize credit cooperatives among vendors. At the time this study was undertaken, there had been three extensive efforts to form cooperatives, and a fourth was in the planning stage. Of the three which had been put into operation, two had already failed. However, the third was solidly established.

Poorer-class, even rural, Filipinos are generally familiar with the basic principles of credit associations, for in the Philippines credit cooperatives have long existed in rural villages (cf. Lewis 1971:147–155), as they do in many peasant communities in most of the monetized areas of the world. It comes as no surprise, therefore, to find such organizations among the marketplace sellers of Baguio City. But the credit cooperatives in the Baguio marketplace are somewhat more complex than the usual village-level credit cooperative.

The usual credit cooperative found in rural villages is the so-called rotating credit association (cf. Geertz 1962b, Ardener 1964). This kind of association is characterized by a limited and (for any given transactional sequence) fixed membership, regular contributions from members, and use of the collective fund by each member according to a turn (hence "rotation") which is determined by agreement, through bids, or by drawing lots. Few rotating associations permit nonmembers to borrow from the fund (Ardener 1964). Furthermore, their ability to function at all depends heavily on the fact that most or all of the members are associated by bonds of long-standing social obligation and trust—which is only to say that they have a social basis.

The credit associations of the Baguio marketplace vary among themselves, but taken as a type they exhibit features which distinguish them from the rotating credit association just described. Unlike the rotating association, in none of the Baguio market cooperatives are regular contributions to the fund a stipulation, and the amounts contributed are fixed only in the sense that there is a minimum acceptable amount—much like purchasing stock from a broker. Moreover, none of them permits the borrowing of money without interest, in no case can one borrow more than a small part of the loan fund, and in only one case are loans limited to persons who are members of the association. In fact, one of the few features which the marketplace and rotating credit associations have in common is their social basis. At the founding of each of the marketplace cooperatives, the membership was initially composed of per-

178

sons who were related through kinship or through long-standing friendships which had previously involved mutual assistance. Thus the cooperative involved not only self-interest, but also trust.

The three credit associations which had actually been in operation were the Batangueño Credit Association, the Vegetable Vendors' Cooperative Credit Association, and the Fish Vendors' Loan and Savings Association. Of these only the Fish Vendors' Association remained functioning at the time of this study. The latter was durable largely because it had full-time management which conducted its affairs in such a way that the core of major investors realized substantial profits.

According to persons who had been officers when that organization was in operation, the Batangueño Association was originally founded by 25 persons, all related consanguineally or affinally. Each member contributed what he could, and the total fund was 10,500 pesos (approximately $2400 US). Loans to members were limited to 500 pesos for 30 days at 2 percent interest. As is customary, interest was deducted immediately, and the principal repaid by daily installments. Interest is said to have been returned to the general fund to increase the size of the working capital, and it was hoped that eventually this amount would provide members with adequate funds to increase profits by making quantity purchases possible.

Loans were not limited to members of the association, but when nonmembers borrowed money much more interest was charged. One nonmember dry-goods seller alleged that he had borrowed 500 pesos from this cooperative, received 400, and paid the balance at 17.50 pesos per day for 28 days, plus 5 pesos for the remaining 2 days. In other words, the interest rate was said to be 20 percent per month.

This operation should have been profitable enough to have been successful, but unfortunately conflict is said to have arisen among its members when the president of the association authorized a loan of 2,000 pesos to one of his close relatives, an amount well above the limit established by the "rule." The situation was all the more divisive because several of the association's other members had warned the president that his relative was an exceptionally poor risk. However, the relative was one whom the president "could not deny," and the loan was made. The relative defaulted, and the aroused membership demanded that the president disband the association. Some of the other members confided that they felt it was a pity that affairs had not gone better, for now that the lines of division were drawn, it would be difficult ever again to induce local Batangueños to cooperate.

The Vegetable Vendors' Association drew its membership from the main vegetable section of the marketplace, and although the group was not kin-based, a number of the founding members were relatives, and the remainder were persons who had known one another for many years. The organization was very like the Batangueño Association, but it was much less well capitalized, and the loan limits were much lower. Loans from the vegetable vendors' group were limited to 300 pesos for four months at 5 percent interest. This association was successful for a time, but then ran afoul of the law. The operation came to the attention of the Bureau of Internal Revenue and the members were warned that they would have to disband or be prosecuted for exceeding the legal limit on interest (12 percent per year).

The surviving credit association, the Fish Vendors' Loan and Savings Association (FVLSA), is said to be the largest and most active of the credit groups ever formed in the marketplace. Its long-term economic significance, however, is another matter. According to informants, it was founded in 1955 by several related persons, all fish sellers who combined wholesale and retail operations. The original founders retained control of the organization, and none of the governing offices had changed hands in nearly ten years of existence. The president of the association has a stall in the fish section, but it is usually operated by an employee, for the president devotes most of his time to management of the association. His wife is also an active trader and is an important wholesale supplier of fish.

FVLSA consists of sixty regular members, each of whom pays yearly dues of 3 pesos and is assessed 15 pesos per year to provide office supplies and to maintain the "death fund" (FVLSA will bury its deceased indigent members). Members make either regular or irregular contributions but may only borrow the amount they have on account at 2 percent interest per month.[2] Larger loans may be obtained but at higher interest rates, providing the borrower can find a coguarantor.

However, according to informants, the loans which FVLSA provides for its members, according to its own bylaws, are a less extensive operation than those it provides *ex officio* to nonmembers. The FVLSA is often alleged to be the "cover" operation for the activities of usurers. This charge is so common that reference to the interest rates charged by these persons is regarded as a source of high humor by other sellers, and some BAMARVA officials suggested that if I wanted to know how best to operate in the marketplace I should consult the officers of the FVLSA.

Interest rates exacted by local moneylenders are not standardized and reflect the lender's assessment of the risks involved in each instance, as well as the market value of capital.

---

[2] While borrowing one's own money (at 2 percent interest at that) may not seem an attractive offer, putting money into a credit cooperative has some other advantages. First, it puts savings into an immediately reclaimable form. Second, it is a means of "hiding" liquid assets from possible excessive demands made by friends and relatives.

The one attribute shared by all interest charges exacted is that they are impressively high. One woman, who alleged that she was in debt to the FVLSA, reported that she had borrowed 1,000 pesos for 28 days and was in the process of repaying it by making daily payments of 40 pesos each, or 12 percent interest per month. A second informant, a man and also a non-member, said that he borrowed 2,000 pesos for 100 days from the same source and was paying 13 percent per month. A third informant, who claimed membership in the organization, said that investments in the FVLSA were so good that they had encouraged some of the town's professional people to invest in the loan fund.

Although credit associations are useful for the provision of cash, they appear to have contributed little to the growth of the marketplace economy. This problem seems to be the result of two related conditions. If interest charges are within legal limits and reasonable, then the amount of the available loan is too small to be useful for commercial purposes. Or in the case of *ex officio* loans, the amounts are of economic proportions, but the interest rates are too high for the capital to be useful commercially. Sellers therefore tend to obtain these loans to cover subsistence and ceremonial obligations (cf. Wolf 1965) and not for use as venture capital. Credit associations, then, exploit conditions of capital shortage for the benefit of a few, well-situated financiers, and are not useful as a source of commercial capital.

As we have seen, usury is not limited to such organized groups, and tends to be widely distributed throughout the economy wherever liquid capital is available. This condition is partly due to demand and high prices for capital, but it is also encouraged by the fact that moneylending is not seen as a base or contemptible occupation. Rather, the reverse seems often to be the case, and vendors occasionally express their gratitude to usurers for a timely loan.

Generally sellers are aware of the commercial limitations of usury sources and try to avoid borrowing money from them. But there are likely to be times in the life of any seller when he must turn to such sources for emergency funds: to meet a social obligation, for example, or to pay some valued supplier when there is no other source. However, sellers characteristically offer a cultural justification for such loans. Weddings, baptisms, confirmations, funerals, beauty contests, and school graduations are all subjectively valued enough to be legitimate justifications for injudicious borrowing. For instance, one stallholder borrowed 800 pesos from a moneylender in order to support his oldest daughter's candidacy in a beauty contest,[3] only to see her defeated when another man invested 1200 pesos to support his own daughter. When some of his neighbors implied that this was a frivolous use of highly-priced money, the stallholder pointed out that it was important to see that even if his daughter didn't win, at least she was not shamed by a lack of support.

Thus, many sellers borrow from moneylenders, and as the buying peak passes in the late afternoon, moneylenders and their agents move quietly about the marketplace making their daily collections. As we have seen, rights to stalls are often used to secure loans, so sellers could lose their principal sources of income if they were obliged to default on a loan. But moneylenders are careful about loaning money, for frequent fore-

[3] As happens often in Hispanizied societies, a beauty contest usually accompanies each Philippine fiesta. The winner of the contest is determined by the number of votes received, but because votes are sold, the girl who gets the most votes is the one whose backers are willing to spend the most money. Therefore, the correlation between wealth and beauty is high.

closures give the lender the reputation of being "hard." This may not only arouse the rancor of the seller community, but worse, it may drive prospective customers elsewhere. Therefore, moneylenders themselves may attempt to dissuade a potential customer who might find repayment particularly difficult.

KINSHIP

Of all the sources of capital utilized by marketplace sellers, the statistically most important was found to be loans obtained from relatives (see Table 6). A number of writers have pointed to the tendency among lowland Filipinos to distinguish members of the nuclear family, and a small number of other relatives, as the main source of support within the greater universe of kin (e.g., Fox 1959, Hollnsteiner 1963, Lynch 1964). The

TABLE 6

Sources of Initial Trading Capital[a]

Source	Number	Percent
Relatives	51	34.0
Savings	43	28.7
Supplier Credit	25	16.7
Credit Assn.	8	5.3
Bank	4	2.7
All Others[b]	11	7.3
No Reply	8	5.3

[a]The sample here is 150 randomly selected stallholders, and does not include open-market vendors, whose capital commitment is low. Moreover, alternatives for obtaining capital are to a considerable degree limited by the nature of the product sold. Where multiple sources were reported, vendors were asked to report which was the most important.
[b]Gambling winnings, inheritance, land sales, pensions, and shares in farm income were mentioned here.

nature of mutual assistance among marketplace sellers supports such a view. Not only were the members of nuclear family categories reported to be important in providing initial operating capital, but members of the same units commonly continue to be sources of support in emergencies, particularly if they are located in geographical proximity to the seller. If a seller has primary kin in the community, he will turn first to them for assistance, unless it is already known that these kinsmen have no resources to spare. Loans of this kind are made without interest, except in rare cases, and some informants were mildly annoyed that such a question would even be raised. It is, however, common for loans from family members to be made for specified periods of time, and the obligation to repay such a loan is felt to be especially strong. It is embarrassing to both borrower and lender when the lender-relative is obliged actively to request repayment. In fact, in such cases some third relative may operate as an intermediary to smooth the path. However, when the creditor-relative is wealthy, he is expected to be more lenient about the terms of repayment, for he can better afford to lose and has an obligation to support fellow members of the network of close kin. Yet the lending of money and goods between kin is looked upon as a relationship of mutuality and not one of unilateral generosity, no matter how wealthy the lender may be.

Relatives other than primary kin, may also be sources of support, but beyond the limits of the nuclear family, requests for assistance are much more selectively made and granted. Individuals do not offer support to everyone to whom they are connected by kinship, nor do they expect it from every kinsman. Rather, one chooses (and is, in like measure, chosen by) those relatives, among the wider network of extended kin, with whom relationships will be validated through exchanges. In this process the ability to provide support is an important element influencing validation of choices, and although "support" involves the exchange of benefits other than economic ones, the latter are clearly powerful factors. From the seller's perspective, it is not only easier to approach a relative than a nonrelative for a loan, but the loan is also more likely to be forthcoming from kinship sources, for the bond of kinship itself can function to reduce risks for the lender. At the ideal level, and usually at the level of action as well, kin are ashamed to default on an obligation to one another.

Yet, as one might anticipate, in practice the honoring of kinship obligations is something less than perfect. Some sellers reported, for example, that they charge interest on loans made to relatives, but charged them less than they would have charged nonrelatives (the clear exception is a loan from parent to child). And it was reported that relatives sometimes renege on their obligations to repay loans. In fact, some of the better known feuds in the marketplace exist between relatives, and some of these have gone into formal litigation—a circumstance regarded as scandalous. In these cases, the disputes most frequently arose from misunderstandings concerning repayment of loans of trading stock made between related marketplace sellers.

Emphasis on the economic support functions supplied by relatives, however, should not lead us to ignore the commercial importance of associations formed solely on the basis of sentiment and mutual appreciation—close friendships. In many cases friends are much more important emotionally and commercially than relatives are. However, where this occurs, individuals who are deeply involved in mutual aid relationships are likely to initiate a bond of ritual kinship, making nonkin relations more morally binding, a circumstance which will be described in some detail below.

The economic support obtained from kin is not limited entirely to the provision of money loans; indeed, other forms of support are often more important than the small amounts of cash that relatives of marketplace sellers are likely to produce. One particularly significant nonmonetary form of assistance is for the relative to function as an intermediary between a seller and persons who control sources of trading goods, particularly when these latter are agents. The use of intermediaries has been often noted as a characteristic of more complex chains of social interaction in the lowland Philippines (e.g., Lynch 1964:12-14), and their appearance in a commercial context is not exceptional. Because livelihoods are often at stake, intermediation roles take on particular significance in the marketplace economy.

Because of the low income level characteristic of marketplace operations, producers and suppliers often seek to facilitate distribution of their stocks by extending credit to the retailers with whom they deal. Moreover, lenders face high risks unless extralegal sanctions can be brought to bear to secure the loan. Such sanctions take many forms—kinship, ritual kinship, etc.—but all involve considerable personal information about the debtor, and usually some kind of valued social relation. Personal relationships of these kinds are so important to the conduct of business in the marketplace that they constitute still another kind of resource. In a number of cases, sellers were initially able to enter marketplace trade only because they knew some agent who provided them with a stock of operating capital.

Because debts are difficult to collect, suppliers are reluctant to extend credit to sellers whom they do not know to be both personally trustworthy and commercially competent. However, agents will extend credit to an unknown seller when some third party, whom they know and trust, will stand "in bond" for the unknown seller; he vouches for the latter's integrity, or even cosigns a note. Nearly always relatives perform these intermediation operations, and it is difficult to overstress the significance of this kind of advocacy in facilitating the flow of credit through the marketplace.

To understand the organization of the marketplace in kinship terms alone would be much too simple, for many sellers have no relatives in the marketplace. Nevertheless, kinship is an important principle of organization, and in nearly every case there is a core of kinsmen among the sellers of particular classes of goods. In fact, all but a few sellers of two classes of products, footwear and *chucheria*, are related. In most cases in which clusters of kin appear, the organizing bond is kinship traced through females, and the typical example is a group of sisters, their husbands, and a few other categories of their consanguineal kin. This emphasis on females follows logically because small-scale marketing is predominantly a female role. On the other hand, there also exist a few groupings based on a core of siblings of both sexes, and at least one based on a group of brothers. The latter involves some Tagalog speakers who set up multistall enterprises from the outset, and is understandable in terms of the generally high correlation between large-scale market activity and male direction of the firm.

Among stallholding sellers surprisingly few kinship units involve two or more generations of lineal kin. In contrast, among open-market sellers mother-daughter units, in particular, are common. The reasons for this appear to be the strong drive for upward mobility among stallholders and the corresponding emphasis upon seeing that children are educated and encouraged to find other kinds of jobs—a condition similar to that reported among more substantial sellers in Haitian marketplaces (cf. Legerman 1962). Far more common are stalls operated by a woman and one or more collateral relatives in junior generations, particularly a sister's daughter or a cousin from a poorer, rural family.

Establishment of the larger kinship units in the marketplace has followed a roughly similar pattern in each case: an individual emigrated to Baguio City for economic reasons, found the situation promising, established a foothold, and sent for some of his (or her) relatives. In some cases the "pioneer" assisted the new arrivals by using his influence to help them obtain stalls (related sellers often occupy adjacent market stalls), and in others they merely provided advice about how to obtain stalls. But in nearly every case reported, the pioneers either provided the newcomer's initial operating capital from their own stocks, or provided the support necessary for the newcomers to establish connections with their own suppliers. The clustering of relatives in particular zones (product specializations) of the marketplace is understandable in these terms: one's "choice" of stocks is often limited to the kinds of goods in which one's relatives deal.

"Support" from relatives may also take the form of loans in kind. Commonly, stocks of commodities are loaned back and forth among kin as relatives seek a foothold in the market, or as periodic shortages occur. These loans are sometimes simply repaid, either in cash or kind; just as commonly, goods are sold by the borrower and the profit divided with the lender. Many of these sharing arrangements are not merely responses to the circumstances of the moment but are deliberately planned to provide optimal use of capital. Sellers must operate with little operating capital, and therefore they can purchase only limited quantities of stock. When they try to obtain savings through quantity purchasing, they can afford to buy only a limited range of goods and thus have little variety in their offerings. Lending stocks as they do gives each seller access to a much larger, more varied inventory than would otherwise be possible. For example, a vendor who specializes in rubber shoes may borrow leather or plastic ones from a relative, and then divide the profit from their sale. Or the vegetable seller who has plenty of vegetables but no fruit may exchange the one for the other. The ability to borrow stock also greatly increases the individual seller's opportunities to stabilize his inventory yet still meet a wide range of his customers' demands. In effect, then, the practice smooths out the flow of supplies.[4]

Finally, relatives also provide a source of labor—often cheap labor. Any city dweller is likely to be approached sooner or later by poorer rural relatives who seek assistance for themselves or for one of their children. Often they request the city dweller to take a child into his household; in fact, the townsman is likely to feel an obligation to do so, depending upon the closeness of the relationship. Many marketplace sellers' households contain such relatives, though sellers are not especially wealthy even by local standards. However, such relatives are not treated as guests, or given equal rights as "members of the family." They are recognized to be relatives, but rather than allocating tasks equally to all members of the household, consistent with age and sex, the poor relation is given a disproportionate share of menial work.

The performance of such tasks as cooking, washing, and caring for children by houshold menials has wider economic implications, for it frees the adult female for increased participation in the marketplace. She may take over the operation of the stall in order to free her husband for additional duty as a carrier, thereby increasing opportunities for income. In

---

[4] In a few cases relatives were found to be the sole sources of supply. For example, all the entrail sellers are poor relatives of the more substantial meat sellers, and a few footwear sellers depend entirely upon their wealthier relatives in the same trade. In effect, these poor relations become additional sales outlets for the less salable products, but the advantage obviously is mutual.

the marketplace stalls large enough to require clerical assistance, clerks are usually relatives of the stall operator. Their wages are commonly no more than food and lodging and a few pesos a month for spending money—and, of course, an opportunity to learn the business. These kinfolk-clerks are often delighted to be in as lively a place as Baguio City, and these arrangements allow the vendor to meet his kinship obligations and provide him with a source of cheap labor. The obligations of kinship undeniably involve give and take, but this hardly implies that the flow of benefits is equal in all directions.

SUPPLIERS

"Suppliers" (whether they are producers, carriers, or agents) must frequently extend credit to their customers, not only to move stock, but also because extending credit is a way of competing with other suppliers. It is common knowledge that the extension of credit to a customer can obligate the customer to make continued purchases. Yet the willingness of suppliers to extend credit, and the amount of interest they charge if they do so, depends on a number of factors. For example, suppliers are in general more inclined to extend credit on perishable items than durable ones, for credit tends to increase the rate at which they move and thus to reduce the risk of spoilage. Or, other things being equal, they are more likely to extend credit on the less salable items than upon those for which demand is high.

Market conditions, however, may create circumstances which take precedence over other considerations. The supplier may prefer to extend credit only on perishables or slow-selling items, and then only to persons he knows well and trusts. But it may happen that demand is low relative to supply, or that he needs cash to meet his own obligations or to take advantage of an opportunity to speculate. He may, therefore, find it expedient to choose a less advantageous strategy, and allow retailers to take goods on credit, or be content with installment payments, or take unusual risks by extending credit to persons whom he does not know well. Additional inducements to lend include the use of credit as a competitive strategy calculated to secure control over retail outlets. Large-scale suppliers sometimes finance sellers in the marketplace by providing them with stocks, in some cases even assisting them by paying market fees. Some captive sellers of a few durable goods such as rice, dry goods, and footwear serve as lower-level wholesale outlets which also extend credit, and which further expand the primary supplier's potential market. Finally, another compelling factor encourages suppliers to extend credit: they realize additional profit through interest charges.

Where loans take the form of loans-in-kind from agents, interest is not usually discussed as such, though it clearly exists in the higher prices charged for goods taken on a loan basis. For example, the footwear seller is quoted one price if he intends to pay cash, and a second if he asks for credit. The difference depends on demand for the goods and the length of time involved. In most cases, if the seller pays for his stocks within a thirty-day period, he is charged only 5 percent interest. But if he goes beyond thirty days, the costs of borrowing rise sharply. Because few sellers can afford to pay within the thirty days following delivery, they pay high interest rates, and many become perpetually indebted to suppliers. Once the debt has been established, the supplier is in a position to exploit the relationship by charging more interest and by persuading the retailer to accept less-salable items in his stock.

Suppliers of some locally-produced goods operate in ways similar to the agents of large firms. For example, the majority of meat and fish sellers obtain their stock on credit from a small number of others who double as suppliers and retailers, for only a few sellers have enough capital to establish connections with primary producers. In order to purchase sizeable quantities of marine fish, for example, one is expected to deal with coastal fishermen, who require a cash deposit before they will release stock. Because only a few local sellers can afford to make such a deposit, they virtually control the flow of marine fish into the local market. Other fish sellers must purchase from them or deal in pond-raised fish supplied by carriers from the lowlands. The situation among meat sellers is similar. At the time of this study only three meat sellers had access to primary sources of supply, and they, too, functioned as both wholesale and retail outlets.

Many marketplace retailers can't afford to purchase even their daily trading stock on a cash basis, and must again rely upon credit. When fish are purchased on credit from marketplace wholesalers, the price is raised 10 centavos per kilogram over the cash wholesale price, and the credit price of meat is raised 20 centavos per kilogram. Given the then-current prices of fish and meat (about 2.50 pesos per kilo for fish and about 4.50 for meat), these charges amounted to approximately 4 percent over wholesale costs. However, in these cases sellers are not dealing with the agents of large wholesaling houses but with other marketplace sellers, and such loans are rarely for extensive periods of time. When one obtains meat and fish from another seller in the marketplace, he is expected to repay the debt later the same day. In other words, the 4 percent credit charges are daily ones.

The capacity of these small-scale sellers to stay in business at all, given the interest charges on their stock, is largely due to the fact that there are so few sources of supply. Thus, suppliers can manipulate prices to levels at which their clients realize small profits, while the suppliers themselves realize relatively large ones, particularly on goods sold at retail. Obviously, none of this profiteering would be possible if transport were good enough and cheap enough to allow goods to come freely to Baguio from competitive lowland markets.

Rice sellers illustrate the same general pattern. Among the rice sellers were seven women who had been established in business by agents representing rice-milling interests in the Cagayan Valley. These women received rice in truckload lots "on consignment" (which implies "on credit" and nothing more), and in addition mill representatives paid their market fees. In turn, these sellers function both as retailers and as local credit wholesalers for other rice retail sellers.

Rice is available in many different varieties, qualities, and grades of milled "cleanliness," each of which usually sells for a somewhat different price, but one example should establish the point. In 1964 a particular kind of rice sold for 1.60 pesos per *ganta* cash wholesale at the mill and was delivered to one of the marketplace wholesalers in Baguio for 1.70 pesos, on credit, delivered. The marketplace seller then sold this rice to her vendor clients for 1.75 pesos cash or 1.80 pesos on credit. Both retailed to consumers at 1.85. Because transport costs from the mill are approximately 4 centavos per *ganta*, the wholesale seller in the marketplace paid approximately 4 percent interest per *ganta*. All these prices were reckoned on 28-day loan periods, and additional charges were made if the debt was not paid on time.

In credit relationships between producers of agricultural commodities and carriers, the carrier is given agricultural produce on credit: first, because he is trusted, and second, because he is providing a valuable service. He collects small quantities of goods which in themselves are hardly worth the trip to market, he provides transport, and he probably obtains higher prices for the goods he carries than the producer would if he acted in his own behalf. Thus he earns his margin, and for producers to extend interest-free credit to him is consistent with their own economic self-interest.

Nowhere in the marketplace economy is the importance of credit from suppliers greater than to the many *sari-sari* (see Appendix I, p. 289, for a list of *sari-sari* items) sellers. At the time this study was undertaken, the principal sources of *sari-sari* commodities were the government-sponsored NAMARCO dealers, the salesmen representing Manila-based manufacturing and wholesale firms, and the large Chinese-operated grocery stores adjacent to the marketplace.

All things being equal, the *sari-sari* vendors would have preferred to obtain their supplies exclusively from NAMARCO outlets, for those subsidized goods offered a slight retail advantage over Chinese competition. But for several reasons NAMARCO outlets were not the sole, or even the most important, sources of *sari-sari* goods. First, the NAMARCO program didn't include a variety of goods large enough to meet anything approaching the entire range of customer demand. Moreover, the more desirable NAMARCO items rarely reached the local-level supplier, being drained off at higher levels in the distributional chain. Thus those goods that did filter down were less marketable and less profitable. Second, the flow of goods in the program was erratic, so sellers didn't know what they would receive or when it would arrive. The principal value of NAMARCO goods, therefore, lay in their function as "lead" items, luring the customer in range of the stallholders' persuasive salesmanship.

But from the viewpoint of the marketplace seller, the greatest problem with the NAMARCO program—the condition most complained about—was that NAMARCO dealers were reluctant to extend credit to lesser-order wholesalers. Distributors limited credit to short periods of time—one week and less—and offered it only on the less-salable items. One can well imagine that distributors who had on hand a supply of government-subsidized, low-cost, high-quality goods which were much in demand would not find the prospect of offering them on credit to other wholesalers very attractive. Large quantities of the more desirable NAMARCO commodities simply went to the highest bidder, often a Chinese, thereby magnifying the problem the program was designed to remedy.

The representatives of the large manufacturers and wholesalers who distributed locally are other possible sources of *sari-sari* supplies both for *sari-sari* sellers in the marketplace and for the Chinese grocers outside it. However, these firms can hardly afford the costs of extending credit to all the sellers who desire it, and they usually instruct their agents to clear requests for credit with their Manila offices. As a result, the organization which emerges is similar to that suggested for the distribution of other classes of goods: a few successful local sellers obtain access to credit and become local-level wholesalers for other sellers. This organization is useful to the large, Manila-based firms, for it allows them to avoid establishing a huge number of high-risk credit relations at the local level. But it creates an opportunity for price manipulation and profit-taking of which the local-level wholesaler is aware.

That prices on *sari-sari* items are not higher has little to do with competition in the marketplace itself and results rather from competition from the Chinese grocery stores adjacent to the marketplace. For the Chinese compete with local *sari-sari* wholesalers, and even with the agents themselves. Their chief manner of competing is through credit. In 1964 over 80 percent of the *sari-sari* sellers in the marketplace reported that stock obtained on credit from local Chinese grocery stores either constituted a major portion of their stock at that time, or had done so at some time within the past year. The primary reason for the popularity of Chinese supply sources is that the Chinese extend greater quantities of credit for longer periods of time than the local Filipino wholesalers can manage. In larger terms, the Chinese grocers carry the burden of providing investment capital for most of the local *sari-sari* sellers.

The economic success of Chinese populations is not unique to the Philippines but is general throughout Southeast Asia. The factors which have led to this superior commercial success are not clearly understood, though they have been much discussed (cf. Dewey 1962b). This success involves many "subjective" elements that impinge upon economic performance. An inquiry into them shows us that the "rules of social organization" may indeed have considerable influence on economic performance.

Two common propositions relate to this issue: first, that Chinese sellers work harder; and second, that Chinese are more clever businessmen. Local Filipino sellers work long and well, given the capacity of the economy to absorb their labor in return for wages or profits. Many sellers are on hand by five or six each morning to receive or purchase stocks and to arrange displays. They are at work literally all day, even taking meals in their *puestos*, until seven at night. In fact, in sheer hourly inputs many Filipinos work harder than do local Chinese shopkeepers. On the second issue—commercial sophistication—it is necessary to depend more heavily on impressions. Moreover, there is considerable variation among sellers in just this respect. Many marketplace sellers know little about conducting commerce and are "inefficient" by any objective standards. However, the many carriers, sellers, middlemen, etc., who have long been in trade are clever about their use of capital. Any carrier, for example, who consistently grosses 10 or 15 percent profit under prevailing local conditions has given an adequate demonstration of commercial ability. Because incentives and commitment seem to be more or less constant, the differences between the Filipino and Chinese performances must result from other factors. These factors appear to be differences in social organization and prevailing political conditions.

Relatives provide useful economic and support functions for Filipino sellers, and the organization of one's relatives is important to a seller's enterprises. But the character of kinship organization as it exists among most Philippine ethnolinguistic groups, and especially lowland Filipinos, presents some problems when viewed in economic perspective.

The typical way in which kinship is reckoned in the Philippines allows for a considerable degree of social "ambiguity": kinship associations are so arranged that they allow for competing claims on the loyalty and support of individuals. Kinship among most Philippine groups is reckoned bilaterally; that is, the kin of both of one's parents are equally important, and true descent groups are generally lacking (see Eggan 1967 for some exceptions). Because the individual "inherits" some relatives from his mother and some from his father, his own kin group is different from that of either parent and is precisely the same only for full siblings. Because kinship is reckoned bilaterally from the individual's perspective, and not from a fixed point of remote ancestral origin, membership in kin groups overlaps considerably, so a given individual is a member of the kin groups of many other persons and ideally, at least, owes support (and gets support) from all with whom he reckons a kinship bond. But such an organization, because it overlaps, does not distinguish a corporate group of relatives with objective boundaries, in which all members owe loyalty to all other members of the group rather than to all of an individual's bilaterally-reckoned kin. Individuals may easily be caught by conflicting claims for support in such a system, and except for the nuclear family, kinship alone does not provide the basis for corporate economic activities. Large corporate kinship units are found in the Philippines at least occasionally, but where they are a second limiting principle—rights in an estate—has been introduced, and membership in the group is limited on an *ad hoc* basis (cf. Anderson 1964).

The Chinese local kin group presents a somewhat different set of characteristics. In ideal terms, the basic unit of Chinese social organization is a group of males who trace descent from a common remote ancestor, together with their wives and children, but minus out-marrying females and their children. Ideally this group should also constitute a household unit, with all its members residing under a common roof (cf. Yang 1945:73–85). Thus, unlike the common lowland Filipino mode of kinship organization, Chinese kinship focuses on males and emphasizes a principle of descent. Such principles of organization define the membership of kin groups discretely: the principle of patrilineal descent results in the formation of corporate kinship groups, and one is a member of only one such group. Because the membership of such groups is relatively small (maternal relatives are ideally not included) and non-overlapping, the kin group can function effectively as a unit, and rights and duties can be unambiguously assigned. Moreover, because it is based on descent and not upon conjugal bonds, the Chinese kin group can endure through time and constitutes a more effective unit than its Filipino counterpart for the management of resources and investments.

But from an economic perspective what is more important is that the corporate nature of the Chinese kin group encourages collective economic behavior. The ideal in the Chinese case is to treat resources controlled by family members as a pool, dispositional rights to which are presided over by a "family manager." Conventionally, this manager is the active senior male in the kin unit, but in the local situation a younger man who has had training in modern business methods may carry out management functions.

The Chinese unilineal form of organization, therefore, provides a basis for retaining the cooperation of the members of the kin group, while at the same time encouraging efficiency through diversification. For example, one local Chinese family had interests in wholesale groceries, rice lands, rice mills, transport, and finance. Each specialized aspect of the entire enterprise was managed by a son of the senior male (or in one case, a son-in-law), while the whole was directed by the elderly man who had founded the firm. Capital, with obvious reservations, was transferred from one of these endeavors to another, consistent with the greatest amount of calculated advantage. This kind of executive direction tends to distinguish the Chinese family sharply from the Filipino variety, and this is perceived and commented on by members of both groups. As one Chinese informant summarized the difference, "Members of Filipino families are always fighting among themselves, but we put someone in charge."

Therefore, the Chinese kin group has several important features like those of stock corporations, with perhaps the greatest difference being that kinship limits participation. The resemblance is so strong that it has been explicitly recognized, and some families have actually issued "stock" shares (informally, without a legal charter) to their members. In one case, for example, thirteen shareholders divided profits at the end of each year. Furthermore, after the death of two of the original shareholders, rather than reapportion the deceased relatives' shares, income accruing to them has been set aside to finance education for the sons of family members.

The organizational differences between Chinese and Filipino kin groups, as these have been enumerated, are by no means absolute. The rules of organization of Chinese families are ideals which are not always realized in practice in the Philippines, as they often are not in China and Taiwan (cf. Wolf 1968:23–35). Moreover, as intimated above, local Philippine Chinese family enterprises frequently incorporate some in-marrying males, which provides them with a bilateral aspect that violates the patrilineal convention. And some Filipino families take on a corporate character by excluding from rights in the estate any relative who is not a descendant of that estate's founder. The claim here, therefore, is simply that Chinese family enterprises are typically more effective units for organizing the use of productive factors and financial affairs than their Filipino counterparts. Moreover, they are especially effective in an economic sector in which stock corporations are very rare. Not that Filipino kin groupings are ineffective as economic units in any absolute sense, but the Chinese family has superior capacity for pooling resources, for the executive management of them, and thus for efficiently undertaking ventures of greater scale.

However, Chinese social organization includes forms of association other than kinship units. It also features a number of goal-oriented interest groups. The most important of these is the Chinese Chamber of Commerce, to which all local Chinese businessmen belong. As we have seen, this organization not only serves a political function, but also regulates economic relationships within the Chinese community. Its officers mediate disputes between Chinese businessmen, encourage economic cooperation within the Chinese business community, and operate as a communication center in the quest for capital to support Chinese-managed ventures. These operations, too, have much to do with the success of Chinese commerce.

The second set of factors influencing Chinese economic performance is the political position of Chinese in the contemporary Philippines. Because of their inferior position in Philippine society, Chinese who manifest any visible sign of wealth are likely to attract more than a fair share of attention from tax collectors, and are apt to be considered fair game for extortion attempts by local politicians. Therefore, when Chinese accumulate wealth, they are well-advised to keep the fact from becoming public knowledge. Moreover, most of the usual modes of converting wealth to prestige and influence which are open to Filipinos, and which among Filipinos absorb large proportions of wealth, are simply not real alternatives to Chinese. Chinese cannot, for example, become landlords and patrons to many share tenants as Filipinos can. They cannot hold public office if they are not citizens, and are unlikely to be elected even if they are; and they dare not consume conspicuously in any way. To a considerable degree, then, the Chinese position in Philippine society imposes upon them a situation of "forced reinvestment." Regardless of the goals which they might prefer, Chinese are, by the nature of their denigrated minority-group status, given powerful inducements to reinvest capital in their enterprises. Like it or not, the Chinese in the Philippines are largely obliged to follow the guiding principle of capitalist development: forego consumption and employ resources as productive capital.

Undoubtedly, minority-group status and pride in Chinese culture are other significant factors, and together these generate a feeling of considerable solidarity within the Chinese community. These, too, are economic assets, for they generate the strong feeling that, other interests being equal, one should assist fellow Chinese in any way possible.

The commercial position of the Chinese wholesale grocers in Baguio City is enhanced by frictions in the local transport network. Local Chinese wholesale grocers share, with other Chinese, access to superior specialized transport, particularly the trucks of the Chinese growers' cooperative. Moreover, their commercial relationships with the large Manila supply houses also provide them with better price information than is available to Filipino stallholders with whom they deal. Their position has a double advantage. In the first place, they are able to take advantage of impending price increases by withholding items in order to obtain higher future prices. Largely for this reason wholesalers are reluctant to provide credit on items on which prices are rising, for they prefer to force buyers to wait for the price increase. Second, they are in a position to speculate, or even to manipulate prices "artificially" by creating shortages. The latter strategy of course depends heavily on the poor quality of the transport available to their competition. For it is possible in this locale to withhold goods, drive the market price upward, and reap the benefits before high prices can call in shipments from other areas.

In one instance local Chinese learned that the price of flour was about to be raised substantially. Accordingly, Chinese wholesalers held their stocks of flour from sale to wait for the increase. In this situation one of the smaller-scale Chinese operators attempted to take advantage of this privileged information by purchasing all the flour he could. However, he lacked the necessary cash. Because his Chinese colleagues would not, for obvious reasons, sell flour on credit, he instead bought 500 cases of tinned beef, which could be purchased on credit. He disposed of the beef by selling it for 3 pesos a case less than the going price, and then used the cash he received to buy flour from Filipino merchants. In three weeks' time the price of flour rose from 9 to 13.50 pesos per sack, and the Chinese had, after repaying his debts, made approximately 8,000 pesos while using money borrowed from other Chinese. In another case, refined sugar was held from the market long enough for the local price to rise from 25.50 to 30.50 pesos per hundredweight, at which point the arrival of a sugar shipment once more depressed it.

More important for day-to-day operations, however, Chinese wholesalers command enough capital to pay cash for goods purchased from higher-order wholesalers and manufacturers. They achieve savings by not having to pay interest and through the price reductions obtained for quantity purchases. It is, of course, important to their competitive position to purchase in sufficient quantity to obtain the maximum possible savings on volume purchase. Furthermore, their ability to obtain cheap transport by using the trucks belonging to the Chinese growers' cooperative permits savings by reducing transport costs. The combination of these factors enables local Chinese wholesalers to offer goods at nearly the same prices as those quoted locally by the manufacturers' agents.

However, the principal means through which local Chinese wholesalers compete with other suppliers is not so much by offering lower prices, but by offering better credit terms. Again personal relationships are vitally important, for one of the advantages which these local wholesalers have over their Manila-based competitors is personal information about individual marketplace sellers. This information allows the local wholesaler to assess risks more accurately than his competitors. In addition, the proximity of the Chinese to the market makes possible the daily collection of payments, a strategy which is another hedge against loss.

However, as a result of the large number of sellers involved, both within and outside the market, *sari-sari* selling is a competitive business. Moreover, risks are increased by two additional circumstances. First, since most *sari-sari* items are edible, stallholders who receive such goods may literally consume their capital. Second, Filipinos are less than scrupulous about repaying debts owed to Chinese, for they know that public attitudes against Chinese make them reluctant to pursue legal means of redress. Chinese wholesalers, therefore, often find themselves in a difficult position in spite of their superiority in capital accumulation: they must extend credit to compete with the representatives of lowland Filipino firms, but they know that their Filipino debtors in the marketplace will repay only the minimum necessary to keep supplies flowing. Thus, long-standing debt relationships are unavoidable, and they must be manipulated cleverly to be profitable.

Chinese pursue several strategies in order to make the most of existing conditions. In the first place, informants reported that Chinese wholesalers will not extend credit to any seller who has defaulted on a loan obtained from any one of them. This effectively implies that the Filipino seller who is deeply in debt to a Chinese supplier must either continue to deal with him, or alternatively must raise enough cash to obtain stock from other sources. Second, Chinese are reluctant to provide credit to any seller who attempts to purchase selectively. Stallholders preferred to use their cash to purchase as much NAMARCO stock as they could and then to purchase from Chinese sources only the more salable commodities not available from NAMARCO outlets. This contradicts the Chinese strategy, which is to use the marketplace seller as an outlet for slower-moving commodities. Thus, in order to obtain credit from Chinese, the *sari-sari* seller must agree to accept a wide variety of items which are difficult to sell. Indeed, selling them involves considerable effort and skill, and usually personal knowledge of one's customers. In many cases, therefore, sellers simply ask for stock worth a certain amount of money without specifying the nature or quantities of the items. This accounts for the seemingly "irrational" choices of stocks carried by *sari-sari* sellers; that is, the high proportion of unusual and slow-moving items which they carry on their shelves.

However, the arrangement is not as iniquitous as it seems at first. Because the Filipino *sari-sari* sellers are his principal customers, the Chinese wholesaler is ultimately interested in their welfare. In effect, therefore, the wholesaler becomes the primary source of operating capital for the marketplace *sari-sari* seller and—less directly—his business manager as well. Thus, although the Chinese may receive the lion's share of the profits, he also maintains some retailers whose businesses would undoubtedly fail otherwise. Above all, the Chinese wholesale grocer is in the position he occupies largely because he provides services which are not so effectively provided elsewhere.

Retailers in the marketplace itself also often perform a supply function for other sellers as well as for the ultimate consumer. In such cases credit is also customarily extended. For example, wandering peddlers carry clothing and knicknacks from the Baguio marketplace to be sold in rural villages and hamlets. These persons commonly obtain trading stock through credit relationships which they have with the more substantial stallholders in the marketplace. In fact, most of them have kin relationships with stallholders.[5] These peddlers, in turn, operate a credit trade in the countryside, a situation possible because peddlers tend to follow the same routes year after year. This peddler trade is relatively small, but it provides the marketplace seller with additional outlets, much as the *sari-sari* stallholders provide outlets for commodities sold by Chinese wholesalers.

Of much greater scale is the external, mixed-vegetable trade with the Manila area which is conducted by Chinese middlemen. In this case, as noted earlier, a large proportion of the produce is collected by the "native" sellers in the Hangar

---

[5] The close association of peddlers and stallholders is sometimes obvious. For example, some of the *chucheria* stalls operated by Batangueños are constructed so that the walls of the stall (on which wares are displayed) are instantly removable for use as sandwich boards by traveling peddlers.

Building. In this example, too, credit is an integral aspect of trade relations, although it is extended somewhat reluctantly. Chinese have a near-monopoly on this trade as a result of their control of market outlets and transport. Therefore anyone seeking an external market for large quantities of vegetables is virtually obliged to deal with Chinese middlemen under conditions largely dictated by the latter. Consequently, although local native peoples have certain advantages when dealing with the lowland Filipinos of the main-market area, they are at a distinct disadvantage when they turn to external markets for their produce. In general, Chinese middlemen take vegetables only on a "consignment" basis, and pay for them after they have been sold in lowland markets. Only when vegetables are in short supply are middlemen willing to pay cash.

Unfortunately for the native vegetable sellers, market conditions usually favor the middlemen, and the latter are quick to take advantage of them by shifting the risk to the sellers. Prices are agreed upon at the time produce is consigned to the middleman. But here the Chinese is at an advantage because his communication network provides him with more accurate information about market conditions. Moreover, native informants consistently complained that they rarely receive the prices agreed upon (the difference is usually attributed by the middleman to "spoilage"), and are not likely to receive payment at all for two months or even longer after the transaction. Thus, the Chinese furnishes transport and market outlets, but the native seller provides most of the capital and absorbs most of the risks resulting from spoilage and market fluctuations. Furthermore, middlemen often have the use of the native sellers' capital for several months' time, thereby realizing additional financial benefits. At one point this problem became so grave that an organized protest was attempted. But it could not be sustained, for the produce was perishable, and the Chinese con-

trolled the market outlets. Yet, again in defense of Chinese activities, it is problematic whether an external vegetable trade
could be sustained at all without the services provided by Chinese middlemen.

In some cases native sellers provide capital to primary producers, motivated by the desire to obtain regular sources of
supply and to assist friends and relatives in rural villages. Cultivation of market-garden crops is much more capital-intensive
than any of the traditional forms of cultivation employed in the
southern Cordilleran region, and capital is scarce and expensive.
A number of local farmers have sought to acquire production
capital by selling immature crops in the field. These sales are
usually to Chinese middlemen, although some member of the
local elite may purchase them if the price is very favorable.
However, such sales are not popular with producers, for production estimates made by the purchaser for pricing purposes
are customarily on the low side. Thus, barring a crop failure,
for the producer to bring his crop to harvest before selling it
is more advantageous. Moreover, if the purchaser sustains a
heavy loss from natural calamity, the producer is under an
obligation to give the purchaser even more generous terms on
a subsequent crop. A crop sale of this sort with Chinese buyers is not likely unless the producer's fields are close enough
to a road to allow frequent inspection, in order to ensure that
none of the crop is sold surreptitiously.

The native vegetable sellers in the marketplace are themselves a source of production capital. Sellers are often so anxious to obtain routine sources of supplies that they approach the
producers. The object is to secure supply sources by obligating
producers through the use of debt relationships. In this instance, the seller lends the producer enough money for the
necessary labor, fertilizer, insecticides, seeds, etc., to bring the
crop to harvest. When the crop is harvested, the producer is

obliged to deliver his produce to the seller, selling to him at prices a few centavos per kilogram under the current market price. The seller limits risks by regulating his source of supply, while the producer gains production capital and a sure market for his perishable produce.

This "crop loan" arrangement, however, is hardly risk free. For in addition to the obvious perils of natural calamity or market fluctuations, there is always the danger that the producer will default. Producers are likely to live in remote regions, well away from the eyes of the seller, and considerable temptation exists for the producer to market some of the subsidized crop to other sellers, who would pay the full market price. Consequently, sellers hedge against such risk by negotiating crop loans only in areas in which they have relatives. In fact, these arrangements are often made with relatives. This kinship factor emerges as significant, for the stocks of native vegetable vendors are invariably obtained from their own villages of origin. The corallary of this general statement is also true: no native vegetable sellers in the marketplace originated in communities which were not vegetable producing. In addition, sellers often noted that vendors who had relatives in many different communities were fortunate, for relatives residing under different ecological circumstances would make a considerable variety of produce available to the native seller.

Vendors reported that as the scale of operations has increased in recent years, encouraged by the growth of lowland markets, sellers have been tempted to offer crop loans to more distant—and less trustworthy—relatives. The result has been that risks have risen sharply. Accordingly, modifications in the crop loan procedure have been instituted which were calculated to hold these risks to acceptable levels. Sellers were beginning to market the crops they financed, deduct the amount of the loan from the proceeds, and then divide the profit equally with the producer. This obviously reduces the seller's profits, but it also hedges against greater losses due to clandestine marketing by the producer.

Lowland sellers in the main vegetable section are also interested in obtaining regular sources of supply, and are willing to invest in such arrangements when opportunities arise. However, lowland sellers typically lack the socially-valued relationships with producers which reduce risks for native peoples. Some lowland Filipinos who have long been in trade have developed such relationships with producers, particularly with some of the larger-scale producers in the Trinidad area. But most find it more practical, and less costly, simply to purchase stocks from the native sellers in the Hangar Building.

Finally, credit is also an important aspect of relationships between sellers and consumers and therefore is a critical factor in competition between sellers. But this is a matter better discussed in the following section.

Chapter Seven

Economic Personalism

I n the preceding chapters two significant dimensions of marketplace economic relationships have emerged. First, credit is widely used as a means of facilitating commercial exchange. In the local marketplace system credit is one of the principal factors which organize different economic roles. Second, credit is not extended so freely as is likely in economies in which contract law can secure debt relations. Credit tends to flow along lines of communication established by highly personal relationships, in which individuals interrelate in terms of more than purely economic role dimensions. Personalistic relationships may carry the use of credit simply because they involve subjective values and extralegal sanctions which encourage individuals to meet obligations to others. The lack of an effective legal system and the corresponding restrictions on credit flow are not exclusively Philippine problems. For instance, Hannah and Krausz find that: "Assuming that a plentiful supply of credit is essential if... resources are to be developed, it is almost an axiom that such credit will not be ex-

211

tended—even for the highest interest rates—unless there is some minimum security under the law" (1960:332).

Because credit relationships in the Baguio market commonly involve a high degree of selectivity and choice, they are generally consistent with the idealized market model. But these personal relationships imply a lack of interchangeability of buyers and sellers which is not consistent with such a model. In the following examination of the several kinds of marketplace relationships, the degree to which buyer and seller roles are allocated in terms of personal, nontransferable attributes will be stressed (see Anderson 1969:452–453 for a similar treatment).

Kinship

As noted, kin relations often facilitate the extension of credit between producers, wholesalers, and retailers. Also, the crop loans extended by sellers to vegetable producers are most commonly based on kinship bonds. In addition, retailers in the marketplace often extend credit to relatives who also happen to be customers. While this is not particularly surprising, it nevertheless raises an issue which has been discussed extensively in the literature of anthropology and economic development: the purported conflict between the social obligations inherent to entended kin networks and the demand to husband resources which is so important to commercial activities. Economic obligations to a large number of relatives are widely held to constitute a major restriction on capital accumulation and growth. For example, referring specifically to the Philippine situation, Golay remarks that:

> . . . as is well known, the extended family system tends to stifle individual initiative. The extension of conjugal responsibilities to remote relatives means that individual economic success may

be followed by an increasing burden of dependency. The weakened relationship between individual enterprise and the material welfare of the individual has retarded the evolution of entrepreneurial qualities essential to economic development" (Golay 1961:16).

Foster (1962:94) accepts a similar proposition as axiomatic and suggests that among the reservation Navaho the drain created by excessive demands on traders' resources kept traders poor. In local terms, this "kinship restraint" hypothesis would imply that sellers' relatives levy frequent claims against the sellers' stock, yet feel themselves under no obligation to repay. Thus, for the seller to have a large number of relatives in the community is an economic liability, for the one-sided flow of material goods may drive him bankrupt.

However, kinship obligations are not inevitably impediments to the commercial success of individual Filipino marketplace sellers.[1] Golay has oversimplified a complex issue. First, the number of mutually-supporting relatives is typically much smaller than many Western scholars believe. The rules of social organization (i.e., bilaterality) governing kinship provide individual Filipinos with a potentially enormous network of kinship relations. However, not all these relationships are actually validated by reciprocally supporting actions. Individuals tend to pick and choose (and, again, to be chosen) on the basis of such criteria as spatial proximity ("being close enough to help"), relative wealth and influence, and personal attractiveness. The result is that the effective "action set" of kinsmen which is abstracted from the kinship network is much

---

[1] Sellers complain about the borrowing habits of relatives—or anyone else, for that matter. Thus, what occurs is here being distinguished from what informants say is their view of the matter. Based on accounts of their entrance into commercial operations, many sellers apparently would not be trading at all if they had not received assistance from relatives.

smaller than the entire kindred, and also changes as old relationships are allowed to lapse and others are activated.

Second, the expectations involved in kinship roles do not necessarily result in an ever-increasing "burden of dependency" for individuals. Though one is expected to assist his relatives (though not all of them), it is not anticipated that he will divide his wealth equally with them. He may, in fact, satisfy his obligation with quite low levels of performance. Nor is it expected that this relationship is one of unilateral generosity, with benefits flowing in a single direction from the entrepreneur to his extended kin. Rather, one's kin are expected to respond to a degree consistent with their own resources. Moreover, although indebtedness among relatives may never be eliminated entirely, it is carefully limited. Sellers often impose an absolute limitation on the amount of credit which they will extend to anyone, including relatives, and refuse to go beyond that point. Sellers are frequently candid with relatives about these limits. Sellers' kin accept and understand such limits, the justification being the hard necessities imposed by the ways in which sellers make their livings.

Finally, the "bad debt" element which is alleged to be so strongly developed in extended kinship relations, and which Golay's proposition raises to central importance, is by no means unique to relationships with kin. An "investment" in one's regular customers is typical, for in an enduring relationship, whatever its basis, the buyer's debt will probably not ever be paid in full. This is so not only between persons who are bound by the bonds of sentiment, but also in more explicitly instrumental relationships, such as those between Filipino *sari-sari* sellers and Chinese wholesale grocers. Chinese informants reported that it was commonly necessary to invest from 100 to 600 pesos in accrued and perpetual debt with each of their marketplace retailer clients. Indeed, this debt is important in binding together particular wholesalers and their customers.

"Bad debts," therefore, represent a constant factor in all varieties of enduring buyer-seller relations, and commercial failures among sellers cannot be attributed to the unilateral claims of relatives. The successful seller is one who, among other things, has learned to keep outstanding obligations to relatives at a minimum, and who knows how to manipulate these—and other—relationships to his advantage. The skillful trader realizes that perpetual indebtedness cannot be avoided and utilizes his "investments" in ways calculated to monopolize a portion of the market. The Chinese wholesaler is successful not because he is in a position, as an outsider, to avoid perpetual debt relationships. Rather, as a principal source of supply he is in an economic position to take advantage of these attachments and the obligations which they establish. He is, for example, able to unload his slow-moving stock and to substitute cheaper brands at prices appropriate to superior goods.

Far from being absolute economic liabilities, then, relatives may perform a number of economically significant functions. They may be the core of the vendor's steady clientele, and if the seller is skillful in dealing with them the relationship can be profitable for him. It is not considered avaricious to take profit from relatives, as long as the profit is modest; and it does not violate cultural values, or produce shame in the debtor to request that debts be repaid, providing that the request is delicately made (Fox 1956:433). Relatives may also advertise the excellence of their seller-kinsman's stock, his reliability, and the quality of his service. They may perform information functions which ultimately connect sellers to suppliers and sources of commercial credit. And they may also provide cheap labor to operate the seller's business. It is, then, entirely possible to meet the obligations of kinship and still realize considerable utility from kin relationships, depending upon how one plays the game. In this sense the mobilization of kinsmen is the initial phase in the development of a commercial enterprise in the marketplace.[2] Thus, it is not that Filipino kin groups cannot be effective economic units, but that the Chinese variety has some structural superiorities.

"SUKI"

Though relations of kinship are of considerable significance in the local economy, the principle of kinship is not adequately inclusive to organize a market economy. In fact, the particular utility of market arrangement is precisely that it facilitates exchanges which transcend the limits of the kindred and local territorial groupings. Thus, in the marketplace economy the greater number of relationships are not among kin.

In theory impersonal relationships oriented toward gain are adequate for commercial market transactions between buyers and sellers, and Polanyi and Dalton draw attention to this theory with their emphasis on the impersonal, conflict-producing character of markets. But the theory is designed for ideal market systems, on which the frictions of inadequate transport, poor communication, monopolistic practices, ineffective legal systems, and other real-life conditions do not impinge. Taking account of these real conditions, sellers in Baguio attempt to reduce risks by building up steady clienteles rather than by attempting to optimize profit returns from each transaction.

---

[2] Arensberg (1937: Chapter V) makes a similar case for the organization of distribution in rural Ireland, where shops depend heavily on relatives to keep them going. The nature of credit relationships is also strikingly similar.

And in the Baguio marketplace obtaining regular customers involves the extension of credit to them. Yet lending risks are high unless the credit relationship also involves the sanctions which attend personalized, multiplex relations. In the marketplace this security is most commonly provided by the formation of social accords referred to as *suki*. These *suki* bonds are noncorporate, essentially dyadic relations which, though economic in orientation, are nevertheless rich in subjective social content.[3]

Thus, in the marketplace economy, even outside relations fixed by kinship, there is surprisingly little random buying and selling. The majority of all transactions take place between persons who habitually trade with one another, and who are said to be one another's *suki*. Each seller then pursues strategies aimed at acquiring as many *suki* as he can manage (the word "manage" has been selected deliberately for reasons which will become apparent). "*Suki*" is probably a word borrowed from Chinese and may be translated as "special customer." The word may be applied to any person or role relationship in the trade network, and does not designate any specific economic function. Nearly every seller has "supplier *suki*" from whom he buys and "customer *suki*" to whom he sells. The usage of the term is reciprocal, each partner referring to the other as "my *suki*." It may be used in direct address, though when it is, it usually implies that the relationship requires reinforcement, for example, if one partner thinks the other is behaving in ways close to violating the norms of the relationship. Local informants reported that in "the Tagalog provinces" it is common for buyers who have not established *suki* relations

[3] The *suki* relationship in the Philippines is similar to Haiti's *pratik* relationship, on which Mintz (1961a) has reported extensively. And the economic context of *pratik* is similar to the situation in the rural Philippines.

with a seller to address him as *suki* in an effort "to gain his sympathy." But it was usually also added that one could only find such behavior locally among "those Batangueños."

Because credit is the essence of the *suki* relation, such relations typically take some time to build as trust and confidence are established between two potential partners and goodwill replaces the tendency toward sharp bargaining. Before committing operating capital to such a relationship, the seller must be assured that the buyer is a trustworthy person and that his clientage will involve enough sales to make him worth the investment. Some *suki* relations "just grow" as buyer and seller are mutually attracted on a friendly basis. Typically, after such a friendship has continued for some months on a casual basis, the seller will one day tell the buyer that he may "just pay later"—that immediate payment is no longer required. The buyer is likely to accept the invitation, thereby initiating the *suki* relationship. But the buyer will be especially careful of the conditions of his next several purchases in order to determine what kinds of privileges are being extended. Similarly, the seller will be concerned to see that the buyer's first payments are made on time and without hesitation. Thus, although there may be no explicit discussion of the terms of the *suki* arrangement, maneuvering occurs implicitly. Moreover, as the bonds of trust grow stronger through longer association, the element of *hiya* (embarrassment) enters the relationship. That is, partners in a long-standing *suki* relationship are careful to meet their obligations in order to avoid shame—a common tension-producing feature of social relations in the Philippines. As Fox (1956:433) points out: "Debts in the Philippines are not purely economic, but have a marked social overtone. The loaning of money and goods establishes an allegiance having some similarity to ritual kinship in which the debtor is in a subordinate position, but in which there are still reciprocal obligations."

Suki relations, however, may be established in ways in which the bond grows more rapidly. A common means of obtaining new *suki* is through the intermediation of older ones. If a trusted *suki*, or a relative, or some prominent figure in the community will recommend a customer to a seller, the customer may become an immediate *suki*, though he is again watched carefully for a time. (This provision of referrals is one of the ways in which relatives may be important assets to sellers). Some *suki* may also be passed along in exchanges of market stalls through the good offices of the old operator, or they may be "inherited" from a relative or friend who is retiring from business. Because they desire credit, buyers may themselves initiate the relationship by singling out some seller with whom they proceed to deal exclusively with the intent of becoming his *suki*.

In the community particular persons are especially prized as *suki* buyers, and there is considerable competition for their trade. Foreigners, especially if they are local residents and likely to be sources of repeat business, are greatly desired, for most of them are wealthy, are inclined to purchase high-profit items, and are generally less demanding than Filipino customers. Even American Peace Corps volunteers, whose means are limited, often are surprised to find that when they deal repeatedly with the same sellers they can purchase goods at slightly lower prices than some local residents—contrary to the notion that marketeers charge what the market will bear.

The Americans, Europeans, and lowland Filipinos who hold administrative positions in the mining communities are also highly valued as *suki*, but for other reasons. They are not only excellent customers in their own right, but their cooperation can open additional trading opportunities with mine employees. As noted earlier, wages paid to mine workers are an important source of local income. However, mines are often well outside Baguio City, where the employees are not readily accessible to marketplace sellers. But if one is fortunate enough to have a *suki* who is also a mine official, he may be persuaded to assist the seller in trading with miners by bringing pressure to bear on delinquent debtors. Accordingly, some sellers are able to carry on a modest credit trade with the mining camps. However, this kind of trading involves still another link in the chain of *suki* relations, for the only available communication with the mines is through the rural passenger bus service. Bus drivers are commonly pressed into service, therefore, to deliver goods to miners, in exchange for a payment or a share of the profits. These bus drivers, too, are considered *suki*. The local seller who is said to be most successful in mine trade happens also to be the wife of a lawyer who represents mining interests, and who, therefore, enjoys special advantages. But other sellers are involved, so there is some competition for these privileges from other sellers, commonly expressed in gifts and special services offered to certain mining company employees.

Political figures are also desirable *suki*, again not only for their personal value as customers, but also for greater advantages. Having an important politician for a *suki* establishes the seller as one whose goods are of high quality. And, just as importantly, the *suki* bond opens a channel of communication through which the politician may be approached directly for special favors. Indeed, *suki* is an especially fortuitous relationship for a seller to have with a political figure, for it facilitates the bestowal of gifts on the political patron with far less likelihood of problems, should the delicate matter of bribery arise. If, for example, one's *suki* meat seller offers him a few kilos of beef or some sausage, it will hardly raise eyebrows in the community, yet it may nevertheless lubricate the wheels of patronage. For the most part, the requests made of politicians by sellers are petty, involving protection from market authorities for one's own interests, or for those of a relative. But for some of the larger stall operators, requests for favors may be much more substantial—as are the gifts involved in the negotiation.

Finally, there is also a valued class of "institutional" buyers, who represent some large firm which has considerable purchasing power. This class includes persons who purchase for wealthy households, local restaurants and hotels, middlemen, and peddlers. Because of the scale of their purchases, these persons, too, are likely to find *suki* relations easy to establish.

The Socioeconomic Dimensions of Suki

Although the extension of credit to the buyer is the most significant economic feature of *suki* relations, there is typically much more to *suki* dyads than credit. The seller is expected to offer price concessions to his *suki* which are not available to nonprivileged buyers and which may take various forms. In some cases, the *suki* buyer receives a direct cost reduction in the prices of goods. The exact amount is determined by the nature of the goods, the quantity, and the maturity of the *suki* bond. In these cases the seller usually quotes the full price and then declares the more favorable price to the *suki* in a way which makes clear the privileged nature of the reduction, for example, "But for *you*, the price is only. . . ."

With perishable commodities other price concessions are more popular than a direct reduction in price. In this case the seller is more likely to provide benefits to his customer by giving him an extra measure (*dagdag*) for his money. This extra measure may be more of the goods being purchased, or it may be a small quantity of another kind. A buyer purchasing vegetables, for example, may find a particularly nice mango or papaya included at no additional charge but with a flourish calculated to draw attention to the seller's largesse. Sellers favor the *dagdag* concession particularly in disposing of perishables because it maximizes liquidity, optimizing cash income while reducing the possibility of perishable stock remaining at the end of the trading day. It is also popular because it "saves the price," that is, it doesn't require the seller to reduce his selling price. To do so would suggest to the buyer that prices were too high in the first place, thereby disturbing the buyer's confidence in his seller *suki*.

Although sellers are expected to reduce prices for their *suki*, the reduction varies with market conditions. Furthermore, the reduced price may still contain a considerable profit margin. If, for example, a seller should enjoy a temporary monopoly on some commodity, his *suki*, too, may have to pay dearly for the seller's advantage. The point, however, is that regardless of the margin of profit, the *suki* would always expect to pay less than non-*suki* buyers. Nevertheless, striking displays of "economic irrationality" occasionally occur between *suki*. For instance, in situations in which prices are generally rising, traders invest heavily in inventory, for relative profit margins are likely to increase. Yet for specially favored *suki*, sellers sometimes calculate their selling prices on actual wholesale costs rather than on the current market prices. In general, then, prices are not as elastic the they would be if such relations did not exist, for *suki* relations make both buyer and seller substantially less free to seek the best bargain of the moment.

In addition to price concessions the seller is expected to provide his *suki* with good quality merchandise and to set aside his best quality items for his *suki*. When supplies are short (again, the rainy season is the best example) sellers are expected to hold back supplies for their *suki*, and may ration these. A good *suki* supplier is not only fair about prices and quality, he is also a dependable source of supply. Preferably, he is also able to carry a wide variety of the classes of goods in which he trades so that customers need not look elsewhere to satisfy their range of wants.

When retailing in the marketplace, the seller is also expected to provide some services to his buyer *suki*. He should package their purchases so that they may be carried easily and will not allow their contents to spill. Many sellers keep a supply of *buri* (woven fibre) bags on hand which they lend to buyer *suki* for portage purposes. If the purchase is bulky or heavy, the seller is obliged either to assist the customer in carrying it to available transport, or to make arrangements with one of the market-place porters to do so. Each seller usually has one or more porters attached to him (who are also *suki* of his) who look after his *suki* customers' needs.

When the buyer is a specially favored customer, the market-place seller may function as an agent, obtaining commodities for him other than those he stocks himself. Because each seller tends to deal in a limited range of goods, under ordinary cir-cumstances shopping is a lengthy process, for buyers must pur-chase goods from a number of different sellers in order to satisfy their wants. One obtains vegetables from a vegetable dealer, rice from a rice merchant, and so on. But for a few of his special customers, the seller may offer the additional con-venience of shopping for them in other areas of the market. Each seller in the marketplace has a number of *suki* of his own among the sellers of products in which he does not normally trade, as well as *suki* who wholesale to him his usual stock-in-trade. The seller may then use his own *suki* relations to obtain goods for his customers. A vegetable seller may obtain meat, fish, or rice, and so on. This service is useful to his customers in several ways. The buyer, in effect, obtains credit for a wider variety of goods than those to which he might otherwise have access, and he is also more likely to obtain high quality wares for his money, for his agent is a skilled professional trader. Finally, he saves a great deal of time which might otherwise be spent shopping. On his side of the transaction, the seller is also realizing benefits. He provides a service which helps to retain the loyalty of his customers, and he receives a share of the profit from such purchases, widening the range of goods in which he deals. Finally, he puts some otherwise unproductive time to good use, and time is a surplus commodity for most sellers. The benefits accruing to the third-party seller are equally evident: he expands his market without having to risk lending goods to a buyer he does not know—all at a partial reduction in profit (a share of which rewards the intermediate seller). Goods may, however, be borrowed in this way through two or three marketplace sellers before they reach the ultimate consumer, thereby reducing profits to small amounts.

As a result of the sentiment which exists between *suki*, the common practice of haggling over prices is much reduced; or alternatively, if haggling does occur, it is done in a much more subdued manner than when randomly associated buyers and sellers negotiate. In a mature *suki* relationship, the buyer should assume that his *suki* is trustworthy and that he will offer the best possible prices without active encouragement to do so. While sellers typically honor their *suki* obligations in this regard—the seller cannot afford to establish a reputation as a person who doesn't—buyers usually do enough surreptitious shopping to provide themselves with information adequate to determine if they are being favorably treated. However, although prices are clearly important in the relationship, the overriding consideration is credit, and minimal discrepancies in prices are tolerated. As long as the seller's prices are more or less consistently on the low side of the current market price range, and his services graciously extended, most buyers would not choose to lose sources of credit by breaking off the relationship. There are many subtle ways in which the buyer may express his dissatisfaction before disagreement on prices will be allowed to terminate the bond.

In reciprocation for the many considerations which his seller *suki* extends to him, the buyer is expected not to patronize any other dealer in the class of goods handled by his seller *suki*. An occasional breach of this is acceptable, as one would anticipate, and is shrugged away. Sometimes buyers who purchase large quantities have more than one *suki* supplying the same kinds of commodities. But if the buyer continues to be inconstant to the degree to which there is little point to investing capital in him, the *suki* privileges will be withdrawn after suitable warnings.

The buyer should also "advertise" for his *suki*, praising him to others and perhaps introducing him to potential *suki*. Above all, the customer should make payments on his account at the appointed times, for the seller depends on cash income at specified times to make payments on obligations to his own suppliers. In practice, the total obligation owed to the seller *suki* is rarely removed entirely, and is not expected to be. This perpetual debt is said to demonstrate the good will which exists between *suki* partners. But at another level the residue of debt also tends to maintain the relationship; perpetuating the debt is treating the affair as an enduring connection, rather than as a series of short-run, discrete exchanges. Payments by *suki* are usually made monthly or bimonthly, a sharp contrast to the daily payments which must be made to moneylenders or to Chinese wholesalers.

While there is in *suki* relations a certain cultural "fit," in the sense that they are in many ways similar to other social attachments common in Philippine society, there are also some excellent pragmatic reasons for their popularity. They are important mechanisms for the reduction of trading risks, and as such they are advantageous to both parties. On his side, the seller obtains a greater measure of control over some important economic variables in the marketplace sector. Most important, the seller is able to achieve secure market outlets for his stock through *suki* relations, and these give him more complete information regarding the minimal size of the market to which he should orient his operation. He is able, by these means, to commit only a minimum amount of his capital to inventory and to use his reserves in other investments which might be more profitable. Many sellers are careful about committing capital to credit investments in slow-paying customers or slow-moving stock. When demand is high and business is brisk, sellers complain privately that conditions oblige them to pursue a strategy which leads to slow turnover of their capital. But at the same time they realize that for the better part of the year their *suki* customers are their salvation. Furthermore, there is a subjective element to *suki*: it has value for its own sake. There is pride and prestige to be gained from a reputation for competent merchandising and satisfied customers, just as there is pride in craftsmanship among artisans. Neither of these loftier values prevents the taking of profit, but both reduce the profit margins at which sellers work.

For his part of the bargain, the buyer receives credit necessary to carry him from one income-event to the next. He receives more favorable prices than he could obtain as a nonaligned buyer, and he receives a number of peripheral services which are a convenience and which may actually provide him with additional savings. Moreover, *suki* relations provide assurances of a continuous flow of supplies. If the buyer is but a consumer, assured supply may only be a convenience; but if he is a trader, such a flow may be absolutely critical to his capacity to service his own customers.

Because the *suki* relationship provides mutual satisfactions, once such a bond is established it tends to endure. In fact, the relationship may last as long as both parties live, or until the buyer moves too far away for the relationship to be continued, or until the seller retires. But some of this durability is the result of noneconomic satisfactions, and not merely material self-interest. Each seller is likely to count some of his *suki* among the persons who are regularly invited to share the seller's important social occasions: weddings, school graduations, baptisms, and other ceremonial episodes. Moreover, it is not unusual for a *suki* relationship to develop into a more formal relationship of a sort which ideally has more social value, such as ritual kinship, which will be discussed presently.

Some *suki* relations have proved to be viable not only through time, but over considerable space. The Manila-based agents of clothing manufacturers, food processors, and other large-scale firms, for example, are careful to maintain *suki* relations locally, for these are very important to the maintenance of distribution outlets. And most of the carriers who regularly travel such long distances to market their stocks in Baguio would not venture the risk if they didn't have *suki* stallholders waiting to buy from them when they arrived.

In the cases cited *suki* relations are maintained by frequent personal confrontations between the two *suki* partners, and these tend to reinforce the relationship. But some *suki* relations endure even the strain of long absences which prevent such personal renewals. These latter invariably involve persons (who were once both local residents and *suki* of local sellers) who have subsequently moved to other locales. Local sellers ship goods to them in accord with previous arrangements, orders received by mail, or perhaps orders carried by friends visiting in the Baguio area. Commodities are sent by bus and the payment made by mail. However, in only one case—an enterprising fresh-flower seller—do relations of this kind constitute a major part of any seller's trade. Nevertheless, one vegetable seller who had a *suki* in Manila had the notion that the development of such a market would be worthwhile, and he recently had some handbills printed which he asked his Manila *suki* to distribute among the latter's friends. This was the only case discovered in the study in which a marketplace seller employed advertising literature.

Suki is not an absolute relationship. Not all *suki* bonds are of the same intensity or value to the participants, and the concessions that sellers make to different *suki* may vary. Indeed, sellers are emphatic in pointing out that the specific contents of particular *suki* relations are among their most closely guarded trade secrets. The benefits which sellers offer to their buyer *suki* represent one of the important forms of inter-seller competition. If the terms of his several relationships became known to all his *suki*, each would demand the same terms as the most favored, thereby making inroads on the seller's income.

Just as *suki* relations vary in their economic concessions, they also vary in the intensity of their more purely social elements. In addition to variations which are understandable in terms of different stages of development in the relationship—from inception to maturity—even mature *suki* relations differ. These differences may be expressed in a continuum of sociability which varies between "self-interested" and "subjective" poles. At the self-interested end of the continuum are *suki* relations with agents who represent large commercial firms. Relations between marketplace sellers and agents are commonly thought of as *suki* relations, and the great importance of these relationships as sources of capital for the local economy has already been noted. Obviously, the more credit the marketplace seller can obtain from such commercial sources, the greater his capacity to service a large number of *suki* buyers. However, agents are only infrequently involved in the more sociable aspects of *suki* and rarely, for example, attend the social events centering on local sellers or exchange small gifts with them. Moreover, unlike other *suki*, agents charge interest on the credit they extend, although they often make rebates if the local retailer can pay in cash within four or five weeks.

The explanation for the paucity of social content in agent-seller *suki* bonds is a dual one. In the first place, agents do not operate independently as individuals. They are the employees of distant firms and must put their firm's interests above their own. To establish *suki* relations locally, so that sales outlets may be retained, is in the firm's interest. But it is also in the firm's interest to manipulate these to its own advantage. The firm is, after all, a narrowly economic institution, not an individual with a multiplicity of interests. Agents are therefore likely to keep their *suki* relations as asymmetrical as possible, consistent with maintaining them: they make heavy demands on *suki* while keeping their own commitments minimal. Second, even if the agent is a local person, his principal source of reinforcement is the firm which employs him, not the local community. As a result, he is less concerned with sociability—except as it is useful to him—and more concerned with his sales quota. He is, accordingly, much less susceptible to the usual local means of social control.

Some Filipino marketplace sellers consider their Chinese suppliers *suki*, and the Chinese wholesaler also falls near the self-interested pole of the continuum. In this case matters are complicated: the *suki* relationship must cross an ethnic boundary typically characterized by considerable hostility. Some Filipino informants debated whether Chinese could appropriately be considered *suki* at all, for they were held to be generally untrustworthy. Chinese wholesalers charge interest on all credit, collect payments daily, and generally behave more like the Filipino stereotype of the moneylender than as "proper" *suki*. But the Chinese can be depended upon to deliver goods on time, and thus meet one of the criteria for *suki*. For their part, the Chinese consistently use the term in referring to their seller-customers in the marketplace.

Near the opposite end of the *suki* continuum, the "subjective" pole, are special *suki*. Most, if not all, sellers have among their *suki* customers some whom they find so personally attractive and so useful that relations with them are strongly social in orientation. The social element, in fact, may depress the economic-interest aspect of the bond. In some cases, the seller may sustain a small net loss in dealing with them over the long term. These special *suki* may be powerful or prestigious persons, so that the monetary loss is countervailed by increased opportunities, competitive advantage, or an increase in personal prestige. Or they may be persons whom the seller is cultivating for use on some future occasion of great need. But for a few persons not related to him by kinship, each seller will sacrifice gain in preference to some more purely social quality.

Nevertheless, the *suki* continuum encompasses only a limited range of possibilities. No matter how great the measure of self-interest may be, they nevertheless retain a generous measure of subjective content. But few *suki* relations are so "subjective" that the interest element is entirely lacking.

THE SITUATIONAL DISTRIBUTION OF SUKI RELATIONS

The creation of a *suki* bond is an obvious exercise of choice, and the decision is made only after advantages and risks have been carefully weighed by both partners. But there are marked differences in the degree to which individual buyers and sellers wish to stress *suki* relationships in their commercial operations.

Thus any interpretation of such relationships is rendered more adequate by considering the conditions under which *suki* relations are likely to emerge.

The supply and sales interests of any individual participant in the marketplace economy are distinct. Buyers, whether they are wholesalers, retailers, or consumers, are uniformly interested in acquiring *suki* suppliers, for routine supply sources reduce risks. Any trader finds interest-free (or low-cost) credit, lower prices, courteous treatment, and stable flows of supplies useful.

However, *suki* customers are not universally valued among sellers—with the qualification that any seller is interested in customers who purchase regularly and in large quantities. All things being equal, the seller of perishable goods is most anxious to create a clientele of *suki*. Because the great majority of sellers in the marketplace deal in perishables, *suki* relations are common. In these cases having assured clients and superior information about projected demand levels are most useful attributes, for miscalculations can mean the loss of scarce capital through spoiled stock. Unless he is fortunate enough to operate from an especially well-located selling site with access to an unusual number of potential customers, the seller of perishables prefers not to stock large quantities of goods above the amounts which he anticipates his *suki* clients will purchase. The preference among produce-selling stallholders is to increase sales slowly by increasing the number of *suki*, rather than by concentrating on attracting the unaligned passer-by. By the same logic, the seller of perishables is likely to extend credit more readily—to make *suki* more rapidly, for example—because his stock must move. Because he can't withhold his stock from the market, toward the close of the day's trading he may even extend credit to non-*suki*, for this is less risky than trying to sell old produce the following day.

Second, open-market sellers are in general much less likely to emphasize *suki* than stallholders are. Because the open-market seller is not in the marketplace daily, he is at a considerable disadvantage in terms of a steady clientele. However, if the seller is a frequent visitor, or even a regular visitor, to the marketplace he will probably develop a few *suki* (the claim was "five to ten," as opposed to the "twenty to thirty" reported by stallholding produce sellers).[4] Open-market sellers also have less capital with which to support *suki* than stallholders. Furthermore, the style of *suki* interaction differs somewhat in the open market, for here one anticipates haggling between *suki* buyer and seller. Otherwise, the extension of credit and other features of *suki* also appear in the open market.

Third, sellers of goods or services which are frequent or habitual purchases are more inclined to favor *suki* bonds as a commercial strategy than are sellers who deal in infrequently purchased items. Sellers of items which are major household expenditures, such as stoves and kitchenware, usually have *suki* suppliers but not *suki* buyers, because individuals purchase these goods only a few times during their lives, and there is little point in attempting to establish a regular clientele under such conditions. Credit on these major purchases is extended with the understanding that the debt will be paid within a brief period of time. Furthermore, some goods are such insignificant purchases that there is little point in establishing credit relationships with purchasers. Periodicals and candy are examples.

Within the marketplace, the location of the seller's *puesto* is a fourth important variable influencing value of *suki* attachments. Some stalls in the interior are difficult to approach

---

[4] These figures are based on estimates which sellers were asked to make about the size of *suki* clienteles maintained by *other* sellers adjacent to them. This was an attempt to obtain information without prying too deeply and directly into sellers' trade secrets.

and have virtually no room for display. Such selling locations are heavy liabilities, in spite of the lower fees one pays for occupying them. All things being equal, sellers operating from such locations rely almost exclusively on *suki* customers. In consequence, the poorly-located seller, like the seller of perishables, is inclined to overextend his capital reserves in the attempt to obtain *suki*. In contrast, sellers with especially favorable locations (particularly corner stalls where walkways intersect) tend to minimize *suki* bonds with buyers. These sellers can save their capital for the few customers they may have who purchase in large quantities, or to invest it in enterprises where the turnover is more rapid and more profitable than are investments in loans to *suki*. Because their locations tend to lower risks, they may pay more attention to immediate gain.

Fifth, *suki* relations tend to be influenced by ethnicity. When ethnic boundaries are crossed there is less sociability, and *suki* becomes more difficult to establish. The origin of *suki* in the Philippines is not known. But it may be derived from Chinese practices, for similar kinds of relations exist in the Chinese community. In any event, Chinese certainly have enough familiarity with it to operate within the limits of *suki* expectations when dealing with Filipinos, if they wish to do so. Unfortunately, Filipinos mistrust Chinese and often accuse them of sharp practices of the most petty kind: for example, of removing a few pieces of candy from each bag, a few matches from each box, or a few ounces of cooking oil from each bottle sold. Native peoples, however, seem to value *suki* little, for they make disloyal buyers, and they do not place great stress on *suki* in their own dealings, prefering to rely on other connections.

Finally, *suki* relationships sometimes do not appear when they might be anticipated simply because they have been superceded by some relationship with greater subjective value. A kinship relation is one of these: two relatives linked in an interdependent trade relationship are not likely to think of, or to refer to, one another as *suki*. To do so would be to suggest that the economic dimension was prominent in the relationship.

Compadrazgo

In the marketplace economy all *suki* are important, but, logically enough, some *suki* are more important to the seller's enterprise than others. A particular supplier, for example, may be an absolutely critical source of credit, or a particular customer may represent an especially significant part of the seller's total market. In such cases relations with these special *suki* have commonly been further stabilized by conversion to a formal relationship: the *compadrazgo*, or ritual kinship. In the marketplace the formation of *compadrazgo* bonds has been so frequently preceded by the existence of a *suki* relationship that one must conclude that the former are the results of deliberate strategies intended to replace one interpersonal relationship with another, ideally more obligatory, form.

Compadrazgo is a common feature of social structure in societies which have been strongly influenced by Catholic Church doctrine, as the Philippines in general have been, and its use as a kind of "all purpose" social bond has been widely reported elsewhere. For example, Mintz and Wolf point out that: "The outstanding characteristic of the compadre [*compadrazgo*] mechanism is its adaptiveness to different situations. As the structure of the situation changes, so may we expect to see the compadre mechanism serve different purposes" (Mintz and Wolf 1950:347). Similarly, Foster notes that in the New World the *compadrazgo*: ". . . appears in very considerable measure to be the result of local elaboration to meet felt needs in the emergent social structure of Post-Conquest America" (Foster 1953:167). In the Philippines specifically, the utilization of *compadrazgo* in organizing various kinds of goal-oriented behavior is mentioned by Lynch (1959), Pal (1959), Fox (1956), and Hollnsteiner (1963), among others. It has been particularly widely discussed in terms of its functions in the political process and as a form of communication between status groups. Moreover, Foster (1961:1182) mentions the role of *compadrazgo* in securing advantages in a narrow economic context in Mexico, so the appearance of this particular kind of relationship as a risk-reducing social device in the Philippine marketplace is not surprising.

In Catholic doctrine, as is well known, it is customary upon some ritual occasions, such as marriage or the baptism of a child, to choose for the initiate one or more pair of sponsors, or godparents. This relationship is then symbolized linguistically in the use of "godchild-godparent" terms between child and sponsor, and "cofather" and "comother" terms between the sponsors and the parents of the initiate. The doctrinaire rationale for the ritual parenthood relation is that it is the godparents' obligation to ensure that children they sponsor are maintained in the faith and guided toward spiritual ideals. The emphasis in doctrine, then, is upon the intergenerational bond. In common Philippine practice, however (as often happens in other areas, as well), the actual behavioral emphasis is not upon intergenerational bonding, but upon the intragenerational connection, that is, the relationship between parents and godparents (cf. Fox and Lynch 1956).

Therefore, parents may often base the choice of their children's godparents on the capacity of the potential godparents to provide future benefits for the parents rather than the child. Thus, instead of persons from the parents' own socioeconomic level, the emphasis is typically upon a godparent with position, power, and wealth. In practice, there is something of a game element, for the object is to choose someone with enough prestige and influence to be able to provide benefits, but who is not so elevated in the social hierarchy that he will not accept the charge, or will not validate later claims against him if he does. Hollnsteiner (1963:73) observes that individuals who choose so highly in the rank order that their requests fall on deaf ears are likely to be objects of ridicule among their peers. The practice of exercising interested choice in selecting godparents is so frequent and expected that often the prospective godparents are fully aware of the impending claim, and in agreeing to sponsor the child they are more or less agreeing to grant the favor. For this reason requests to sponsor children are not usually made until the prospective godparents' willingness to serve has been indirectly determined. The procedures of choice may be reversed, and one may establish a bond with a child's parents by volunteering, in some subtle way, to sponsor the child. As one might imagine, candidates for elected offices are inclined to pursue this strategy as an aid in their quest for votes.

In some cases, the conflicting functions of *compadrazgo* relations are reconciled by the recruitment of two pairs of sponsors. One pair is chosen on the basis of the prestige their presence will lend the ceremony and for their ability to provide potential future benefits. But the other pair is chosen from among the parents' peers and may be expected actually to perform the godparent functions which doctrine demands.

This is hardly to suggest that all ritual kinship relations among Filipinos serve only material interests, but the relationship is established optionally, and it can, therefore, provide opportunities to build useful social connections. Informants were often candid in their assessment of the self-interested aspects of such relations. In response to queries, for example, it was pointed out that only rarely were relatives chosen to be godparents, for "that would be a waste." The implication was that kinship relations already provide avenues of approach to relatives, so that adding the ritual dimension to the relationship is unnecessary. Moreover, in the marketplace, in *compadrazgo* relations between retailers and their suppliers, the retailer (debtor) is far more likely to have initiated the relationship than the supplier (creditor) is. It is difficult, for cultural reasons, to approach a ritual kinsman to request repayment of loans. The marketplace seller may, therefore, gain valuable time to raise payments to creditors by the judicious use of the ritual kinship relation.

In spite of the important role which *compadrazgo* plays in ordering economic, political, and social relationships in Philippine life, it would be a gross oversimplification to suggest that *compadrazgo* relations are always honored by culturally proper action. In the course of a lifetime virtually every Catholic Filipino becomes a ritual coparent many times, particularly if he is in a position to grant favors. But few persons have the resources necessary to validate all such relationships, and careful choice must be exercised to select those persons who are valuable enough to make transactions with them worthwhile. Once *compadrazgo* relations are initiated, there are no formal means of terminating them, but they may be validated at low levels of performance or simply allowed quietly to fall into disuse. Moreover, they may be manipulated, just as *suki* bonds may be, so that one partner gains substantially more from them than the other.

Compadrazgo relations, however, involve an explicit declaration of intention to establish a formally ritualized association of

237

which, ideally, mutual obligation is an integral aspect. Accordingly, convention demands that the obligations ideally inherent in the relationship should be more deeply felt and more carefully honored than those of *suki*. Thus, though the norms of *compadrazgo* are often violated, violation usually involves more of a sense of shame and guilt than violations of *suki* norms do. The sanctions which tend to maintain the *compadrazgo* bond are, therefore, somewhat different from those which operate in the *suki* case. The latter is more a relationship of self-interest, and the purely subjective elements are less prominent. It is primarily mutual interest and advantage which maintain *suki* ties. Ritual coparents, however, have formalized their relationship institutionally in the Church and have explicitly undertaken common obligations to a child. Thus, aside from any common interests, the local interpretation of Church doctrine tends to bring to bear the weight of public opinion—a third party—to support the relationship. This element is not as prominent in the essentially dyadic *suki* bond.

In sum, *compadrazgo* relationships are more likely to be validated over time than the *suki* bonds are. Such relations have, therefore, become means of stabilizing highly valued economic relationships. Once one identifies any seller's most important suppliers and customers, it may be predicted that he has also identified at least some of that seller's ritual coparents. Neither *suki* nor *compadrazgo* relations are necessarily the most important social attachments which individuals form, but they both have great social and economic utility, and they both are enormously significant for the organization of the marketplace economy.

Thus, personal, noninterchangeable relationships are the dominant organizational feature of marketplace behavior. From the most prosperous wholesaler to the lowly marketplace porters, subjectively-valued social relationships are the principal mode through which buyers and sellers interact. But they are also the major elements in the process of competition, as we shall see.

Chapter Eight

Economic Personalism and Competition

INTERFIRM COMPETITION

As a result of the personalistic economic relations typical of the marketplace sector, the structure of the marketplace economy may be thought of as a number of specialized sellers, each of whom is connected to an enduring quasi-group of buyers. Although sellers are pleased to deal with random buyers, the greatest number of marketplace transactions occur with customers who are linked to sellers through long-standing personal relationships. The strategy of each seller, therefore, is to secure, through manipulation of social relationships and economic inducements, a monopolized portion of the local market.

Such commercial strategies obviously have important implications for the nature of economic competition. In the first place, the various types of social relations which have been described exert considerable influence on individual persons to pursue particular kinds of distributional roles and to trade particular kinds of goods. Second, they have a significant impact on the manner in which sellers compete with buyers and with each other.

Because personalized social relations are so important in obtaining capital, market outlets, and market information, one's social relations, rather than superior commercial ability or the lure of highest possible profits, often determine the economic specialty he will pursue. Because the ability to form obligatory social relations or to activate those already existing reduces risks in trading, traders are inclined to specialize in the kinds of roles and commodities which can be obtained through them. Primarily for this reason trade in particular classes of goods tends to be monopolized by particular kin groups or regional-ethnic groups.

Some of the most significant examples of the effect of personal relationships on economic specialization have already been mentioned in other contexts. For example, the native vegetable sellers in the Hangar Building established themselves as vegetable wholesalers through the use of crop loans made to their rural relatives and neighbors. And Chinese wholesalers used their ethnicity as a basis for cooperation which provided advantages over competitors. These two cases, however, are noteworthy only because of their scale and not because they are unique. At a less spectacular level, the small-scale poultry trade exemplifies the same process. Most fowl sold locally originate in Pangasinan, and correspondingly nearly all poultry sellers in the Baguio marketplace also originated in Pangasinan. Similarly, fish sold in Baguio are from two principal sources, Damortis in La Union Province and Dagupan City in Pangasinan. Likewise, the carriers who are so important to the fish trade have also come from these two municipalities. In the case of *chucheria*, most of the local supply originates in Batangas Province, and all the local *chucheria* sellers are Batangueños. In fact, all but one of them originated in the same *municipio*, and more than half came from the same *barrio* (village).

Nor is the trade in manufactured products exempt from the influences of personalism. For example, most of the ready-to-wear clothing sold in the Baguio marketplace is manufactured in Batangas Province. By coincidence, in the days during which Baguio City was governed by appointed officials, one of the town's councilmen was a Batangueño. It is alleged that he was active in assisting some of his relatives to obtain market stalls and in arranging contacts between them and the representatives of the small factories which produced the clothing. This combination of factors provided the Batangueño element with competitive advantages, and they remain by far the largest ethnic or regional group represented among clothing sellers. In turn, most of the rural peddlers who deal in clothing are also relatives of these persons.

Since Batangueño clothing sellers are able to obtain better credit terms and lower prices, it is difficult for other sellers to compete with them. As a result, non-Batangueño clothing dealers have begun to shift their attention from distribution to manufacturing. Some have converted their market stalls to tiny tailor shops. A few have taken a new entrepreneurial step: they have become *costareras*, minor manufacturers who operate by organizing five to ten seamstresses in a cottage-industrial type assembly line similar to the "putting out" system popular in Europe in the early stages of the Industrial Revolution (cf. Pirenne 1925). These latter have put particular emphasis on producing shirts and work trousers, but their products have few qualities superior to the clothing available through Batangueño outlets, except for, perhaps, better stitching. Prices are similar.

Additional examples of the influence of personal relationships on marketplace specialization are easily offered. Most of the footwear sellers are relatives from a single community in Nueva Ecija—the same community from which the sales representative of the principal local supplier of footwear originated. American "imports" (i.e., Post Exchange goods) are exclusively sold by Pampangans, for the main source of supply is Clark Air Force Base which is near Los Angeles, Pampanga Province. Tobacco is supplied by Iloco-speaking carriers from La Union Province, where it is grown by Iloco-speaking farmers. Similarly the primary local source of Ifugao woodcarvings is a wholesaler who has an Ifugao wife. One could go on, but the point seems established: in this sector of the economy utilization of personal relationships to establish a commodity specialty in the market is the rule not the exception.

To turn to the second aspect of competition, because buyers tend to be bound to particular sellers, competition between sellers is not as keen as one would anticipate and tends to take forms other than price competition. Offers of lower prices do not easily attract *suki* buyers to other sellers unless differences are marked. Sources of credit are highly valued, and buyers are not likely to jeopardize them frivolously. Moreover, in the case of many commodities, the absence of standard measures of quantity and quality render it difficult for the average buyer accurately to determine real price differences unless they are of considerable magnitude. This explains why, when his prices are questioned by *suki*, the seller's first line of defense is to justify his prices on the grounds of higher quality. That is, he plays on the buyer's self-doubts and lack of information. Moreover, the strong social element in the relationship means that when sellers are faced with irrefutable evidence that their prices are higher than some competitor's, they may appeal to the long-standing nature of the relationship, to more generous transactions made in the past, and to the bonds of sentiment which buyer and seller share.

Thus, once a seller has established a regular clientele, these customers tend to exhibit a high degree of loyalty to the seller over considerable periods of time. This is so, however, not only because of interest and obligation, but also because of marketplace norms external to the immediate buyer-seller relationship. In many cases adjacent sellers in the marketplace have long-standing associations of cooperation and restrained competition. The marketplace, like other enduring social associations, has become constrained by a system of norms which, though not explicitly or precisely agreed upon, influence behavior. Directly relevant here is the tacit proscription against any overt attempt to alienate another seller's *suki*. Persons who have adjacent selling locations in the marketplace sell much the same kinds of merchandise, and therefore know one another's operations well. Moreover, because the stalls are open, they know most of their neighbors' *suki*. If a buyer initiates a transaction with a seller other than his *suki*, he is fair game: his *suki* seller is not entitled to complain if the second seller deals with the buyer. But ideally no neighboring seller takes the initiative. Those who violate this norm are termed *baratillos* (rascals), with the implication that they are unethical and given to sharp practices.

The minimal expression of overt competition between sellers encourages considerable cooperation. Neighboring sellers often borrow stock from each other, watch one another's stalls against theft, and in the event a customer appears at a nearby stall during a neighboring seller's absence, the good neighbor may actually make sales for his colleague. One's neighbors should also be willing to help him change bills of large denomination and generally be approachable for small favors. Above all, the good neighbor does not take advantage of some particularly fortunate wholesale price to lower his prices below those of his colleagues. Sanctions which may be applied for violation of these norms include the termination of all mutual services which neighbors usually provide one another, and various degrees of public scorn and verbal abuse. Furthermore, if an individual makes repeated attempts to alienate other sellers' *suki* in spite of warnings, his neighbors eventually will attempt "to convince him that he is wrong," a popular local euphemism for physical violence. Ignoring this "rule" was the common explanation offered for the unpopularity of the Batangueño contingent. In fact, the Batangueños were obliged to start a collective contingency fund to cover legal fees because they were so frequently involved in disputes.

All things being equal, at any given moment in the marketplace there is little price difference among sellers. Several classes of goods exhibit this uniformity because everyone uses the same few sources and pays approximately the same wholesale price. The only significant exception is the occasional seller who can afford to buy in large enough quantities to receive price reductions on volume purchases. Rice, meat, several kinds of fish, most kinds of clothing, footwear, and packaged groceries are all commodities with limited supply sources. This also implies that suppliers of these commodities are in an excellent position to influence the price structure.

But even when sellers are able to obtain stocks at advantageous wholesale prices, the structure and norms of the marketplace economy in general tend to encourage them not to reduce retail prices. The usual reason for competitive price cutting is to attract more customers and to increase thereby the rate of capital turnover, that is, to decrease the profit per transaction with the intent of increasing the number of transactions. However, where buyers tend to be clients and friends of specific sellers and to give priority to maintenance of credit sources over small price savings, it is felt that the potential profits from an increase in customers resulting from underselling are less than one is likely to make by maintaining the price. This is especially so because failure to maintain price uniformity arouses one's neighbors. Furthermore, the alternative—seeking to align new customers—would involve extensions of credit, and there are limits to the seller's willingness to do so. This is not to deny that prices fluctuate in the marketplace, for they clearly do. But the greater variations in price structure occur in locally-produced agricultural commodities for which there are a large number of suppliers. Competition in trading these commodities more closely approaches the "free market" model.

Moreover, there exist other exceptions to the generalizations just stated. First, any seller who is badly in need of cash (for example, to meet the demands made on him by his own suppliers) may slash prices in order to increase cash sales. A seller's suppliers are crucial to his enterprise, and it is absolutely necessary for him to make at least token payments on his accounts when they fall due. Sellers will even borrow from moneylenders in order to make payments to suppliers if there is no other alternative. Second, sellers who are newly establishing marketplace operations, and who are anxious to acquire a steady clientele, are also apt to cut prices. Unless they have unusually fine locations, sellers need *suki* to remain in business and are likely to obtain them only through offering more inducements than their colleagues offer. The anxiety of new sellers to get customers, and their inclination to extend credit somewhat recklessly to do so, encourages them to lend money to some of the very persons whom established sellers consider poor risks. Neophyte sellers, therefore, often become involved in an excessive number of bad debts, and the failure rate of new stallholders is high. Another advantage of sellers who have relatives who are also traders is that they can use their kinsmen as sources of information and instruction.

As long as price cutting is clearly done under conditions of personal duress, the offending seller's colleagues are usually patient. But if he continues these activities, it is likely that a group of his fellows will visit him to persuade him to cooperate. If the miscreant continues to be unconcerned, and especially if he manages to entice some of his colleagues' customers, stronger sanctions, such as those mentioned above, will be applied.

Alienating *suki* solely through offers of modest price advantages, therefore, is not readily accomplished. In an interesting example of a potential new seller in the marketplace (and of some impressive entrepreneurial activity), one vendor attempted to develop a market for woven bamboo baskets (of a type regularly used locally as containers for shipping fruit and vegetables) which were produced by the seller, his siblings, and their families. His offer was 60 centavos per basket, well under the then-current market price of 75. Although he tried for several weeks to attract *suki* customers, he obtained little interest and soon gave up his efforts. All of the sellers who regularly used such baskets in volume were already *suki* of two other suppliers, and most of them were not willing to transfer their loyalties. The lower price interested them, but they were not sure that the new supplier could supply adequate quantities of baskets, or that he could continue to supply the kind of credit terms already offered by their *suki*. The price advantage was not adequate inducement to convince vegetable sellers to break away from old and tried suppliers and friends.

The overall uniformity of sellers' prices, however, does not imply that competition is lacking in the marketplace. Similarity

of retail prices is somewhat misleading, for it obscures different margins of profit. Moreover, some seller's enterprises visibly
accumulate capital more rapidly than others, a fact which provides an objective indication of competition. However, competition is especially likely to be implicit in such elements as a
superior ability to provide customers with regular supplies of
a large variety of good-quality commodities, skill in locating
new markets (such as in the mines and lumber camps, or shipments to *suki* in the lowlands), or in providing more and better
peripheral services: shopping, packaging, and shipping. Above
all, however, competition is expressed in clever use of credit,
that is, greater amounts for longer periods of time, with losses
through bad debts kept at a minimum.

Suki relationships involve the seller in delicate and complex
situations in which he must weigh the buyer's reliability and his
commercial and social value against the amount of credit
necessary to preserve the buyer's loyalty. At the same time,
the seller attempts to minimize his credit commitments in order
to keep an optimum quantity of his operating capital in liquid
form. Therefore, each seller must not only know local marketing conditions well but also have a considerable amount of
information about his suppliers and customers. By no means
are all sellers successful in manipulating relationships to produce gain consistently. Bad debts are a major concern of marketplace sellers, a common topic of conversation among them,
and an important cause of business failure.

The competitive ideal is to have as many *suki* (or other kinds
of aligned customers) as one can successfully manage, given
his resources. The number of aligned customers a seller has,
however, is subject to the principle of rising marginal costs,
for the number of persons one may know well enough to deal
with them effectively has a low upper limit, though this number varies for each seller. There is, therefore, an equilibrium

point in *suki* relations, which is the largest number of *suki* relations which each vendor may have without extending credit to persons not known to be reliable, and with whom bonds of trust do not exist. Of the sellers sampled 60 percent suggested the "twenty to thirty" category as an average, and no seller indicated a clientele larger than forty-five attached buyers. In their desire to realize profits, individual sellers press hard against this optimal number, and it is a rare seller who does not have uncollectable debts resulting from bad judgment in selecting *suki*.

Once he has become established, a fear of bad debts encourages the seller to expand his monopolized portion of the market rather slowly while he is establishing relations of trust with, and obtaining information about, yet other potential *suki* (unless he chooses to become a wholesaler, whose strategy is different). Because the seller's secured market tends to increase slowly, there is considerable temptation to find ways of realizing more income from the seller's already-established clientele. He may provide additional services for his *suki*, such as shopping for them in other areas of the market, in exchange for a "commission" from the other sellers from whom he buys for his own *suki*. Or he may extend the range of the customer's demands which he attempts to satisfy, which implies increasing the range of goods offered. Pursuit of this last strategy is one of the paramount inducements tempting sellers to ignore the Zoning Ordinance. Ambitious sellers can transcend the limitations on growth occasioned by the necessity to have personal knowledge of one's customers, but doing so requires a different kind of commercial strategy. Rather than attempting to expand the size of one's clientele to the point of incurring high credit risks, the more clever sellers have accepted limitations on the size of the personally-controlled retail market and have become wholesalers. Realizing the limitations on his own information, the ambitious seller may choose to concentrate on selling to other sellers, thereby allowing the latter to bear most of the risks of dealing with consumers. In short, he arranges to use other sellers' *suki* by dividing profits with those sellers.

Any moderately successful seller can pursue this strategy simply by providing commodities to other sellers on credit, usually on an equal-share, profit-sharing basis. When this study first began, I was surprised to find sellers lending stock to one another to the degree that they were, for it seemed "irrational" to lend stock to a seller who was ostensibly a competitor. But the lending of stocks usually involves an agreement to share equally any profit made on their sale, and because the seller who borrows the stock is dealing with his own monopolized clients, the two sellers are actually appealing to different markets.

Difficulties in expanding the number of one's aligned customers, together with the subjective value placed on the bonds involved, also help to explain another marketplace phenomenon: the seemingly infinite replication of similar economic units. The question is: "How does it happen that large-scale firms don't absorb the many petty sellers who are providing the same services?"

This issue has received some attention and excellent analysis by Barbara Ward (1960). Ward sought to explain the large number of "middlemen" in Chinese markets in Sarawak and the New Territories, Hong Kong, by focusing on two factors: the need for credit and the limited quantities of available capital. She found that relations between buyer and seller typically involve a credit relationship which produces debts that are never entirely obliterated. However, she argues that because the resources of each trader-creditor are limited, each can carry only a small number of buyer-debtors. Thus, because of the small quantities of operating capital controlled by each seller, there is demand for a large number of traders, each doing more or less the same thing.

The similarities between the situation reported by Ward and the one being described here are apparent. There is, however, a critical difference, for limits on available capital are much less stringent in the Baguio case than in the cases cited by Ward. There appears to be a more systematic articulation between the large-scale sector of the economy and the local marketplace in the Baguio example. Thus, many of the sellers in the Baguio marketplace operate on capital obtained from much larger firms. These firms are capable of increasing the supply of capital available to the local seller if there is concrete demand for it. Theoretically, therefore, it should be possible for larger firms to absorb the functions of smaller ones, thereby eliminating large numbers of intermediaries from the marketplace, and creating economic units which are fewer in number but much grander in scale.

However, because large firms which attempt to work at the local level immediately encounter rising marginal costs in the form of uncollectable bad debts, it is preferable to work through local sellers. In other words, because credit is carried by personalized associations between traders, for any large-scale firm to eliminate the small marketplace intermediary is difficult. No commercial firm is willing to assume the heavy risks involved when subjectively-valued social relationships are absent. Social relationships, therefore, are of considerable importance in accounting for the relatively large number of traders in the marketplace sector. Thus, traders offer nearly identical goods and services, but they offer them to different sets of persons.[1]

---

[1] Additional reasons for the large number of functionally repetitive marketplace intermediaries were furnished in Chapter V. The wide dispersal of sources of supply and demand and the difficulty of learning

An example may clarify several of the points concerning the nature of competition. At the time these data were collected a certain Chinese family in town had segregated itself from the Chinese community and appeared, in terms of the life styles of its members, to be on the way to assimilation into Filipino society. The family name had been Filipinized (here they will be referred to as the Reyes family), and two (of five) sons and a daughter had become Philippine citizens. Since the man who had founded the family enterprise was too old to be active in business, the oldest son had become "chairman of the board," and much of the family's property was held in his name (largely because he held Philippine citizenship and could own property). In accord with his role as a successful Filipino businessman, the eldest son was a regular at the local chapter of Knights of Columbus, and was a member of all the more important local service associations. He was, in short, a model progressive young Filipino and was widely accepted as such in spite of the fact that the older generation of his family was strongly Sinitic in cultural orientation.

Although the Reyes family's wealth was already substantial, it's members had one additional commercial goal: they wanted to control the flow of wholesale grocery items into Baguio City, and ultimately throughout Mountain Province. This was not a frivolous scheme, but a plan which was explicitly formulated and which was in the process of implementation. That such goals were at all realistic has to do with the limited number of supply sources. However, it is not the goals which are important here, but the strategy by which the Reyes family sought to attain them, for their procedure was precisely to take advantage of the social constraints on free association in the marketplace.

---

the details of market conditions in more than a few classes of goods are other factors.

The initial step in the plan was an effort to become the main source of supply for 80 percent of the marketplace *sari-sari* sellers. They hoped to accomplish this by offering commodities wholesale on ninety-day credit terms, but without reducing prices. Because the Chinese wholesalers offered credit for thirty-day periods, the Reyes' willingness to offer better terms was a decided advantage. Furthermore, this credit was dispensed primarily through a marketplace operation managed by one of the Reyes' daughters, and secondarily through other lesser-order wholesalers throughout the marketplace. The use of marketplace personnel was calculated to take maximum advantage of the binding features of personal social relationships: to spread the risks involved in debt collection and to deal with petty traders in terms familiar to them.

The operating assumption was that once the family "controlled" a majority of grocery sales outlets, the producers and packagers of these items would have only two choices: they could either allow the enterprising Reyes group to become brokers for them, or they, themselves, could enter into the credit business in competition with the Reyes family. The Reyes family was gambling that the processors would choose the first alternative, thus leaving the Reyes firm in a position to manipulate prices to its own advantage. However, the Chinese wholesalers guessed what the Reyes group was attempting and not only refused to buy from them, but also threatened to undersell them, thereby producing a stalemate.

What seems clear in this example is that the strategy pursued emphasized the necessity to know one's debtors on a personal basis. It was this feature of local economic organization which offered opportunities for monopsonistic control. Moreover, only this factor prevented the heavily-capitalized processing firms from dealing directly with the *sari-sari* retailers in the marketplace, thereby eliminating the need for storage-credit functions supplied by the opportunistic Reyes family and by Chinese wholesalers. We see emerging here a tendency which is probably significant in all market systems, but which because of particular local sociocultural features may be more prominent in the Philippine marketplace than typically elsewhere: the attempt to compete by controlling exchange networks in the market, rather than by providing goods and services more efficiently and cheaply.

INTERETHNIC COMPETITION

Specialization and competition in the local internal marketing system, however, cannot be dealt with adequately solely at the level of competing individuals and firms. One must also take into account competition between the major ethnic units into which the personnel of the marketplace economy are divided. The members of each of the several ethnic categories share certain advantages, tend to occupy certain distinctive kinds of economic niches, and to a considerable degree, also tend to compete with one another as groups.

Participants in the marketplace economy are ethnically diverse. However, although many different ethnic units are present, the principal lines of division and competition are those between Filipinos of lowland Christian origin, indigenous hill peoples, and Chinese. Although the members of these categories deal commercially with each other, there is considerable antagonism among them, and each has an area of concentrated economic activity from which its members attempt to exclude others.

Each broad ethnic category is internally differentiated into lower-order ethnic units, and only the Chinese constitute a group with formal organization and representative leadership.

However, if the issues are significant enough, the official organizations of government may be counted upon to support lowland Filipino interests. Only the indigenous mountain populations in the marketplace, then, lack any form of corporate unity.

In theory, the Chinese category is the only absolute one, for it is extremely difficult to cross the ethnic boundary and become Chinese thorough any means other than birth. Otherwise, individual members of these units can change affiliation by identifying with, and accepting the cultural norms of, an alter category. Interestingly enough, such identity changes always seem to involve taking up one of the economic specialities of the group with which affiliation has occurred. However, in practice, transfers of ethnic identification have been almost entirely in the direction of affiliation with the lowland Filipino category. The priority of the lowland Filipino ethnic model is understandable in pragmatic terms: lowland Filipinos have more prestige than native populations and a wider range of political and economic rights than the Chinese. When individuals have transferred ethnic identification, the most common means of doing so has been through intermarriage. Yet as Barth (1969:9–10) has indicated, one of the interesting things about interethnic relationships is that the boundaries of division remain in spite of the transfer of persons across them.

In Baguio City the lowland Filipinos constitute the dominant political majority. They not only greatly outnumber indigenous mountaineers and Chinese, but many members of the latter two categories cannot vote in city elections. Chinese, by virtue of their economic resources, are able to exert considerable influence on political decisions through judicious contributions and gifts to political parties and politicians. But anti-Chinese sentiment is so powerful that this influence must be cautious and clandestine. It is politically ruinous for any politician to fall under suspicion of representing Chinese interests, and exactly that occurred in Baguio City in the celebrated case of the ex-vice mayor who had helped Chinese investors lease lands adjacent to the marketplace. Native mountain peoples are citizens and can vote, but so few are town residents that their interests are not well represented. As a consequence of these conditions, local policy and policy implementation are strongly biased in favor of lowland Filipino interests.

This concentration of political power is widely used to structure local interethnic economic relationships. Political power has been employed, for example, to exclude Chinese from the marketplace, to prevent indigenous peoples from obtaining adequate selling facilities in the marketplace, and to afford lowland Filipinos a competitive advantage in trading through the use of the NAMARCO program, which was subsidized by tax revenues. For Chinese, it is illegal to sell in the public marketplace, and even to conduct large-scale retail operations at all. Furthermore, Chinese are subjected to additional penalties: special taxes and fees are legislated against them, and petty extortions often must be paid to officials. Unlike the Chinese, the native peoples are admitted to the marketplace, but with only a handful of exceptions, they occupy the inaccessible Hangar Building, leaving the more choice locations almost entirely in lowlanders' hands. It also happened that no local native seller was a NAMARCO distributor, another considerable advantage for lowlander populations.

Moreover, such relationships as *suki* and *compadrazgo* are vastly more common among lowlanders than among other categories, binding together lowlander Filipino buyers and sellers with loyalties not easily alienable by competition from members of other ethnic categories. From this perspective, both of these relationships associate roles and interests usually thought of as being inherently in opposition—buyer and seller—and orient them in a common direction favorable to the lowlander population: the maintenance of economic specialties for lowland peoples.

Although the other ethnic categories lack the political power associated with lowland Filipinos, they, too, have attributes which have enabled them to gain and protect niches in the marketplace economy. In addition to the more effective organization of Chinese family-firm units, the principal advantages that Chinese share are access to relatively large quantities of low-priced capital and efficient transport and communications. Chinese have been able to employ their capital for volume purchasing, thereby realizing savings, and to extend credit on a scale which no local Filipino firm has been able to match. Through these advantages the Chinese have been able to secure their roles as wholesale suppliers of groceries for the marketplace. Chinese middlemen have been able to employ capital to capture, again through generous extensions of credit, outlets for mid-latitude vegetables in lowland markets—thereby both creating and controlling the external trade in vegetables. Access to truck transport is an advantage in both these endeavors, for Filipinos have available to them only the transport resources furnished by public conveyors. These are of limited utility, for they were intended for passenger use, not freight. It is also alleged that on occasion Chinese merchants close ranks to drive Filipino competitors from the market, principally by dumping commodities at low prices. Suffering as they do from a lack of political power, Chinese have been obliged to exploit a number of marginal opportunities, or to create new ones. They have pursued both strategies impressively well.

The general economic position occupied by the native populations is, by any objective measure, inferior to those held by the members of the other two categories. Indigenous peoples have neither the power and wage-earning potential enjoyed by lowland Filipinos, nor the access to capital and transport used so effectively by Chinese. For the most part, natives are small-scale agricultural producers, or the more poorly paid laborers. Yet those who have become produce traders have some resources which they use to advantage. Most of the nearby agricultural land is owned by native peoples, and control of that basic resource has allowed natives to become the primary producers and first-stage wholesalers in the important mid-latitude vegetable trade. The production of these vegetables commonly involves a mutualistic, capital-sharing "crop loan" relationship between farmers and the native sellers who have intruded upon the market. Because the social relationship which carries production credit is essentially kinship, it is difficult for persons who are not native to interpose themselves in the first stages of the vegetable trade network. The net effect, therefore, is to allow indigenous peoples to defend their specialized roles as producers-wholesalers of the varieties of local produce most in demand.

Thus the pride expressed by Chinese in their culture and their willingness to extend credit to retailers; the *suki, compadrazgo*, and political patronage relationships common to lowland Filipinos; and the crop loans extended by native sellers —all such features of the marketplace economy are reinforced through competition. They are more thoroughly understood when it becomes clear that members of different ethnic categories compete with one another and make occasional sallies on one another's positions. In fact, interethnic economic competition has much to do with intra-category cooperation, as ranks are closed against outsiders. The degree to which this situation is unique in the Philippines, however, can only be assessed as comparative data become available. But strong elements of subjective sociability exist among the members of the ethnic groups that staff the marketplace. Furthermore, these elements are most completely understandable in a framework that draws attention to both cooperation and competition.

Chapter Nine

Reciprocity in the Marketplace

THE PROBLEM OF SOCIABILITY

Substantive economic theory holds that the economic relationships in primitive economies and market economies are different not in degree, but in kind (cf. Dalton
1961:20). Briefly put, economic relationships in the primitive
economy are presumed "embedded" in the sociocultural ma-
trix and therefore constrained by public morality. They are
"sociable." Relationships which characterize the market are
impersonal, atomistic, and conflict-producing. They exist solely
because exchange partners seek gain. But the Baguio marketplace example indicates that in a market of the type commonly held to be purely competitive, personal obligation and
sociocultural constraints are common features of economic
relationships. At issue here, therefore, is the degree to which
primitive economic relationships and market relationships dif-

fer in prestational content—whether this difference is, indeed, one of "kind."

The subjective intensity of social relationships—such things as sentiment, sociability, and prestation—are notoriously difficult to measure objectively, for it is only possible to know them through extrapolations from expressed behavior. However, Marshall Sahlins has recently offered a formal model of reciprocities which he holds also to be a measure of the sociability content of exchange relations (Sahlins 1965:144). Sahlins focuses on exchange in primitive societies, but because he includes such elements as bargaining for gain his model is general enough for the analysis of exchange relations in more commercialized settings. He measures the approximation of balance (or "equivalence") of returns in transactions, the immediacy of returns, and "like material and mechanical dimensions of the exchange" (Sahlins 1965:145). This model assumes that the structural distance between exchanging units determines the form and content ("social distance") of the relationships between them. Thus, one form of exchange occurs between members of the same family; another when partners are not members of the same family, but are members of the same tribe; and still another when partners are members of different families and different tribes. However, although the model is basically formal-structural, its social structural dimensions are isomorphic with such subjective factors as the degree of morality, impersonality, self-interest, and compassion which are also expressed in exchange.

The "sociable," or subjectively valued, end of Sahlins' continuum of reciprocities is the ideal type which he calls "generalized reciprocity," in which there is no element of self-interest and in which the debtor's obligation to return a countergift is so vague and temporally distant that it may never be fulfilled. In its most ideal form, generalized reciprocity consists of a unilateral flow of benefits which is not terminated by failure to provide countergifts, and is not, therefore, reciprocity in the usual—mutualistic—sense. Empirically, Sahlins suggests, most examples of exchange in primitive societies would cluster around a midpoint on the continuum, a point which Sahlins terms "balanced reciprocity." Balanced reciprocity involves returns of commensurate value (an "equivalence") and a time interval between gift and countergift which is more or less fixed. In this case, partners to the exchange "confront each other as distinct economic and social interests," and "the material side of the transaction is at least as critical as the social" (Sahlins 1965:148). At this point there is an attempt at more or less precise reckoning of gifts and countergifts, and "for the main run of balanced exchanges, *social relations hinge on the material flow*" (1965:148, emphasis supplied) rather than the reverse.

At the unsociable, self-interested pole, Sahlins places "negative reciprocity," the attempt to get something for nothing: "transactions opened and conducted toward net utilitarian advantage" (1965:148). Here participants confront each other as separate and *opposed* interests, and each seeks to maximize his own gain at the other's expense. According to Sahlins, behavior such as haggling in a marketplace is an overt expression of an exchange relationship which falls near the negative pole, although it is, of course, not so unsociably negative as that most rational economic act, theft. A Plains Indian horse raid (Sahlins 1965:149) is an example.[1]

[1] This raises another point, for rational, or "negative," treatment of exchange partners is not limited to market contexts. "Strangers" are apparently legitimate objects of exploitation in most societies. But the problem goes beyond that. To return to a "typical tribal society," that of the Trobriand Islanders, Powell (1960) has pointed out that *pokala* and *urigubu* (other forms of social exchanges) were both employed pragmatically by ambitious persons seeking to improve their political and economic positions.

Sahlins' provocative and useful model is a creditable effort to bring objective measurement to subjective social relations. But it is difficult, nevertheless, to fit empirical cases to it precisely, and several problems bear on the immediate issue.

First, the negative extreme has an empirical referent (e.g., theft or piracy), but that the sociable extreme (the disinterested pure gift) exists is doubtful. Some scholars argue that if it did, the psychological costs incurred by the recipient would eventually produce hostility and not sociability (cf. Gouldner 1960, Hynam 1966). Second, it is difficult accurately to measure "equivalence" at the subjective level. Even when precisely the same quantities of the same things are being exchanged, the participants may perceive their value differently, depending upon such things as the commonality of values and the individual's relative position in terms of access to resources. Gouldner (1960:171-172), for example, notes that relative need is an important variable which colors the way any individual perceives and evaluates a transaction. This is an especially significant consideration in the Philippine case, for giving something to a needy exchange partner at the time of need may establish an obligation whose intensity is out of proportion to the quantity of benefits exchanged (cf. Kaut 1961).

However, there is yet a more significant problem: the actual kinds of transactions which collectively comprise any particular exchange domain (these are often named) may individually express different degrees of sociability. This makes careful comparison of data more difficult. For example, in the classic case of the Trobriand Island *kula* transactions (Malinowski 1922), this category actually consisted of a number of different kinds of exchanges. Moreover, there was also a considerable range of motives and styles in the way in which individuals expressed any given form. In short, in *kula* one exchanged in terms of different "material and mechanical dimensions" with different partners in different places. The nature of *kula* exchanges was conditioned by such things as one's relative social position, the length of time he had been participating in the transaction, and the valuables controlled (cf. Uberoi 1962, Firth 1957). As it happens, most scholars have stressed the "balanced reciprocity" aspects of *kula*, and have pointed to the "sociable lapse of time" which occurs between gift and countergift, citing Malinowski's own remark that, "The two gifts of the kula . . . are distinct in time . . . any valuable received on such an occasion cannot be exchanged at the same time" (Malinowski 1922:353). But a few lines later Malinowski clarifies his remark, noting that, "there must be an interval between the two gifts, *of a few minutes at least*" (1922:353, emphasis supplied).

It therefore seems that even in primitive society the time interval alleged to be the harbinger of sociability is not necessarily a long one. In fact, a protracted interval between gift and countergift appears to be characteristic of only the *uvalaku* type of *kula*, and these were special affairs of state, not the main run of *kula* exchanges at all. Therefore, it is difficult to substantiate that *kula* exchanges fall at the midpoint (balanced reciprocity) of the reciprocity continuum. Rather, they seem to overlay a wide range on the continuum. If other categories of Trobriand Island exchanges were added to our considerations (e.g., *wasi, vava, urigubu*, the several kinds of *pokala*, and *gimwali*), their distribution along the continuum would be as thoroughly continuous as one is likely to find in empirical cases.

The market relationships which have been described here are clearly not "atomistic" (Dalton 1961:2–3) or "fundamentally antagonistic" (Polanyi 1957:255) in any critical sense of those terms. Rather, the organization of the marketplace economy consists principally of ego-centered exchange networks in which the social content of relationships is fundamental. Each such network consists of a seller and his associated suppliers and buyers, most of whom are bound to the seller by relationships which are enduring, sociable, and largely obligatory in nature. Above all, they foster the development of trust. These units tend to be bounded by, and maintained by, the higher "costs" of transactions beyond the limits of the network: the antagonism which follows from the termination of personalistic relationships, the increasing hostility one encounters as he deals more and more with strangers, higher risks, and higher prices. From this perspective, the high interest rates charged by moneylenders are understandable, for these relationships are antithetical to the prestational conventions of the marketplace exchange network, and lack the mutual confidence which characterizes relationships in the latter. In brief, it is largely the lack of trust which justifies the usurious rates of interest.

The mutual obligations and advantages in buyer-seller relationships within these marketplace network units make it apparent that buyer-seller relations are reciprocal in the general sense of that term. They are mutualistic to a high degree. However, in terms of their prestational content the market relationships described here cover the entire range of Sahlins' continuum—including approximations of the ideal polar types. More importantly, their distribution thoroughly overlaps those of economic relationships presumed typical of primitive economies, including the tribal example singled out by Polanyi (1957:252–253), Dalton (1961:9, 1969:72), and Fusfeld (1957:345) for its subjective, disinterested content: the Trobriand Island *kula* trade.

In order to render the data as precisely comparable as possible, it is useful to apply Sahlins' measures to the marketplace relationships which have been described here. First, there is the sticky problem of equivalence, or balance, in marketplace exchange relationships. Ideally all market relationships involve the seller's attempt to realize gain. But "gain" is reckoned in price increments over costs. The buyer does not necessarily feel that he did not receive a fair measure for the price. In fact, although Polanyi treated bargaining behavior as inherently antagonistic, bargaining can also be viewed as the regulation or dampening of conflict which may result from incomplete information about market conditions. Khuri (1968) has recently argued that spirited bargaining is especially likely in those market areas, and in regard to those products, in which information concerning quantity, quality, and current price structure is most lacking. The buyer frequently bargains in order to obtain information, not necessarily to drive down the price. Moreover, the buyer's conventionalized expectation (one of the "rules of social organization" of the marketplace) is that the seller will make a profit from the transaction. There is no resentment of this fact, for it is accepted as the seller's just due. The buyer is, of course, concerned that his seller treat him fairly. In the Philippines a man who allowed a seller to take great advantage of him would expose himself to ridicule. But the seller also knows that if he "shames" a buyer, there is little likelihood the buyer will return.

Bargaining may involve antagonism. Sellers may misrepresent the quality of their wares or seek to take great advantage of the buyer's lack of information, and buyers may insistently seek unrealistically low prices. But this rarely occurs in the examples discussed, as long as the seller is a professional and the buyer is a regular customer or is being solicited as a potential regular customer. Much local bargaining behavior, therefore, is a mechanism for ameliorating antagonism by assuring that the interests of both parties are represented in the price. Thus, the price approaches a condition of balanced exchange. Furthermore, bargaining may not occur at all between fixed trading partners, such as *suki*, for the buyer often trusts his *suki* to keep the profit margin to a minimum. Finally, additional indications of the sociable dimension of marketplace exchange relations are that sellers tend to offer favorable terms to customers who have sustained heavy losses on previous transactions and that nearly every seller has some customers from whom he does not attempt to realize gain. The "special" *suki*, who are valued for nonmaterial reasons, are also cases in point. Relations of these latter varieties move across the balance point on the continuum toward the sociable end of the scale. In sum, in terms of equivalence, market relationships fall from pole to pole all along the continuum of reciprocities.

The second dimension is "material likeness and mechanical dimensions of exchange"; that is, whether similar things are exchanged in similar ways. The economy described here is monetized, so that with a few exceptions exchanges involve the transfer of money for things unlike money, namely goods and services. However, the same circumstances are not unusual in primitive societies (e.g., Bohannan 1955, Pospisil 1963), so this cannot be held to be unique to market economies. Thus, "material likeness and mechanical dimensions" seem to be of little diagnostic significance in classifying economies. Moreover, although all societies appear to have some things which cannot properly be bought for money, that money is used in an exchange does not preclude sentiment and moral obligation. The use of money is not, in itself, an index of negative reciprocity. And the exchange of goods for money is only one dimension of the multiplex relationships between a seller and the buyers associated with him. Buyer and seller may exchange a whole series of "things" which are of mutual interest and benefit: small gifts, political support, attendance at social events, and personal affect, among other possible gains. In any event, it is not demonstrated that exchanges of different kinds of utilities (say, goods for political patronage) are any less sociable than those involving the same kinds of gifts and counter-gifts (cf. Foster 1963).

The third dimension is the "interval of sociability," the lapse of time between gift and countergift. This is a particularly difficult category, it has two kinds of variation. Relations between the seller and different buyers are variable, and there is also variation in the several kinds of transactions which may occur between the seller and any particular buyer. For example, while the money-for-goods aspect of the exchange may be completed within a few days, it may be some time before the buyer has an opportunity to advertise his seller's good qualities or send him referrals. Installment payments for goods received are usually paid within a time period fixed by agreement, but in practice these are only approximate time limits, and sellers actually demand only that something be paid on the account at that time. Furthermore, although the random, un-aligned buyer must usually pay in full at the time of the transaction, the aligned buyer customarily has a perpetual debt relationship with the seller. As in the more typical *kula* exchanges, there is no closure subsequent to each transaction. Each sale in the market is only one episode in an enduring set of transactions. Indeed, the whole point in the use of credit by the Philippine petty trader is that it obligates the recipient to future transactions with the same seller.

Finally, there is the qualitative "inner state," the "spirit" or degree of compassion which accompanies marketplace transactions (Sahlins 1965:145). *Suki* relationships differ from one another. In the first place, they pass through a period of development and therefore differ in maturity; and second, they differ in intensity, or subjective value. Inevitably, some "obligatory" relationships are not honored, for they have become too socially or economically demanding. This may be because they no longer yield satisfactions adequate to encourage their maintenance or perhaps because they were never structured on a solid basis of mutual warmth. A prime example of the latter is the "agent" who attempts to use his position as a valued supplier to establish and manipulate local ritual kin and *suki* relationships to enhance his (and his firm's) position. But local norms oppose such negatively reciprocal behavior, and buyers and sellers ideally meet mutual obligations. Accordingly, buyers and sellers exchange pleasantries, and they commonly carry their association beyond the context of the marketplace. *Suki* relationships may endure for decades and over considerable distances. Indeed, when confrontations over prices occur, it is usual for one partner or the other to recall their past association as reason for overlooking some current slight. Last, many of the persons selling the same classes of goods are related through kinship. This fact, together with the tendency each seller has to monopolize a portion of the market, encourages cooperation between sellers and reduces tension between sellers and buyers. It is clear, then, that these are not simply commercial relationships, but social bonds held firm by subjective values.

Reciprocity and Interpersonal Relations in Philippine Society

The marketplace relationships described here have many features which position them close to the "balanced reciprocity" midpoint of Sahlins' continuum. Furthermore, Filipinos interact in the marketplace much as they interact in the wider range of social relationships. In fact, the creation and maintenance of mutually advantageous, dyadic relationships on a pragmatic basis seems to be one of the most prominent features of lowland Philippine social structure. From this perspective, prestational relationships of the *suki* type are distinctive only because there is a specific word for them, and because they occur in a commercial context.

The formation or selection of social relationships in an optative fashion is clearly not unique to Philippine social structure. For example, in analyzing social relations in a Mexican village community, Foster (1961, 1963) went beyond the consideration of norms and formal roles to deal with interaction between specific persons. He noted that beyond the limits of the nuclear family individuals exercise a considerable degree of choice in selecting the social relationships which will actually be validated by interaction and exchange. Foster indicates that persons organize their social relationships in terms of "a special form of contractual relationship" which he terms a "dyadic contract" (1961:1174). These relationships are informal and implicit; they are not sanctified by ritual or maintained by law, and are therefore not legally enforceable. Dyadic contracts exist only at the pleasure of the "contractants," and they are specifically noncorporate because they obligate individuals, and not groups, to one another. They may exist between persons of roughly the same status or rank ("symmetrical" dyadic contracts) or between persons who are related in a superordinate-subordinate manner ("asymmetrical" dyadic contracts). But all dyadic contracts are defined by, and find overt expression in, a mutual exchange of goods and services. They are the components of a pragmatic system of interpersonal reciprocities.

Foster suggests that "dyadic contracts" are the organizational counterparts, in "bilaterally" organized societies, of the corporate relationships found in "unilineally" organized societies (Foster 1961:1173). However, the corporate relations of unilineal descent groups and the "dyadic contract" are structural explanations directed to different levels of behavior.

"Unilineal organization" exists at the level of the "rules of social organization," while dyadic contracts are at the inter-personal, interactional level. The latter can be pursued quite as productively in societies with unilineal organization. Additionally, a "contract" which is informal and extralegal is a strange contract indeed. Moreover, any attempt to deal with social structure and interaction solely in dyadic terms is overly simple, for one person may influence another's behavior through a large number of intervening individuals. For example, sellers in the Baguio marketplace influence the behavior of suppliers whom they may never meet, but with whom they interact through intermediaries. We do better, therefore, to treat patterns of interactions as complex linkages, or "social networks" (cf. Barnes 1954, 1968).

It is useful to think of the economic relationships of the marketplace economy as a network of optionally-established relationships involving the transaction of goods, services, and subjective values. But the same structural model is equally useful in considering the typical modes of lowland Philippine *social* interaction. For example, Kaut (1961) has shown that individuals choose those relatives (outside the immediate family) and associates with whom social relations will be actively maintained. These choices are then confirmed by the presentation of some gift or favor symbolic of the implicit *utang na loob* ("debt of deep obligation") relationship which then exists. Additionally, Hollnsteiner (1964), in a more inclusive typology of lowland Philippine reciprocal relationships, has added "contractual" (reciprocal exchanges of a specified sort at specified times) and "quasi-contractual" (the terms of repayment are not explicitly stated, but repayment is expected) categories to the less explicit obligations of the *utang na loob* type. But all of these common forms of interpersonal association involve the exercise of choice and the reciprocal transfer of goods and

271

services. As a result, they are strongly reminiscent of the "align-ment" relations of the marketplace. In brief, the social rela-tional categories which result from the exercise of choice in the different domains of social action—whether we speak of the seller and his aligned buyers or of the individual and the "per-sonal alliance" of friends and relatives that cluster about him (cf. Lynch 1959, Hollnsteiner 1963)—are similar. Such rela-tionships are also basic to the organization of institutions, for in the Philippines as in Mexico (Foster 1961:1175) the roles appropriate to the social system are supported by mutually advantageous exchanges. In fact, as minimal units of social or-ganization, such relations as *suki*, *compadrazgo*, and *utang na loob* are doubly significant. They allow individuals a range of options with which to create social universes more closely ap-proaching optimal utility than any sort of ascribed relationship (e.g., kinship) is likely to accomplish. They are, moreover, especially important in allowing individuals to cope with new situations, for they provide accepted modes of establishing support relations on more flexible grounds than those of kin-ship or community.

Economic relationships in the marketplace, therefore, are far removed from being "atomistic," or "impersonal," and clearly are not necessarily antagonistic. They typically involve buyer and seller in role relationships with a number of dimen-sions. Indeed, Alice Dewey, commenting on an earlier descrip-tion of interaction in the Baguio marketplace (Davis 1968), suggests that adding new dimensions to interpersonal relation-ships is one way of adjusting to changing external conditions—in her case to "urban adaptation." In her view, buyer and seller initially meet in terms of those roles only, but are likely to widen the bases of the relationship as the economy encourages them to do so. In Dewey's terms:

The suki relationship has economic advantages for both parties, but such advantages can only be assured when the purely commercial roles are supported by the sanctions which govern the other roles which have been involuted into the cluster. . . . This summation and involution thus reverses the process of disembedding which Polanyi felt to be inevitable in self-regulating market relationships" (Dewey 1968:37).

Thus, in the Baguio example there appears to have developed little of the "conflict of economies" (cf. Bohannan 1963: 259–265). The economic rationality of the self-regulating market has not driven socially solidary forms of association from commercial relationships. Instead, local populations have infused the formally rational market with subjective values. The sociable content of market relationships appears to *increase* with the degree of commitment to the market. The difference in these respects between transient relationships of the open market and the intricate network of mutualistic relations of the main market is a case in point. On the whole it is the more marginally committed marketeers of the open market who attempt to maximize returns on each transaction, while the stallholders of the main market are much more concerned with long-term involvement with their clients.

This point has somehow been lost in discussion, but it is not news, for Dalton asserts that Polanyi himself was aware all along of the "reembedding" tendencies of market organization:

Polanyi's principal concern is to show the uniqueness, historically, of uncontrolled market exchange as the integrating transactional mode of nineteenth century national and international economy, and to show why the structure and performance of the market economy were socially divisive and inevitably led to extensive social control" (Dalton 1965b:2–3).

In other words, both Polanyi and Dalton appear to feel that market organizations necessarily tend toward the introduction of subjective constraints on freely competitive behavior. Markets inevitably become embedded in social institutions just as other forms of exchange are embedded in primitive societies. We have here "the little red wagon painted blue" problem which often plagues attempts to demonstrate empirically the validity of functionalist arguments: the view that there is an inherent tendency for some institution to express a dysfunctional attribute, whereas the true nature of the institution and its attribute are suppressed by corrective social mechanisms. But a more significant question here is: if markets tend to be embedded in social control mechanisms, how is it possible that an organizational "gulf" exists between the primitive (reciprocal) economy and the Western (market) economy? Likewise, on what grounds may we suggest that, "it is not impossible to say where the usefulness of economic theory ends" (Dalton 1961:18)? If all economies are embedded, the only chasm between them (as opposed to a continuous distribution of varients) is between economies considered as ideal types.[2] In this case, verification may inflate minor conceptual distinctions until they seem empirically significant (cf. Cohen 1967:115), but there is little which is either substance or "substantive" about the latter analytical procedure.

There are consequential organizational differences between the most common economic relationships in modern market systems and those most typical of tribal economies. Sahlins'

[2] Weber defined an ideal type as a "one-sided accentuation ... by the synthesis of a great many diffuse, discrete, more or less present and occasionally absent concrete individual phenomena, which are arranged into a unified analytical construct. In its conceptual purity, this mental construct cannot be found anywhere in reality" (Weber 1949:90–93). Ideal-type constructs are designed to emphasize differences which in empirical cases may be slight. It is conceptually dangerous, then, to attribute cause or "conflicts" to slight differences in constructs which cannot be found in reality.

measures make tribal economic relationships appear typically to express more sociability than those of the marketplace. However, the same measures assure us that the degree to which this is so is considerably less than Dalton and Polanyi have argued. Furthermore, once we move beyond the level of the "rules of social organization" to consider interpersonal behavior, the fundamental similarity of relations in both kinds of economy becomes apparent. The data now available, therefore, do not sustain the view that differences between primitive and market economic relations are those of kind, not degree, as Dalton (1961:20) asserted. Correspondingly, the cross-cultural applicability of formal theory cannot be ruled out solely on logical grounds. The influence of social and cultural constraints on economic behavior in the marketplace is powerful, and some marketplace relationships involve as strong elements of prestation as some classic examples of "noneconomic" exchanges mentioned in the literature on tribal economies. At the same time the explanation of these personalized market relations is enhanced by analysis in terms of such notions as scarcity, choice, a profit motive, supply and demand, resource mobility, and efforts to reduce risks. Logically, then, tribal economic relationships should be understandable in the same terms.

All societies manifest some constraints on formally rational economic behavior. That social ends may be chosen over purely economic ones, that choice-making is an exercise of groups rather than of individuals, or that choice may not be exercised in some areas of behavior does not imply that decision-making models are necessarily inapplicable (cf. Joy 1967:35). The factors which according to substantivist scholars constrain the free exercise of choice—law, custom, etc.—may be dealt with usefully as elements which actors must consider while determining a course of action. In the short run, for example, it is economically irrational for a farmer to offer lower-than-market prices to the seller who suffered a loss on a similar transaction previously, as often happens in the case under discussion. But the obligation to do so which is imposed upon him by the expectations of his fellows can certainly be incorporated as an element in the decision-making process.

STRUCTURE AND PROCESS

Relationships in the Baguio marketplace economy typically involve subjective elements which, from the perspective of maximizing immediate gain from the transaction, appear economically irrational. Nevertheless, in the long run the concessions which sellers offer to buyers and the social attachments they form provide some benefits which influence both individuals' ability to accumulate capital and the growth potential of the local economy as a whole.

In the brief passage alluded to earlier, Belshaw (1965:77) suggests that marketplace systems in general do little to encourage the accumulation of capital. That they do not, he contends, relates primarily to the scale of the activities of individual participants and to the severity of competition which is characteristic of such systems. Because participation is typically undertaken on a small scale, substantial quantities of risk capital are not necessary before participation is possible, and nearly anyone may play the game. The result is a multiplicity of sellers among whom competition is so intense that profit is likely to be realized only as the result of "frictions," such as those which result from temporary advantages and windfalls. Thus, new opportunities are incentives for more and more participants to enter the market. The gross quantity of trade may grow, but income remains thinly distributed among the ever-increasing number of individuals who participate. In the local case this would imply, for example, that the tourist trade would have little impact on individual accumulation, for although gross local income may increase, the long-term effect would be to call out ever-increasing numbers of sellers among whom additional income would be widely shared.

The literature on Haiti (Mintz 1956, 1961a, 1964a; Legerman 1962), Jamaica (Katzin 1959, 1960), Mesoamerica (Tax 1953), Mexico (Foster 1948; Malinowski and de la Fuente 1957) and especially Java (Dewey 1962a, 1962b, 1964; Geertz 1962a, 1963) supports Belshaw's suggestion (as does the Baguio example to a considerable degree). However, although the lack of quantified data in all cases makes precise comparison difficult, the Baguio example presents a somewhat more encouraging set of conditions. Operations in the open-market sector of the Baguio marketplace closely resemble descriptions offered of other marketplace systems in a number of ways: small quantities of operating capital, a large number of small transactions, a tendency for buyers and sellers to be associated only for purposes of gain, and so on. At the same time, the stall-holding sellers of the main market, who are much more numerous, present a different picture.[3]

Profits in the Baguio marketplace are not impressive in any absolute sense, but relative to other marketplace systems local stallholders as a class do well. Moreover, an occasional local seller does well even by absolute standards. Some own their own homes and some property, and a few families even own automobiles. Furthermore, in at least three known cases, men

[3] For example, although marketplace organization is much the same as in the Philippines, the average investment in the Baguio marketplace approximates the figure ($500) offered by Mintz (1964a) as the upper limit of investments among Haitian marketeers. Simple comparisons are rendered difficult by the different wider economic conditions obtaining in the two nations.

who began their careers as vendors in the marketplace have managed to expand their holdings beyond the marketplace and have become wealthy. The local Baguio economy, therefore, is clearly not characterized by the minute scale of investments and transactions or the degree of poverty commonly associated with marketplace economies elsewhere.

Obviously, the relative prosperity of the Philippine case is partly a result of better general economic conditions than exist in, say, Java or Haiti. Yet the performance of the local Philippine economy is also strongly influenced by the nature of economic organization. More specifically, this organization has the potential to ameliorate some of the more common limitations on capital accumulation which afflict marketplace systems. The ways in which personalized, subjectively valued, economic relations effect modifications in marketplace competition and how these modifications provide opportunities for additional savings and accumulation remain to be discussed.

In the first place, by removing some risks inherent in market trading, it is likely that the personalistic, noninterchangeable local trading relationships operate to maintain prices at higher levels than would otherwise exist. Bonds of kinship, *suki*, and *compadrazgo* all establish enduring social relationships which in a market context are advantageous, for they result in more predictable market conditions. Through these relationships sellers are able to depress some of the greater fluctuations in supply and demand, for such relations enable the seller to know how many secure market outlets he controls and to obtain a better assessment of the types and quantities of goods he may sell readily. Such information helps the seller to avoid overstocking (or overproducing), and to reduce the possibility of having to sell under distress conditions. Furthermore, the desire of the buyer to maintain a secure source of credit encourages him to be less receptive to competitive prices than he probably would be otherwise. In short, as the result of these long-standing social attachments among buyers and sellers, risks are considerably reduced, and this reduction is reflected in the price structure. Now, this kind of functional argument is difficult to support, for it suggests that existing conditions *would* be different if not for the presence of some critical variable—in this case, the social attachments which exist among buyers and sellers. Because we have no situation in which the variable is lacking to use for comparative purposes, it is difficult to mobilize hard data to test the proposition. However, when buyers remain loyal to their *suki* sellers in spite of more attractive prices offered elsewhere, and when potential competitors are forced out of the market as the result—as in the instances recounted above—the interpretation offered seems consistent with the facts. Therefore, it seems reasonable to assume that *suki* and other similar relationships have a direct impact on price formation.

Second, the personalized nature of economic relations tends to limit the number of sellers who participate in the market and, in turn, increases the income return to those who do manage to obtain stalls. Because the extension of credit is a customary aspect of local commercial operations, each seller requires more capital to participate than merely the amount required to obtain trading stock and to pay market fees. Particularly among stallholders, each seller must initially have enough operating capital to establish a clientele. This implies adequate resources to carry buyers until their accounts first fall due and the seller begins to receive a return on his investment. It is possible to participate in the small-scale carrying trade, or as an open-market seller, with small investments of capital. But the professional stallholder normally operates with intolerable risks if he is not able to secure a clientele early in his career. Once the stallholder has become established in the marketplace, these bonds of personalism operate in his favor by limiting competition and reducing risks. But the initial cost of forming them and supporting them is greater, initial investment in unknown persons is risky, and failure is a real possibility if the seller lacks adequate capital to carry him through his developmental period.

This same set of circumstances produces an economic sector in which an intermediate-sized economic unit is characteristic. The small-scale seller tends to be eliminated from anything more than occasional participation until he can acquire adequate capital to obtain a stall and to support clients. And the necessity of relations of trust with one's buyers makes it difficult for any particular seller to absorb the functions of another and to combine these into larger (and fewer) economic units. As long as personalistic relationships carry the distributive process, the ambitious seller's opportunities for growth tend to be limited to wholesaling—to dividing the fruits of his efforts and ingenuity with retailers who themselves control sets of clients.

In a real sense, therefore, the personalistic relationships of the marketplace economy function as analogs to contractual legal systems. Within the context of such relations commercial activity is stimulated by the substitution of credit for one's own capital. Outside the universe of personalized relations credit is expensive or not available at all. In fact, the degree to which credit is employed in this Philippine example appears to render the situation distinctive in comparison to other such systems which have been described. The effective restriction of local-level credit to the individual's network of prestational relationships provides a limited commercial universe, and the institution of an effective legal system would encourage a wider utilization of credit and the expansion of sellers' clienteles. Moreover, in eliminating the primary utility of personalistic relationships, a more effective legal system would also enable more heavily-capitalized units to absorb smaller, less well-capitalized ones. But in the absence of universalistic legal sanctions, and lacking widely disseminated information concerning individual credit ratings, such as those on which Western credit systems depend, personalistic market relations are extremely useful.

Additionally, personalistic relationships occasionally carry enough force and utility to facilitate the expansion of marketing opportunities by encouraging long-distance trade. In the local economy unaligned traders are limited because they must deal personally with their customers and because they must accompany their goods in transit. Those sellers who have obligatory relationships with persons in other areas, however, may draw on a wider market, for such persons will represent the seller's interests in their own locales. Such activities occur in the trade between Baguio City sellers and their buyers in the mining and lumbering camps. Indeed, for the carrier roles described earlier, personalistic relations make possible the extension of interregional trade without the prior accumulation of capital which such trade usually involves. Where interregional bonds of kinship, *suki*, or *compadrazgo* exist, therefore, the technical quality of transport is a more significant trade-restricting factor than the lack of capital or effective legal sanctions.

Thus, relationships which appear in the short run to be economically-irrational concessions to sociability, in the long term offer a number of pragmatic advantages both for the individual and for the "system." *Suki*, *compadrazgo*, and kinship all establish socially-valued relations which afford the chief means of introducing order and regularity into the local marketplace system. At the same time, they are the major source of the small-scale monopolistic-monopsonistic tendencies—the "frictions"—which provide sellers in the marketplace with the opportunity for profit taking. In contrast to a strategy intended to maximize the profit from each transaction, Filipinos pursue a strategy aimed at optimizing economic stability and long-term income. There is here, to be sure, a "security" orientation such as has been held typical of non-Western economies, and which is often contrasted with the "expansive," risk-taking quality of Western entrepreneurship (cf. Boeke 1953). But the same behavior might also be interpreted as an inclination among Filipino marketeers to forego immediate gain in favor of more extensive future rewards, a strategy which—far from indicating an orientation toward economic conservatism—is the *sine qua non* of capitalist development. A strong infusion of "sociability" in economic relations is not necessarily irrational, even when considered in purely economic terms.

PERSPECTIVES ON SUBSTANTIVE THEORY

In summary, the main points at issue in the substantivist-formalist controversy in economic anthropology result not so much from different notions concerning the motivations underlying economic action as from the fact that the two approaches emphasize fundamentally different levels of analysis. In substantive theory the "reality of society" is not the individual, but the "rules of social organization" of the economy. Polanyi expressly states that the study of economies is most appropriately concerned with "institutional analysis" (1957:242). The substantive viewpoint emphasizes the dominant institutional pattern of the economy, and this pattern is considered the "substance" of economic action.

In practice, the substantive approach has led to a consideration of economies as ideal types, and the "forms of economic integration" (reciprocity, redistribution, and integrative exchange) are typologies of gross features of economic organization, not concepts with which decisions, strategies and social processes may be investigated. Substantive analysis is more than a little Veblenesque in orientation, for its concern is the way in which the economy, defined as a social subsystem delimited by materialistic criteria, relates to other subsystems— what Polanyi (1957:250) and Dalton (1961:10) have termed "the place of the economy in society." Their point of view is evidence in support of the charge which Berliner (1962) has leveled against anthropology in general: that anthropology is more concerned with relations between institutions and the comparison of institutions cross-culturally, than with hard in-depth analysis of specific institutions. When Dalton (1961: 10–11) lists "the matters of interest to the anthropologist (studying primitive economies)," he does not mention that anthropologists might be concerned with nonnormative alternatives or with the degree to which resources might be committed to their realization.

A large number of anthropologists (see Chapter I) have found emphasis upon the normative order and dominant patterns to be unsatisfactory, and now focus their attention on individual actors (or corporate units of them), the choices they make, and the strategies behind these choices. In general, these scholars hold that it is through an understanding of the way actors view alternative courses of action and choose among them that it is most possible to attain models of behavior adequate to explain a wider range of data and permit probablistic prediction. Obviously, they share this view with formal economic theory.

Since Radcliffe-Brown most anthropologists (cf. Firth 1954, Levi-Strauss 1963) have treated social structure as an analytical abstraction, not as "the reality of society." Not that the view of social structure as the outcome of decisions made in interaction contexts is any more "real" than a view which stresses "the rules of social organization." But a concentration on the former provides an analytical strategy (Cancian 1966) which can deal effectively with *both* the rules *and* expressed interpersonal behavior, and which can also account for variation and change. Theory properly deals with "substantive" data. But the issue here is not a distinction between the empirical and the logical, as the substantivists claim. Rather, the issue concerns which of these levels of analysis has the greater utility: which permits the student to deal more adequately with problems?

Above all, if the analyst goes beyond institutional structures, what Barth (1967a) refers to as "ideal aggregate patterns," to consider how individuals actually interact, it becomes difficult to distinguish the social relations which characterize market systems from those exchange relations which have been described as typical in primitive economies. Because of these basic similarities the charge that a general economic theory must be founded on institutional patterns, rather than upon individuals and the choices they make, simply cannot be sustained. For if the formal theory is capable of dealing adequately with the one, it must as surely be useful in explaining the other.

To this point the present discussion has had a negative, polemical orientation with respect to substantive theory. Yet the proper relationship between formal and substantive viewpoints in economic anthropology is complementary—though not in the way substantivist scholars have suggested.[4] Unfortunately, some confusion arises when one attempts to determine precisely how complementary these views are, for it is not clear what the empirical referents of the "forms of economic integration" are. It has not been specified whether these are to be treated as the objective ("etic") categories of

[4] The substantivists see the two theories as complementary in a different sense. They argue consistently that formal theory is adequate for the analysis of market systems, but useless elsewhere.

the observer, or as the action-governing ideals held by the actors themselves ("emic" categories). Dalton's emphasis on the "rules" which govern social organization suggests that he, at least, interprets "transactional modes" to be sets of the latter. Obviously, it makes some difference.

To the degree that the substantive categories of analysis are to be thought of as objective modes of ordering data, they represent the observer's system of classification. They are, therefore, potentially as useful as any other such system of classification. From that viewpoint any assessment of their usefulness must focus on how well drawn the defining criteria are. As a system of classification, the "forms of economic integration" order data, and by displaying features which are consistently associated, they suggest hypotheses concerning relations between variables. In some areas of anthropological inquiry, like cultural history and archaeology, the investigator is simply not likely to have adequate data to deal with behavior from the perspective of individuals, the choices they make, and the strategies they pursue. In these cases a sound classification system may serve important heuristic functions, suggesting the context in which recovered elements occurred. Substantive theory originated in the attempt to deal with historical and archaeological data, has been most impressively applied to problems of that type, and is as admirably suited to the analysis of such issues as the substantivists have insisted that formal theory is suited to the analysis of markets. An emphasis on choice and strategy is probably not possible in historical contexts, and even in ethnographic work with living populations it is tantamount to a call for an unusually meticulous collection of data.

If the "forms of economic integration" are not the observer's categories but the rules understood by the actors themselves to govern behavior, then we may think of them as ends, or values, toward which behavior is, or at least ideally should be, oriented. Many writers, among whom Firth (1954, 1967) and Barth (1966) are prominent, have noted that studying the decisive action of individuals is not such an "individual" matter after all. Action and choices tend to be oriented toward attainment of goals which are widely shared by the members of the same social aggregate, so that even if we focus on "atomistic individuals," we necessarily incorporate the social nature of human behavior. To the degree that the "forms of integration" are rules charged with subjective meaning, it is important to consider them if we have any hope of being predictive, for they are factors which actors consider in choosing alternatives. It is important to know what people do, as opposed to what they ought to do, but it is important to know the hierarchy of values as well. If we have no knowledge of the latter, we have no means of assessing what actors may do in changing circumstances. We cannot assume without additional investigation that what people *do* is what they *value* (contra Epstein 1967). For example, few marketplace sellers in Baguio City make any attempt to stand for city election, and this particular alternative has little impact on the choices they make. Yet if incomes were increased so that campaign costs could be met, it is a near certainty that marketeers would become much more active in seeking public offices for a high value is placed on such activity. Clearly, then, we cannot afford to ignore the "rules of social organization."

Finally, considerable potential benefit can be obtained from a concern, as is expressed in the substantive approach, for the ways in which production and distribution systems interrelate with other subsystems of behavior: for example, the ways in which different forms of economic integration influence values and relationships in other cultural and social domains. This interest, in fact, has potential humanist significance which is surely of equal value to a precise analysis of economizing strategies. I have not, therefore, taken up this discussion because of any commitment to the view that substantivism, like Carthage, must be destroyed. Rather, I have joined the argument because the substantivists have attempted to discredit an approach which has much to offer the development of general economic theory: a systematic consideration of the decisive actions of "atomistic individuals" and the patterned variations in behavior which rise from them.

Appendix I

CONTENT OF MARKETPLACE ZONES
City Ordinance No. 172

A. *Vegetables*: all fresh vegetables, dried beans, root crops, local fruits, and forest products (e.g., rattan, "native" woven baskets, and tiger-grass broomstraw).

B. *Sari-sari*: canned goods, lard, sugar, paper bags, candy, tinned biscuit, cigars, cigarettes, eggs, flour, imported ham, bacon and sausage, cooking oil, soap, tea, matches, imported vinegar patis (fish sauce), dried onions and garlic, writing paper, pencils, pomade and hair oil, ribbons, thread, needles, pins, face powder, toothbrushes, toothpaste, mirrors, rings, earrings and trinkets, imported fruits and nuts, and shoe polish.

C. *Dry goods*: new and second-hand clothing, hats, blankets, umbrellas, raincoats and jackets, ready-to-wear Ilocano jackets, handkerchiefs, towels, and belts.

D. *Footwear*: shoes, slippers, boots, sandles, leather goods, stockings, and shoe laces.

E. *Meat*: all dressed flesh of cattle, pig, sheep, goat, chicken and turkey, local ham, sausage and bacon, and roasted pig.

F. *Fish*: all fresh fishes from sea, pond, or freshwater origin; all shellfish and molluscs.

G. *Salt, Bagoong (fish sauce), and Pottery*: salt, sealed and unsealed bagoong, pottery vessels, jars and earthenware stoves, coconut oil, charcoal, and vinegar.

H. *Rice*: all types of rice, rice husks, rice bran, maize, and other cereal grains.

I. *Caldero*: all kinds of kitchenware except earthenware types, bolos, knives, urinolas, lowland winnowing baskets, buri mats, and basins.

J. *Curios*: woodcarvings, tablecloths, napkins, handbags, ash trays, silver jewelry, and wooden tableware.

K. *Periodicals*: newspapers and magazines (except those deemed obscene or immoral), books, stationery, writing supplies, cigars and cigarettes, and comic book and magazine rentals.

L. *Carinderia*: all cooked food, providing it is served on the premises to customers.

M. *Cakes*: all home-made cakes, bread, peanuts, and boiled corn-on-the-cob.

N. *Entrails*: all kinds of entrails.

O. *Halo-halo*: refreshments, soft drinks, and *halo-halo* (ice and fruit).

P. *Coffee*: all ground coffee.

Q. *Surplus Goods*: all military goods except surplus shoes.

R. *Dried Fish*: all kinds of dried fish.

S. *Flowers*: fresh and artificial flowers, flowering plants, flower baskets, vases, and dried flower decorations.

T. *Fowl*: all types of live fowl, and eggs.

Section III of this ordinance provides that: whenever any article shall be exhibited or displayed out of the proper zone as if it were intended for sale, whether sold or not, this display will be interpreted as an exposure for sale and is, therefore, a breach of this ordinance.

Section IV states that any stallholder found guilty of violating any of the provisions of this ordinance three times is to be deprived of his right to sell anything on the city market premises.

The official classification of zones, which appears here varies from the one utilized by the city treasurer's office in the collection of market fees, and both differ from the zoning classification utilized by the market superintendent's office. Thus, there are some discrepancies in the tables of fees and fee delinquencies.

Appendix II

The following mimeographed handbill was distributed among City Market Vendors one week prior to the Baguio City elections of 1963. It has been altered here only to obscure the individuals and political party involved:

Fellow Citizen:

We, of the......... Party present to you a program which calls for the return of a greater portion of the market fees back to our market vendors, in the form of various improvements, as well as measures designed to enhance the welfare of the market vendors. Among other things, we pledge:

(1) *Beautification* of our market to maintain its reputation for cleanliness, to include: repair and painting of stalls and buildings; putting up awnings and similar structures to protect merchandise in the stalls; elimination of congestion and relocation of vendors now temporarily occupying makeshift structures and areas in permanent buildings to be constructed by the City within the market compound; and development of the upper market areas by construction of a road, and making provision for gardens, parking areas, and open spaces above the present market.

(2) Improvement of sanitary facilities by providing for more decent public comfort rooms, concealed garbage receptacles and cuspidors, repair of market streets and open areas; and by provision of additional men to ensure the regular cleaning of the market.

(3) Construction of uniform mezzanines where the same is desired and practicable, to provide for additional display and storage space for stallholders.

(4) To ensure peace, order, and safety in the City Market, provision shall be made for police within the market around the clock.

(5) Housing in connection with our city-wide housing program, to set aside a portion of the city for housing projects for a Baguio City Market Vendor's community to accomodate at least 750 of our resident market vendors who do not yet own homes in Baguio.

We, of the . . . . Party appeal for your support to enable us to carry out a program designed to improve the position of market vendors as the backbone of the City's economic life. On my personal account, may I thank you for your treasured vote this coming Tuesday, November 12th, and may I reiterate my fervent wish to reciprocate your kind assistance, by serving you with sincerity, humility, and dedication, in the years to come.

Very Sincerely yours,
(A candidate for Vice-Mayor)

Bibliography

Agpalo, Remigio E.
  1965. Pandango sa ilaw: the politics of Occidental Mindoro. Manila: University of the Philippines, Benipayo Press.

Anderson, James N.
  1962. Some aspects of land and society in a Pangasinan community. Philippine Sociological Review 10:41–58.
  1964. Kinship and property in a Pangasinan barrio. Unpublished doctoral dissertation, Dept. of Anthropology, University of California, Los Angeles.
  1969. Buy and sell and economic personalism: foundations for Philippine entrepreneurship. Asian Survey 9:641–668.

Ardener, Shirley
  1964. The comparative study of rotating credit associations. Journal of the Royal Anthropological Institute 94:201–229.

Arensberg, Conrad
  1937. The irish countryman. New York: Macmillan.
  1957. Anthropology as history. In Karl Polanyi, Conrad Arensberg, and Harry Pearson, eds., Trade and markets in the early empires. Glencoe: The Free Press.

Arnaldo, Marcelo
  1955. The agrarian problems of the Philippines and their solutions. The Silliman Journal 2:31–50.

Barberra, Alfredo
  1963. Soils and natural vegetation. In Robert E. Huke, ed., Shadows on the land. Makati, Rizal: Carmelo and Bauerman.

Barnes, John A.
  1954. Class and committees in a Norwegian island parish. Human Relations 7:39–58.

1968. Networks and the political process. *In* Marc Swartz, ed., Local level politics. Chicago: Aldine.

Barnett, Milton L.
1967. Subsistence and transition of agricultural development among the Ibaloi. *In* M. D. Zamora, ed., Studies in Philippine anthropology. Quezon City: Alemar Phoenix.

Barth, Fredrik
1959. Segmentary opposition and the theory of games: a study of Pathan organization. Journal of the Royal Anthropological Institute 89:5–21.

1963. The role of the entrepreneur in social change in northern Norway. Oslo: University of Oslo Press.

1966. Models of social organization. Occasional Paper No. 23, Royal Anthropological Institute of London.

1967*a*. On the study of social change. American Anthropologist 69:661–669.

1967*b*. Economic spheres in Darfur. *In* Raymond Firth, ed., Themes in economic anthropology. Association of Social Anthropologists Monograph No. 6. London: Tavistock.

1969. Introduction. *In* Fredrik Barth, ed., Ethnic groups and boundaries. Boston: Little, Brown.

Befu, Harumi and Leonard Plotnicov
1962. Types of corporate unilineal descent groups. American Anthropologist 64:313–327.

Belshaw, Cyril
1965. Traditional exchange and modern markets. Englewood Cliffs: Prentice-Hall.

1967. Anthropology and economic theory. *In* Maurice Freedman, ed., Social organization: essays presented to Raymond Firth. Chicago: Aldine.

Benet, Francisco
1957. Explosive markets: the Berber highlands. *In* Karl Polanyi, Conrad Arensberg, and Harry Pearson, eds., Trade and markets in the early empires. Glencoe: The Free Press.

Berliner, Joseph S.
1962. The feet of the natives are large. Current Anthropology 3:47–61.

Beyer, H. Otley
1953. The origin and history of the Philippine rice terraces. Proceedings of the Eighth Pacific Science Congress 1:387–398.

Boeke, Julius H.
  1910. Tropisch-koloniale staathuishoudkunde: Het problem. Amsterdam: Leiden University, dissertation.
  1953. Economics and economic policy of dual societies. New York: Institute of Pacific Relations.

Bohannan, Paul J.
  1955. Some principles of exchange and investment among the Tiv. American Anthropologist 57:60–70.
  1959. The impact of money on an African subsistence economy. Journal of Economic History 29:491–503.
  1963. Social anthropology. New York: Holt, Rinehart, and Winston.

Bohannan, Paul J. and George Dalton, eds.
  1962. Markets in Africa. Evanston: Northwestern University Press.

Briñas, Amado
  1954. Tax policy in relation to new capital investments. Economic Research Journal 1:115–119.

Bruner, Edward M.
  1961. Medan: the role of kinship in an Indonesian city. *In* Alexander Spoehr, ed., Pacific port towns and cities. Honolulu: Bishop Museum Press.

Buchler, I. R. and H. A. Selby
  1968. Kinship and social organization. New York: Macmillan.

Burling, Robbins
  1962. Maximization theories and the study of economic anthropology. American Anthropologist 64:802–821.

Cancian, Francesca
  1960. Functional analysis of change. American Sociological Review 25:818–827.

Cancian, Frank
  1966. Maximization as norm, strategy, and theory: a comment on programmatic statements in economic anthropology. American Anthropologist 68:465–470.

Cohen, Percy S.
  1967. Economic analysis and economic man. *In* Raymond Firth, ed., Themes in economic anthropology. Association of Social Anthropologists Monograph No. 6. London: Tavistock.

Conklin, Harold C.
  1954. An ethnoecological approach to shifting agriculture. Transactions of the New York Academy of Science 17:133–142.
  1964. Ethnogenealogical method. *In* Ward H. Goodenough, ed.,

Explorations in cultural anthropology. New York: McGraw-Hill.

Cook, Scott

1966. The obsolete "anti-market mentality": a critique of the substantive approach to economic anthropology. American Anthropologist 68:323–345.

1969. The "anti-market" mentality re-examined: a further critique of the substantive approach to economic anthropology. Southwestern Journal of Anthropology 25:378–406.

Corpus, Onofre D.

1965. The Philippines. Englewood Cliffs: Prentice-Hall.

Coser, Lewis A.

1957. Social conflict and the theory of social change. British Journal of Sociology 8:197–207.

Dahrendorf, Ralf

1959. Class and class conflict in industrial society. Stanford: Stanford University Press.

1965. Out of utopia. American Journal of Sociology 64:115–127. Reprinted *in* Lewis A. Coser and Bernard Rosenberg, eds., sociological theory: a book of readings. New York: Macmillan.

Dalton, George

1961. Economic theory and primitive society. American Anthropologist 63:1–25.

1965a. Primitive money. American Anthropologist 67:44–55.

1965b. Primitive, archaic, and modern economies: Karl Polanyi's contribution to economic anthropology and comparative economy. Proceedings of the American Ethnological Society. Seattle: University of Washington Press.

1967. Bibliographic essay. *In* George Dalton, ed., Tribal and peasant economies: readings in economic anthropology. Garden City: Natural History Press.

1969. Theoretical issues in economic anthropology. Current Anthropology 10:63–102.

Davis, William G.

1968. Economic limitations and social relationships in a Philippine marketplace: capital accumulation in a peasant economy. *In* Robert Van Niel, ed., Economic factors in Southeast Asian social change. Honolulu: Asian Studies at Hawaii Program, University of Hawaii, Publication No. 2.

Dewey, Alice G.

1962a. Peasant marketing in Java. Glencoe: The Free Press.

1962*b*. Trade and social control in Java. Journal of the Royal Anthropological Institute 92:177–190.

1964. Capital, credit, and saving in Javanese marketing. *In* Raymond Firth and B. S. Yamey, eds., Capital, saving, and credit in peasant societies. London: George Allen and Unwin.

1968. Restructuring roles as a strategy in urban adaptation. *In* Robert Van Niel, ed., Economic factors in Southeast Asian social change. Honolulu: Asian Studies at Hawaii Program University of Hawaii, Publication No. 2.

Diaz, May N.
1967. Introduction: economic relations in peasant society. *In* Jack Potter, May Diaz, and George Foster, eds., Peasant society: a reader. Boston: Little, Brown.

Dobby, Ernest Henry George
1960. Southeast Asia. London: University of London Press.

Dozier, Edward P.
1961. Land use and social organization among the non-Christian tribes of northwestern Luzon. Proceedings of the American Ethnological Society. Seattle: University of Washington Press.

1967. Mountain arbiters. Tucson: University of Arizona Press.

Edel, Matthew
1969. Economic analysis in an anthropological setting. American Anthropologist 71:421–433.

Eggan, Fred
1960. The Sagada Igorots of northern Luzon. *In* George P. Murdock, ed., Social structure in Southeast Asia. Viking Fund Publication No. 29. Chicago: Quadrangle.

1963. Cultural drift and social change. Current Anthropology 4:347–355.

1967. Some aspects of bilateral social systems in the northern Philippines. *In* M. D. Zamora, ed., Studies in Philippine anthropology. Quezon City: Alemar Phoenix.

Epstein, Trude Scarlett
1962. Economic development and social change in south India. Manchester: Manchester University Press.

1967. The data of economics in anthropological analysis. *In* Arnold Leonard Epstein, ed., The craft of social anthropology. London: Tavistock.

Erasmus, Charles
1956. Culture structure and process: the occurrence and disap-

pearance of reciprocal farm labor. Southwestern Journal of Anthropology 12:444–469.

Firth, Raymond
1939. Primitive Polynesian economy. London: George Routledge.
1946. Malay fishermen: their peasant economy. London: Kegan Paul, Trench, Trubner.
1951. Elements of Social Organization. London, Watts.
1954. Social organization and social change. Presidential Address, Journal of the Royal Anthropological Institute 84:1–20.
1957. The place of Malinowski in the history of economic anthropology. *In* Raymond Firth, ed., Man and culture: an evaluation of the work of Bronislaus Malinowski. New York: Harper and Row.
1959. Economics of the New Zealand Maori. Wellington: R. E. Owen, Government Printer.
1964a. Capital, saving, and credit in peasant society. *In* Raymond Firth and B. S. Yamey, eds., Capital, saving, and credit in peasant societies. London: George Allen and Unwin.
1964b. Essays on social organization and values. London School of Economics Monograph in Social Anthropology, No. 28. London: Athlone.
1967. Themes in economic anthropology. *In* Raymond Firth, ed., Themes in economic anthropology. Association of Social Anthropologists Monograph No. 6. London: Tavistock.

Fisher, Charles Alfred
1964. Southeast Asia: a social, economic, and political geography. London: Methuen.

Fortes, Meyer
1953. The structure of unilineal descent groups. American Anthropologist 55:17–41.

Foster, George M.
1948. The folk economy of rural Mexico with special reference to marketing. Journal of Marketing 13:153–162.
1953. What is folk culture? American Anthropologist 55:159–173.
1960. Interpersonal relations in peasant society. Human Organization 19:174–178.
1961. The dyadic contract: a model for the social structure of a Mexican peasant village. American Anthropologist 63:1173–1192.
1962. Traditional cultures: the impact of technical change. New York: Harper and Row.

1963. The dyadic contract in Tzintuntzan, II: patron-client relationship. American Anthropologist 65:1280–1294.

1964. Treasure tales, and the image of the static economy in a Mexican peasant community. Journal of American Folklore 77:39–44.

1965. Peasant society and the image of the limited good. American Anthropologist 67:293–315.

1967. Introduction: what is a peasant? *In* Jack Potter, May Diaz, and George Foster, eds., Peasant society: a reader. Boston: Little, Brown.

Fox, Robert B.

1956. Social organization. Area handbook on the Philippines, vol. 1. Chicago: University of Chicago for the Human Relations Area Files.

1959. The study of Filipino society and its significance to programs of economic and social development. Philippine Sociological Review 7:2–12.

Fox, Robert B. and Frank Lynch, S. J.

1956. Ritual co-parenthood. Area handbook on the Philippines, vol. 2. Chicago: University of Chicago for the Human Relations Area Files.

Freeman, J. Derek

1955. Iban agriculture. Colonial Research Studies, No. 18. London: Her Majesty's Stationery Office.

Fusfeld, Daniel B.

1957. Economic theory misplaced: livelihood in primitive society. *In* Karl Polanyi, Conrad Arensberg and Harry Pearson, eds., Trade and markets in the early empires. Glencoe: The Free Press.

Geertz, Clifford E.

1962a. Social change and modernization in two Indonesian towns. *In* Everett Hagen, ed., On the theory of social change. Homewood, Ill.: Dorsey.

1962b. The rotating credit association: a "middle-rung" development. Economic Development and Cultural Change 10:241–263.

1963. Peddlers and princes. Chicago: University of Chicago Press.

1964. Agricultural involution. Berkeley: University of California Press.

Glaser, Barney G. and Anselm L. Strauss

1967. The discovery of grounded theory: strategies for qualitative research. Chicago: Aldine.

Gluckman, Max
   1955.   Custom and conflict in Africa. Oxford: Blackwell.
Golay, Frank H.
   1956.   Economic aspects of Philippine agrarian reform. Philippine
           Sociological Review 4:20–32.
   1961.   Public policy and economic planning in the Philippines.
           Ithaca: Cornell University Press.
Goodenough, Ward H.
   1956.   Residence rules. Southwestern Journal of Anthropology
           12:22–37.
   1961.   Review of George P. Murdock, ed., Social Structure in South-
           east Asia. American Anthropologist 63:1341–1347.
   1964.   Introduction. *In* Ward H. Goodenough, ed., Explorations in
           cultural anthropology. New York: McGraw-Hill.
   1965.   Rethinking status and role. *In* Michael Banton, ed., The rele-
           vance of models for social anthropology. Association of
           Social Anthropologists Monograph No. 1. London: Tavi-
           stock.
Goodfellow, D. M.
   1939.   Principles of economic sociology. London: Routledge.
Gouldner, Alvin W.
   1960.   The norm of reciprocity: a preliminary statement. American
           Sociological Review 25:161–178.
Grossholtz, Jean
   1964.   Politics in the Philippines. Boston: Little, Brown.
Hannah, Harold W. and N.G.P. Krausz
   1960.   The role of law in the development of land resources. *In* Land
           Economics Institute Editorial Committee, eds., Modern Land
           Policy, Papers of the Land Economics Institute. Urbana: Uni-
           versity of Illinois Press.
Hart, Donn V.
   1955a. The Philippine plaza complex: a focal point in culture change.
           Yale University Southeast Asia Studies, Cultural Report Series,
           No. 3. New Haven: Yale University.
   1955b. The Philippine co-operative movement, Parts I and II. Far
           Eastern Survey 24:27–30 and 24:45–48.
Heilbroner, Robert
   1961.   The worldly philosophers. New York: Simon and Schuster.
Herskovits, Melville J.
   1952.   Economic anthropology. New York: Alfred Knopf.

Higgins, Benjamin
  1957. Development problems in the Philippines: a comparison with Indonesia. Far Eastern Survey 26:161–169.
Hollnsteiner, Mary R.
  1963. The dynamics of power in a Philippine municipality. Quezon City: Community Development Research Council study series no. 7, University of the Philippines.
  1964. Reciprocity in the lowland Philippines. *In* Frank Lynch, S. J., ed., Four readings on Philippine values, Institute of Philippine Culture Papers, No. 2. Quezon City: Ateneo de Manila University Press.
  1965. Tagalog social organization. Unpublished essay.
Homans, George C.
  1958. Social behavior as exchange. The American Journal of Sociology 62:597–606.
Howard, Alan
  1963. Land, activity systems, and decision-making models in Rotuma. Ethnology 2:407–440.
Huke, Robert E.
  1963. Shadows on the land: an economic geography of the Philippines. Makati, Rizal: Carmelo and Bauerman, Inc.
Hynam, C. A. S.
  1966. The dysfunctionality of unrequited giving. Human Organization 25:42–45.
Jocano, F. Landa
  1966. Rethinking "smooth interpersonal relations." Philippine Sociological Review 14:282–291.
Joy, Leonard
  1967. One economist's view of the relationship between economics and anthropology. *In* Raymond Firth, ed., Themes in economic anthropology. Association of Social Anthropologists Monograph No. 6. London: Tavistock.
Kaplan, David
  1968. The formal-substantive controversy in economic anthropology: reflections on its wider implications. Southwestern Journal of Anthropology 24:228–251.
Katzin, Margaret F.
  1959. The Jamaican country higgler. Social and Economic Studies 8:421–435.
  1960. The business of higglering in Jamaica. Social and Economic Studies 9:297–331.

Kaut, Charles

1961. Utang na loob: a system of contractual obligation among Tagalogs. Southwestern Journal of Anthropology 17:256–272.

Keesing, Felix

1962. The ethnohistory of northern Luzon. Stanford: Stanford University Press.

Khuri, Fuad

1968. The etiquette of bargaining in the Middle East. American Anthropologist 70:698–706.

Knight, Frank

1956. On the history and method of economics. Chicago: University of Chicago Press.

Kunstadter, Peter

1967. Introduction. *In* Peter Kunstadter, ed., Southeast Asian tribes, minorities, and nations, Vol. I. Princeton: Princeton University Press.

Lande, Carl

1964. Leaders, factions, and parties: the structure of Philippine politics. Yale University Southeast Asia Studies Monograph series No. 6. New Haven: Yale University.

Leach, Edmund R.

1945. Jinghpaw kinship terminology: an experiment in ethnographic algebra. Journal of the Royal Anthropological Institute 75:59–71.

1954. Political systems of highland Burma. Cambridge: Harvard University Press.

LeClair, Edward E., Jr.

1962. Economic theory and economic anthropology. American Anthropologist 64:1179–1203.

LeClair, Edward E., Jr. and Harold K. Schneider

1968. Introduction. *In* Edward LeClair and H. K. Schneider, eds., Economic anthropology: readings in theory and analysis. New York: Holt, Rinehart, and Winston.

Legerman, Caroline J.

1962. Kin groups in a Haitian market. Man 62:145–149.

Levi-Strauss, Claude

1963. Structural anthropology. New York: Doubleday.

Lewis, Henry T., Jr.

1971. Ilocano rice farmers: a comparative study of two Philippine barrios. Honolulu: University of Hawaii Press.

Bibliography

Lynch, Frank X., S. J.
1959. Social class in a Bikol town. Research Series No. 1, Philippine Studies Program. Chicago: University of Chicago.
1964. Social acceptance. *In* Frank Lynch, S.J., ed., Four readings on Philippine values. Institute of Philippine Culture Papers, No. 2. Quezon City: Ateneo de Manila University Press.

Malinowski, Bronislaus
1922. Argonauts of the western Pacific. New York: E. P. Dutton.
1926. Crime and custom in savage society. London: Routledge and Kegan Paul.

Malinowski, Bronislaus and Julio de la Fuente
1957. La economia de un sistema de mercados en Mexico. Acta Anthropologica, Epoca 2, Vol. 1, No. 2.

Mauss, Marcel
1950. The gift. Glencoe: The Free Press.

Mayer, Adrian C.
1966. The significance of quasi-groups in the study of complex societies. *In* Michael Banton, ed., The social anthropology of complex societies. Association of Social Anthropologists Monograph No. 4. London: Tavistock.

Mintz, Sidney W.
1953. The folk-urban continuum and the rural proletarian community. American Journal of Sociology 59:136–143.
1956. The role of the middleman in the internal distribution system of a Caribbean peasant economy. Human Organization 15:18–23.
1959. Internal market systems as mechanisms of social articulation. Proceedings of the American Ethnological Society. Seattle: University of Washington Press.
1960. A tentative typology of eight Haitian marketplaces. Revistas de Ciencias Sociales 4:15–58.
1961a. Pratik: Haitian personal economic relationships. Proceedings of the American Ethnological Society. Seattle: University of Washington Press.
1961b. Standards of value and units of measure in the Fond-des-Negres marketplace. Journal of the Royal Anthropological Institute 91:23–28.
1964a. The employment of capital by market women in Haiti. *In* Raymond Firth and B. S. Yamey, eds., Capital, saving, and credit in peasant societies. London: George Allen and Unwin.
1964b. Peasant market places and economic development in Latin

America. Occasional Paper No. 4. Nashville: The Graduate Center for Latin American Studies, Vanderbilt University.

Mintz, Sidney W. and Eric Wolf

1950. An analysis of ritual co-parenthood (compadrazgo). Southwestern Journal of Anthropology 6:341–368.

Murdock, George P.

1949. Social structure. New York: Macmillan.

1960. Cognatic forms of social organization. *In* George P. Murdock, ed., Social structure in Southeast Asia. Viking Fund Publication No. 29. Chicago: Quadrangle.

Murphy, Robert F.

1955. Credit vs. cash: a case study. Human Organization 13:26–28.

Nadel, S. F.

1957. Theory of social structure. London: Cohen and West.

Nash, Manning

1964a. The organization of economic life. *In* Sol Tax, ed., Horizons of anthropology. Chicago: Aldine.

1964b. Southeast Asian society: dual or multiple? Journal of Asian Studies 23:417–23.

1966. Primitive and peasant economic systems. San Francisco: Chandler.

1967. The social context of economic choice in a small society. *In* George Dalton, ed., Tribal and peasant economies: readings in economic anthropology. Garden City: Natural History Press.

Neale, Walter C.

1957a. Reciprocity and redistribution in the Indian village: sequel to some notable discussions. *In* Karl Polanyi, Conrad Arensberg, and Harry Pearson, eds., Trade and markets in the early empires. Glencoe: The Free Press.

1957b. The market in theory and history. *In* Karl Polanyi, Conrad Arensberg, and Harry Pearson, eds., Trade and markets in the early empires. Glencoe: The Free Press.

1964. On defining "labor" and "service" for comparative studies. American Anthropologist 66:1300–1307.

Pal, Agaton P.

1959. Barrio institutions and their economic implications. Philippine Sociological Review 7:51–63.

Parsons, Talcott

1947. Introduction. *In* Talcott Parsons, ed. and translator, Max Weber: The theory of social and economic organization. New York: The Free Press.

1951. The social system. Glencoe: The Free Press.
Philippines, Republic of
   1956. Annual climatological review. Manila: Department of Commerce and Industry.
   1960. Population and housing, Mountain Province. *In* Census of the Philippines. Manila: Department of Commerce and Industry, Bureau of Census and Statistics.
Pirenne, Henri
   1925. Medieval cities: their origins and the revival of trade. Garden City: Doubleday.
Polanyi, Karl
   1944. The great transformation. New York: Rinehart.
   1947. Our obsolete market mentality. Commentary 3:109–117.
   1957. The economy as instituted process. *In* Karl Polanyi, Conrad Arensberg, and Harry Pearson, eds., Trade and markets in the early empires. Glencoe: The Free Press.
   1966. Dahomey and the slave trade. American Ethnological Society Monograph No. 42. Seattle: University of Washington Press.
Polanyi, Karl, Conrad Arensberg, and Harry Pearson
   1957. The place of economies in societies. *In* Polanyi, *et. al.*, eds., Trade and markets in the early empires. Glencoe: The Free Press.
Pospisil, Leopold
   1963. Kapauku Papuan economy. Yale University Publications in Anthropology No. 67. New Haven: Yale University.
Powell, H. A.
   1960. Competitive leadership in Trobriand political organization. Journal of the Royal Anthropological Institute 90:118–145.
Radcliffe-Brown, Alfred R.
   1940. On social structure. Presidential Address to the Royal Anthropological Institute. Reprinted in Structure and function in primitive society. London: Cohen & West.
   1950. Introduction. *In* A. R. Radcliffe-Brown, and C. Daryll Forde, eds., African systems of kinship and marriage. London: Oxford University Press.
   1952. Structure and function in primitive society. London: Cohen & West.
   1957. A natural science of society. Glencoe: The Free Press.
Redfield, Robert
   1956. Peasant society and culture. Chicago: University of Chicago Press.

Rivera, Generoso F. and Robert T. McMillan
  1952. The rural Philippines. Manila: Office of Information, Mutual Security Agency.
Rottenberg, Simon
  1958. Review of Karl Polanyi, Conrad Arensberg, and Harry W. Pearson, eds., Trade and markets in the early empires. American Economic Review 48:675–678.
Sahlins, Marshall D.
  1960. Political power and the economy in primitive society. *In* G. F. Dole and R. L. Carneiro, eds., Essays in the science of culture. New York: Crowell.
  1963. Review of G. P. Murdock, ed., Social structure in Southeast Asia. Journal of the Polynesian Society 72:39–50.
  1965. On the sociology of primitive exchange. *In* Michael Banton, ed., The relevance of models for social anthropology. Association of Social Anthropologists Monograph No. 1. London: Tavistock.
Salisbury, Richard F.
  1962. From stone to steel. Melbourne: Melbourne University Press.
  1968. Anthropology and economics. *In* O. von Mering and Leonard Kasdan, eds., Anthropology and the neighboring disciplines. Pittsburgh: Pittsburgh University Press.
Schumpeter, Joseph A.
  1950. Capitalism, socialism, and democracy. New York: Harper and Row.
Scott, William H.
  1958. A preliminary report on upland rice in northern Luzon. Southwestern Journal of Anthropology 14:87–105.
  1966. On the Cordillera: A look at the people and cultures of Mountain Province. Manila: MCS Enterprises.
Skinner, G. William
  1964. Marketing and social structure in rural China, Parts I and II. Journal of Asian Studies 24:2–43 and 24:195–228.
Service, Elman R.
  1962. Primitive social organization. New York: Random House.
Smelser, Neil J.
  1959. A comparative view of exchange systems. Economic Development and Cultural Change 7:173–183.
Stine, James
  1962. Temporal aspects of tertiary production elements in Korea. *In* Forrest Pitts, ed., Urban systems and economic behavior.

Eugene: University of Oregon School of Business Administration.

Stigler, George J.
1946. The theory of price. New York: Macmillan.

Tawney, R. H.
1926. Religion and the rise of capitalism. New York: Mentor Books.

Tax, Sol
1953. Penny capitalism: a Guatemalan Indian economy. Smithsonian Institution, Institute of Social Anthropology, No. 16. Washington, D. C.: U. S. Government Printing Office.

Uberoi, J. P. Singh
1962. Politics of the kula ring. Manchester: Manchester University Press.

Uchendu, Victor C.
1967. Some principles of haggling in peasant markets. Economic Development and Cultural Change 17:37–50.

van den Berghe, Pierre L.
1963. Dialectic and functionalism: toward a theoretical synthesis. American Sociological Review 28:695–705.

Van Riper, Joseph
1962. Man's physical world. New York: McGraw-Hill.

van Velsen, J.
1967. The extended-case method and situational analysis. *In* A. L. Epstein, ed., The craft of social anthropology. London: Tavistock.

Ward, Barbara E.
1960. Cash or credit crops? An examination of some implications of peasant commercial production with special reference to the multiplicity of traders and middlemen. Economic Development and Cultural Change 8:148–163.

1965. Varieties of the conscious model: the fishermen of south China. *In* Michael Banton, ed., The relevance of models for social anthropology. Association of Social Anthropologists Monograph No. 1. London: Tavistock.

Weber, Max
1947. The theory of social and economic organization. Glencoe: The Free Press.

1949. The methodology of the social sciences. Glencoe: The Free Press.

Wernstedt, Frederick L. and Joseph E. Spencer
1967. The Philippine island world. Berkeley: University of California Press.

307

Wolf, Eric
   1965. Peasants. Englewood Cliffs: Prentice-Hall.
Wolf, Margery
   1968. The House of Lim: a study of a Chinese farm family. New
          York: Appleton-Century-Crofts.
Wrong, Dennis H.
   1961. The oversocialized conception of man in modern sociology.
          American Sociological Review 26:184–193.
Wurfel, David
   1958. Philippine agrarian reform under Magsaysay, Parts I and II.
          Far Eastern Survey 27:7–15 and 27:23–30.
   1964. The Philippines. *In* George M. Kahin, ed., Governments and
          politics in Southeast Asia. Ithaca: Cornell University Press.
Yang, Martin C.
   1945. A Chinese village. New York: Columbia University Press.

Index